Wherever I go I am asked, "How do you hear the voice of God?" In this book, Cindy Jacobs shares the joys and pitfalls of learning to hear God's voice. The Lord has appointed her as a prophet over nations and kingdoms. Her zeal comes forth as if it were fire shut up in her bones — fire flamed by the Holy Spirit of revival for this hour. This is a much needed book.

ELIZABETH ALVES
President, Intercessors International

God's voice is active today, but Christians must learn to rightly discern it. In my 40 years of prophetic ministry I have found the principles, truths and life experiences presented by Cindy Jacobs to be biblical and true to the activity of the Holy Spirit. This book should be required reading for every Christian.

DR. BILL HAMON
Bishop, President and Founder, Christian International Ministries

This should be required reading for every pastor in whose church intercessors and prophets are arising. It should also be studied carefully by any who feel led to respond to the Holy Spirit's promptings in intercession and prophecy. I agree fully with everything Cindy Jacobs says in **The Voice of God.**

JOHN LOREN SANDFORD
Founder, Elijah House

When we started our church 34 years ago it seemed that we had all kinds of unusual people coming in trying to prophesy. I felt like throwing up my hands in dismay, but God gave me Hebrews 5:14, "But strong meat belongeth to them that are of full age, even those who by reason of use have their senses exercised to discern both good and evil"(*KJV*).

What Cindy Jacobs has brought in this book is strong meat, birthed through her walk with God and her experiences with Him, through her mistakes, through practice. It certainly helps us discern what is spirit, what is truly of the Holy Spirit, and what is satanic.

I love this book. It's a winner!

MARILYN HICKEY

I have great admiration for Cindy Jacobs and the ministry God has given her. She is a dynamic voice for the Kingdom in the world today. Cindy speaks forth God's word and calls believers around the world to powerful intercession, and to effectively and responsibly use the gifts the Lord has given them.

DEE JEPSEN
Director, Women of Faith

Years ago the person who first convinced me by both word and deed that our sovereign God could and would speak directly to His children was my friend Cindy Jacobs. She taught me many important truths that I had never learned in seminary. That is why I am thrilled to see Cindy's dynamic ideas in this inspiring book, **The Voice of God.** I cannot recommend it highly enough for Christian leaders of whatever theological tradition.

C. PETER WAGNER
President, Global Harvest Ministries

Experiential insight, biblical teaching and practical application are elements of Cindy Jacobs's newest book that make it one that will answer questions many have had concerning the role and function of the gift of prophecy in the church today. In her easy-to-understand style, Cindy expresses several principles that will benefit those who are just beginning to step out in their gifting as well as those who are more mature in the prophetic ministry.

I have been blessed personally to receive God's expression of encouragement through this choice vessel. Cindy is a unique gift to the body of Christ, one whom God is using powerfully to impact His people in this vital hour.

JANE HANSEN
International President, Women's Aglow Fellowship International

Filled with supernatural adventure and deep insight, this timely book is essential reading for today's spiritual leader. The chapter on spiritual protocol should be particularly helpful to pastors struggling to govern wisely in the midst of the turbulent winds of revival.

JOHN DAWSON
Director of International Urban Missions, Youth with a Mission

With her first book on prayer and now with this dynamic book on prophecy, Cindy Jacobs has done the Christian community a wonderful service. I believe these truths will take us deeper into the heart and ministry of God. This book has the gift of being simple without being simplistic. Don't miss it!

BOBBYE BYERLY
U.S. National Board President,
Women's Aglow Fellowship International

I slept little the entire night in anticipation of dealing with a serious ministry conflict later that morning. Minutes before confronting the problem my secretary received a phone call. It was Cindy Jacobs calling from between airline connections at an airport 1,500 miles away. As her plane was landing, God had told her exactly what I was about to face and had given her a passage of Scripture to give to me confirming exactly what I was to do. The conflict was resolved in ways I couldn't have imagined.

The Voice of God by Cindy Jacobs is for real. Although the subject of the prophetic is sometimes confusing and often controversial, this book provides an invaluable tool to help us understand God's ways of speaking to and through His children in this, history's greatest hour of harvest.

DICK EASTMAN
International President, Every Home for Christ

The Voice of God is very timely, very instructive and very much needed. Through it, Cindy Jacobs has done a great service to the Body of Christ. I believe her practical approach to the subject, her backlog of rich personal experiences and her corrective words will make The Voice of God a textbook manual for the whole Body of Christ for many decades to come.

DICK MILLS

THE VOICE OF GOD

Cindy Jacobs

Regal Books
A Division of Gospel Light
Ventura, California, U.S.A.

Published by Regal Books
A Division of Gospel Light
Ventura, California, U.S.A.
Printed in U.S.A.

Regal Books is a ministry of Gospel Light, an evangelical Christian publisher dedicated to serving the local church. We believe God's vision for Gospel Light is to provide church leaders with biblical, user-friendly materials that will help them evangelize, disciple and minister to children, youth and families.

It is our prayer that this Regal Book will help you discover biblical truth for your own life and help you meet the needs of others. May God richly bless you.

For a free catalog of resources from Regal Books/Gospel Light please contact your Christian supplier or call 1-800-4-GOSPEL.

Library of Congress Cataloging-in-Publication Data
Jacobs, Cindy.
    The voice of God / Cindy Jacobs.
       p. cm.
    ISBN 0-8307-1741-2 (hard)
    1. Prophecy—Christianity. 2. Spiritual warfare. I. Title.
BR115.P8J33 1995
234'.13—dc20   95-9074
                                                                        CIP

1 2 3 4 5 6 7 8 9 10 11 12 / 02 01 00 99 98 97 96 95

Rights for publishing this book in other languages are contracted by Gospel Literature International (GLINT). GLINT also provides technical help for the adaptation, translation and publishing of Bible study resources and books in scores of languages worldwide. For further information, contact GLINT, P.O. Box 4060, Ontario, CA 91761-1003, U.S.A., or the publisher.

This book is lovingly dedicated
in memory
of my dad
Albert S. Johnson
August 28, 1923—July 5, 1973
A Southern Baptist church planter
who taught me how to love God by the way he lived

CONTENTS

FOREWORD

■

The words "and God said to...," followed by the name of a human being involved in the biblical record, are so common we are struck with a double wonder.

The first is that the sovereign of the universe not only designs to stoop so gently to communicate with His frail creatures, but also that He is always so completely and fully in touch with the details of each of their circumstances.

The second is that given the grandeur of His being and the grace in His revealed nature, anyone would doubt His willingness and regularity at doing that—*speaking* to each of us, *personally.*

That God *today* talks with His people is so basic to the Bible's promise and so abounding in the healthy and healing evidence of its fruit among believers, it should never be doubted or rejected. But it is. It is denied by those who fear that an uncontrolled access to or an unpatrolled wall against such a warm, interactive relationship with God might surrender the subject of "divine revelation" to unlimited, hopelessly subjective definition. They fear, in short, that if anyone can say, "God told me," then anyone can usurp the role of God, either through intentional deception or innocent ignorance of His true Word.

That is not an unjustified fear. The history of mankind is littered with the carcasses of multitudes who have fallen prey to such deception. From the time of the Fall of man until the most recent headlines describing the destruction of a band of cultists, either emotionally damaged or physically dead by reason of the influence of an erratic "voice," the danger of deceptive "revelations" has continued.

Still, the Lord Jesus Christ gave pointed instructions encouraging our expecting to know an ongoing personal communion with God. Even more than an "allowance" of this blessedness in intimacy and confidential communication between the Father and His redeemed children, Jesus promised it! And He gave the specific terms upon which such interaction of a human with the Almighty may be founded.

> He who has My commandments and keeps them, it is he who loves Me. And he who loves Me will be loved by My Father, and I will love him and manifest Myself to him (John 14:21).

A love for the Savior and a constancy of obedience in following Him are both the touchstone and the wellspring from which any of us may become candidates for "hearing" the Voice of God. The very meaning of the words "I will manifest Myself" clearly incorporate personal interchange—as the old hymn says, "He walks with me, and He talks with me."

Thus, the Bible encourages those who *love* and *obey* the living Lord to expect to hear from Him. And further, as the writer of this handbook on biblical prophesying elaborates, God often speaks *to* us that He might speak *through* us. What follows is an effort at helping us, as disciples of Jesus Christ, not only to expect to *hear* God's voice, but also to recognize those occasions He may want us to speak to others in His behalf. We are also helped to know how to go about that without violating Scripture, sanity or just plain practical good sense.

I see Cindy Jacobs as a trustworthy servant of the Body of Christ. Though we have had few occasions to converse together, my observations of her life and ministry over the years have distilled to a conclusion: This lady *walks* with God and she *hears* from Him.

Besides the fact that her prayer life and intercession have brought her to a place of insight into the *ways* of the Lord's speaking with His people, I like the way she conducts herself in relating to others the things God speaks to her for sharing or ministry. There is a happy, yet holy, humanness in her style that defies the notion that a person must be "mystical" to be in intimate touch with God.

My encounters with the writer of this practical guide to hearing God and speaking His heart have evidenced a wisdom that remains childlike, and a spiritual maturity that has remained unaffected—untainted by airs of supernaturalistic pretentiousness or the "slick" sophistication of professionalized piety. She doesn't hold herself aloof, as though somehow beyond the kin of ordinary people, yet, she neither reduces the preciously holy to its becoming the province of casual or glib pretenders.

Prophesying—with the experience of dreams, visions and hearing of "words" from God—is not a parlor game nor a marketable skill to be acquired. But it *is* a promised resource the living God has offered each of us who (1) have been born again through the cross of Christ, and (2) chosen to walk with Him in loving obedience.

> "'And it shall come to pass in the last days, says God, that I will pour out of My Spirit on all flesh; your sons and your daughters shall prophesy, your young men shall see visions, your old men shall dream dreams. And on My menservants and on My maidservants I will pour out My Spirit in those days; and they shall prophesy'" (Acts 2:17,18).

Thus has God spoken in His changeless, eternal Word of absolute and conclusive authority—the holy Scriptures of the Bible. And it is there we always find the guidelines and controls for prophesying, as well as the plumb line and criteria for evaluating the truth or trustworthiness of any "prophecies" or "words from the Lord" in the Church today.

I think you'll find personal encouragement and spiritual insight here. You'll read of people who have learned to trust God's Voice to them, and remained sound in God's Word and sensible in serving His people. And, with me, you'll find helpful pointers intended to prod us to listen for and discern His dealing with us. We can learn how He wants to use us in "prophesying," not to elevate our egos or establish our notoriety as "prophets," but to help us serve the Church of our dear Lord Jesus as encouragers, as uplifters to the fallen and broken, and as edifiers to those for whom He gives us "a word in season" to be "a word fitly spoken."

May the Holy Spirit draw your heart nearer to Christ with a hunger to serve Him and His people in this pure way—as one who loves Him, who walks with Him and who hears His tender voice of caring—speaking love and truth to His own.

Jack W. Hayford, D.Litt.
Senior Pastor
The Church On The Way
Van Nuys, California

ACKNOWLEDGMENTS

■

I want to first thank the Lord for helping me finish this book. It's been tough. Writing a book is just plain hard work, but the end result is extremely rewarding. My family has been just extraordinary. I love you Mike, Mary and Daniel.

Some wonderful people helped me look good—people such as Kyle Duncan, Gary Greig, Kim Bangs and Virginia Woodard. God bless them. Kyle, thanks for your encouragement when I was frustrated. Gary, your knowledge of the Greek and Hebrew was a big addition to the book. To those at Regal who prayed me through, a special blessing is waiting in heaven for you!

Thank you, Joy Anderson, for cleaning up the manuscript. Thank you, Darla's friends, for helping with the index. Thanks also to Becky, Lani, Sue, Beth and various others who would read it. Thanks, Mom and Tom, for your work and love. Bernie, you cleaned my house when I couldn't stand the way it looked. I love you for that. Perry and Arlys, you kept me properly adjusted! Lorna, you've been great.

John Sandford, your insights were very helpful. Thank you.

I also want to thank Peter Wagner for the *many* times I called to get a point clarified and for giving me some great stories he could have used in his books. Also, thanks to Doris for patiently faxing information to me.

To all of my prayer partners, I am forever grateful to you for seeing me through these days of writing. All of you know I'm a Type A person and it's extremely hard for me to sit still long enough to write a whole book. Kay Hoffman and Juana Soloarez have especially prayed and fasted long hours.

Finally, to my pastor, Dutch Sheets, and the intercessors at Springs Harvest Fellowship who prayed and stood with me, I love you all. Thanks from the bottom of my heart.

INTRODUCTION

This book has been on my heart for a long time. I didn't exactly know it would take this form, but the message is interwoven throughout my life's fabric. I really believe God wants His children to know His Voice and that He still speaks in an intimate, individual way today. Jack Deere writes in his *Surprised by the Power of the Spirit* that the most difficult transition in his pilgrimage of believing the gifts of the Spirit are for today was *not* that God heals and does miracles. Rather, the thing he resisted most, was most afraid of and that took the most convincing, was accepting that God still speaks today.[1]

In terms of writing on the prophetic gifts, I do not presume to be one of the major prophetic voices of our time. Actually, writing this book was quite difficult for me. I kept hoping someone else who had many more years of experience would write it. Although I do not feel I have said what is in the following pages any better than any of those who have gone before me, or my peers, it is my belief that the simplicity and practicality of this book will address many questions that are on the heart of the Church. One of my friends read part of the manuscript and commented, "Cindy, you've answered those questions we feel too stupid to ask but have always wondered about."

You'll also note I've been vulnerable in my writing. I've made many mistakes as I've been learning to know and hear the Voice of God throughout the years. Many of the mistakes have also been painful. It is my earnest desire that those of you reading these pages won't suffer some of the things I have, because you will understand many things about which I didn't have a clue.

I hope you will sense the love of God as you read *The Voice of God*.

That has been my goal and genuine heart's desire. You are valuable and special. The Lord and I want you to feel that way as you read. I want you to be encouraged, to laugh with me and to feel uplifted. This has been my prayer for you, my brothers and sisters in Christ.

If you have ever been confused by a prophecy someone gave you, this book is for you. Maybe you didn't have any idea what to do with a prophetic word that was given to you. You'll find some answers between these covers. Some of you have longed for confirmations to things you've thought about, or wondered if anyone else like you exists on God's planet. I hope you will chuckle and remark to a friend, "Hey, remember when I told you so and so? Look at this!"

You don't have to be prophetic to read this book because it is for the whole Body of Christ. Even if you are a brand-new Christian, you will find something for yourself here. The book (in terms of stories, illustrations, the prophetic and the area of spiritual warfare), however, begins with simple addition, proceeds to multiplication, then division, and ends with some calculus for those who are more mature.

I hope this is one of those books you'll want to underline, mark up and use as a manual. I pray it is a blessing to you and that you will take it, use what you've learned and be a blessing to others.

In Christ's love,

Cindy Jacobs
Colorado Springs, Colorado

Note
1. Jack Deere, *Surprised by the Power of the Spirit* (Grand Rapids: Zondervan Publishing House, 1993), p. 212.

CHAPTER ONE

THE VOICE OF GOD

■

In 1955, a little four-year-old girl crept up into her mother's lap. "Mama," she said, "I want a baby sister." The young mother smiled, amused by the child's request. "Sweetheart," she chuckled, "we're not having any more children. You are the last one!" However, the four-year-old was insistent. She just knew Mama was going to have a baby girl. And she was right!

I was that four-year-old child, and the next year my baby sister, Lucy, was born as a present for my daddy's seminary graduation.

Of course, at the young age of four, I had no idea that this "knowing" I sensed about my little sister's birth was a prophetic word (i.e., spontaneous, divinely given understanding or foreknowledge about a person or an event). It would be a long time before I would learn anything remotely connected with prophecy.

Does the Bible have anything to say about children prophesying? The powerful passage in Acts 2:17 refers to sons and daughters (boys and girls) giving prophetic words. "'And it shall come to pass in the last days,' says God, 'that I will pour out of My Spirit on all flesh; your sons and your daughters shall prophesy.'"

The fact that I had foreknowledge of my sister's birth would be "slim pickins" (as we say in Texas) or small substantiation of a prophetic call on my life if this were the only such occurrence I ever had. I remember other times, however, when the phone would ring and someone had a serious message, such as death, and I would know before the phone rang what had happened. I now realize this was part of my being used of the Lord in the area of prophecy and prophetic intercession. At that time, however, I did not understand why those things happened or what to do with the knowledge I received.

WHAT THE BIBLE SAYS ABOUT PROPHECY

I hope this book will help others understand what to do with such "knowing" when it is received and how to know whether or not it is from the Lord. Much of what I describe in this chapter—and this book, for that matter—has to deal with my own introduction to what is called personal (or private) prophecy and corporate (or public) prophecy, as well as prophetic intercession. But what exactly do these terms *really* mean? Before we get too far into our examination of the prophetic gifts, let's take a look at what God's Word has to say.

Personal and Corporate Prophecy
First Corinthians 12–14 lays out much of the biblical basis for both personal and corporate prophecy. Personal prophecy is delivering a prophetic word from God to an individual. Corporate prophecy is delivering a prophetic word to a body or congregation of believers. (I will explore these definitions further in chapter 4.) Some believe that 1 Corinthians 12–14 only has in view corporate prophecy and not personal one-to-one prophecy. However, 1 Corinthians 14:24,25 clearly speaks of prophecy for an individual revealing the secrets of the heart so that the individual confesses "God is really among you!" (v. 25, *NIV*).

First Corinthians 14 (especially vv. 30,32,33) indicates that New Testament prophecy is due to the specific revelatory activity of the Holy Spirit prompting a New Testament prophet to prophesy. New Testament prophecy is to be tested to discern whether a given prophecy is from God or not (see 1 Cor. 14:29; 1 Thess. 5:19-21). New Testament prophets only prophesy "in part" (1 Cor. 13:9).

Although New Testament prophecy never has authority equal to Scripture in our lives, it can carry with it revelation for the hour about which the Holy Spirit wants the Church to know.[1]

Prophetic Intercession
Scripture also gives us some specific models and examples of what I will call "prophetic intercession"—the ability to pray and intercede with prophetic insight and empowering from God's Spirit for specific issues God brings to mind at specific times.

Joel 2:28 and Acts 2:16-21 clearly say that in the Messianic Age the Lord will pour out His Spirit with a prophetic anointing on His people, the Church.

Zechariah 12:10 (*NIV*) mentions that a "spirit of...supplication" will also be poured out on Jerusalem and the people of God in the Messianic Age (compare Zech. 12:10 with John 19:37; Rev. 1:7). In this sense, a spirit of supplication is an anointing of intercession, denoted by the Hebrew word *takhanunim*, which means "supplication, petition." Interestingly, this word *takhanunim* is the same Hebrew word used for intercession in 2 Chronicles 6:21 (see also Dan. 9:3,17,18,23).

God's Word is full of examples of prophetic intercession when His servants prayed with prophetic insight from Him. Examples include Abraham (see Gen. 18:20-23), Moses (see Exod. 32:7-14), Asaph (see Ps. 50,73-83 [see 2 Chron. 29:30, which mentions "Asaph the seer"]), Daniel (see Dan. 9:1-4,20-22), Anna the prophetess (see Luke 2:36-38), Jesus (see Luke 22:31; John 17), Ananias (see Acts 9:10-17) and Paul (see Acts 22:17-21). All these biblical figures prayed with insight, direction and empowering from God's Spirit for issues that God revealed to them when they prayed.

This gives us just a taste of personal prophecy, corporate prophecy and prophetic intercession. My goal in the following chapters is to explore with you the way God uses the prophetic gifts to build, edify and expand His Church—and the role you play in His plan.

As you will see, the first few chapters stress preparation for the prophetic person, including a person's prayer life and personal walk with God. In these chapters, you will notice an emphasis on the role of prophetic intercession. The later chapters shift focus to the application of the prophetic gifts, and the place of personal and corporate prophecy in today's Church.

And as I mentioned earlier, an understanding of God's ways in regard to prophecy was a slow process for me. However, even as a young girl, He gently guided me—never abandoning me along the way.

INKLINGS OF THE PROPHETIC CALL

As years passed, the Lord began to make it clear to me in various ways that He was calling me to "something"—such as the time when I was at junior church camp in Prescott, Arizona, at nine years of age. One day our counselor encouraged each of us to find a quiet place to "talk with God." I remember crawling up on a huge rock outside the chapel. As I was lying back on that rough granite rock, surrounded by the visible manifestations of God's artistry of blue sky and towering trees, I began to pray, "Lord, what do You want from my life?" At first, all I heard was the sound of the wind and trees harmonizing with the birds in the woods. Then I quietly heard another sound—it was the Voice of God saying, "Cindy, I have something I want you to do for Me." At the sound of His Voice spoken so sweetly in my soul, I responded with my heart beating a staccato along with the wind and trees, "Here am I, Lord, send me." I can still hear the words as strongly as the day He spoke them to me.

A couple of years ago, I went back to renew that experience with God. Although that "huge rock" seemed much smaller than it had when I was nine years old, I felt a renewal of the call of God. The Lord met me there again during a time of deep discouragement. That rock became an altar of remembrance in my life of God's call and the affirmation of His presence and anointing. I promised the Lord there that I would never turn back from His call. He planted His covenant within my heart that He would never leave me nor forsake me in the call. The mark of the Voice of God was once again planted deeply within my soul. I pray that God will give each of you who are reading this book and are discouraged a place such as my "huge rock" so you will be affirmed by and touched with the comfort of your maker.

Why didn't God let me know what "the call" meant when He spoke to me in Prescott? I have a theory. Absolutely nothing in my worldview could have remotely given me an inkling of a prophetic call on my life. Maybe some of you can relate to this in your life. It seems God is opening up many new vistas for us in the Body of Christ. There is a hunger across denominational lines to understand personal prophecy. The revelation that God sometimes uses a prophetic word to speak to us is becoming increasingly accepted and understood.

Other inklings of the prophetic call occurred from time to time as I was growing up. At times during conversations, people would stop and say, "How did you know that?" To this day my friends say, "Cindy, it's kind of different traveling with you; you often answer my questions before I ask them." Of course, I cannot read people's minds nor do I have knowledge of everything. At times, I would like to know something specific from the Lord for a person but He is silent. There are various possible reasons for this. Perhaps the Lord has chosen to use someone else to speak His word to that person or He wants the person to personally seek Him for an answer. I realize this sounds strange—even downright weird to some people. How do I know it isn't ESP or some occultic counterfeit gift in operation? This is a legitimate question and one I will touch on in chapters 3 and 4.

A CALL TO PROPHETIC INTERCESSION

This book will not give you a specific formula describing the prophetic call and the way to hear the Voice of God. God's methods are unique. However, I hope to give you some signposts to follow. One thing I have learned through the years is that not all prophetic calls are alike. Each person is unique in his or her gifts and abilities. The ways of God, kneaded into our lives through Holy Spirit-appointed visitations and circumstances, have molded each of us in a different fashion.

Many of these special *kairos* times (a Greek word meaning "time, season," used to refer to strategic times of visitation) reveal the gift-mix of the person. By this I mean some are psalmists or singing prophets and prophetesses, seers and so forth. (I will explain these terms later.) The types of prophetic people in the Bible were widely varied as were the ways by which God called and appointed them for service. I will amplify this theme in chapter 9.

An experience that marked me for life and revealed part of the gift-mix in which God has me function came one hot summer when I was 12 years old. Just as God spoke to Joseph in a dream, He used a series of dreams or night visions, as they are sometimes called, to indelibly etch the call to evangelism along with the prophetic call in my life. We were living in Phoenix, Arizona, when I began having a remarkable series of dreams. They were similar and dramatic. I dreamed about hell. For about a week in the middle of each night, I began to "see" people being tormented in eternal judgment. Hearing their anguished screams was terrifying and I had a sensation of total hopelessness, loneliness and despair. No more chances to change or repent! I watched as their flesh was burned and seared with a fire that was never quenched.

You can imagine the effect of such dreams. Night after night I would awaken, weep and walk back and forth across the floor, crying out to God to use me to win the lost for His kingdom. Dear readers, hell is a very real place. One such experience marks you with a passion to stop people from going there eternally. Little did I understand the call of the prophetic that stirs revival praying—the kind that pours from your spirit and says, "Lord, give me direction and lead me today to some person who does not know You. Lord, give me the harvest for Your kingdom."

The coming worldwide revival is causing more and more people to pray in this manner to see salvation come to their neighbors, cities and the unreached people groups of the earth. Many are being called into prophetic intercession who have never been used in that way before.

The specific call to prophetic intercession was made clear to me when I was 20 years old. (I will write more about this in the next chapter.) At the time, I did not fully understand what had happened to me, but the gift of prophecy was definitely stirred up, amplified and poured out in a greater measure during a deep time of seeking the Lord.

The only glimpse of the future assignment the Lord had for me to travel and prophesy in the nations came one day when my husband, Mike, and I were newlyweds and living in California. The Lord didn't speak to me because I was feeling super spiritual or because I was attending church. I was sitting in our car, waiting for Mike to pick up some of the best Mexican food in the world. While I waited, I pulled my little red Bible out of my purse and flipped it open to read. My eyes fell on the passage in Psalm 2:8: "Ask of Me,...the nations for Your inheritance, and the ends of the earth for Your possession."

I remember thinking, *Well, it says to ask and so I will! Lord, I am asking You for the nations for my inheritance.* Something stirred within my heart. Tears sprang into my eyes. *The nations, Lord? Would You ever send me to the nations?* The possibility seemed as remote as the moon.

It would be many years before I understood that the stirring in my heart that day was a small indicator of the ministry the Lord would someday give to me. Every time I ventured to question what the Lord had meant when He said to me as a nine-year-old girl, "I have something I want you to do," I ended up with the same four-letter word, "Wait." Nothing else, just w-a-i-t. Finally, in time, I stopped asking.

Have you ever noticed how God sometimes seems to take forever to answer? You pray and pray and the heavens seem like brass—He is simply not talking to you about that certain subject. Of course, it took me years to understand that I needed to focus on what I was to be doing at that particular point in time. When I finished that specific step, He would then tell me what the next step was to be. I know He is always on time and never late, but He sure misses a lot of wonderful opportunities to be early!

Ten more years passed in my life; I was then 30 years old. Mike and I had two children, Mary and Daniel, and lived in El Paso, Texas. I began to study intercession—what I would call Abraham-type prayer, when a person "stands in the gap" for another person or group of people (such as a city or nation). At this point in time, I started regularly waking up in the middle of the night to intercede, as I describe in my book *Possessing the Gates of the Enemy* (Chosen Books).

One night, when Mike was out of town on business, I took the children and went to our midweek church service. As I slipped into the back of the church and sat down, I noticed a tender presence of the Holy Spirit. After a short time, the power of the Holy Spirit enveloped me and I quietly put my head down. Something was happening to me but I wasn't sure what it was. After a few minutes, one of the leaders asked if we would pray for the people who were attending the meeting. When it was my turn to pray, the prayer became a prophecy! The person I prayed for started to weep and weep. "You don't know what a confirmation your prayer was to me!" he exclaimed. Confirmation? Why, I had just prayed a simple prayer. Later, after I picked up my children, people stopped to give me their prayer requests, and when we prayed together, the same thing happened. I now understand that the Lord was releasing the gift of prophecy in me.

The prophetic gift had actually been there all along, but the touch of the Holy Spirit upon me stirred it up and loosed it. Dr. Bill Hamon, a respected prophet in the United States, calls this "activating the gift." Even after this incident happened, I still did not have a clue that God would use me to prophesy. I certainly never thought I would eventually travel around the world and teach about prophecy!

"Here Am I, Lord, Send Someone Else!"

The next year, our family moved to Weatherford, Texas. Suddenly, God decided it was time to let me know what He had meant when He said, "I have something I want you to do for Me." Frankly, His plan came as a big shock in my life. I thought I had my life's calling all figured out. By this time, I had done my undergraduate and graduate studies in music, had led church choirs, played the piano, led worship, taught Bible studies and was happy being a mom. Surely this was enough, right? I was spending two or three hours a day in prayer and was feeling fulfilled. Right in the middle of my wonderful fulfillment, the Lord interrupted my peaceful life.

It happened late one night when I was up praying and everyone else was asleep. By this time, the word was getting around that I had a gift of intercession. Many people were asking me to pray for their needs, so I would stay up late some nights to finish my intercession. This night started the same as many others, and I cannot tell you why the Lord chose it rather than others, but it was simply His timing and choice.

Suddenly, in the middle of my prayers, I began to sense a heavy presence of the Spirit of God. It was so deep that I began weeping. Having tears rolling down my face, I said to the Lord, "Father, what do You want?"

I was not at all prepared for what the Voice of God spoke to me. The Bible says, "My sheep hear My voice" (John 10:27), and there was no mistaking it. It was the same Voice I had heard in my heart when I was sitting on that rock in Prescott, Arizona, at nine years old. "Cindy," He said, "I want you to take up your cross and follow Me. I am calling you to take the gospel to the nations of the world."

Truthfully, I cannot tell you I was thrilled. Surely, I must have misunderstood. He must have meant that Mike should go. I tried negotiating. You know the old, "Here am I, Lord, send somebody else." Well, I offered to send Mike in my place and I would be his best intercessor. No deal. Have you ever noticed how persistent God can be? Again He spoke to me, "Cindy, I am not asking Mike. I am asking you. I am calling you, like I called Jeremiah, to the nations." Talk about dropping a bomb on a person's worldview!

I struggled for nearly two years as I walked the floor, weeping night after night. The Scripture from Matthew 10:37-39 kept ringing in my head.

> "He who loves father or mother more than Me is not worthy of Me. And he who loves son or daughter more than Me is not worthy of Me. And he who does not take his cross and follow after Me is not worthy of Me. He who finds his life will lose it, and he who loses his life for My sake will find it."

During these times of struggle, I found it was one thing to say yes to the call of God but quite another to embrace it. At last, one dark night I cried out, "Lord, why me?" The answer came as I opened to the passage in Joel 2:28,29. I gave the fulfillment of the passage in Acts 2:17 earlier, but didn't complete it. The next part reads as follows, "And it shall come to pass afterward that I will pour out My spirit on all flesh;....And also on My menservants and on My maidservants I will pour out My Spirit in those days" (Joel 2:28,29).

The quiet Voice of God gently said, "Cindy, if that prophecy is going to be fulfilled, I need some maidservants [or handmaidens, as some translations say] and I have chosen you." Somehow the Lord has the ability to brush away all of our fears and doubts. That night, I knelt and said what I had said as a nine-year-old child, "Here am I, Lord, send me. I will be Your handmaiden to the nations."

ANSWERING THE CALL

I shared this episode with Mike and we did a lot of praying together. Mike sought the Lord for Scriptures, studied and blessed me. In a short period of time, the doors flung open for me to minister. Since then, I have had the privilege of traveling to many countries of the world, teaching and prophesying to the nations. Mike and I have learned many great lessons through the years. Mike is a protection and a covering for me. Sometimes we tease that we will write a book together about our journey. Throughout this book, I will share more details about my ups and downs, my mistakes and the blessings of learning to prophesy.

When I started to write this chapter, I wondered how others were led into—or called into—prophetic ministry. Did they all have prophetic beginnings as a child? As I interviewed several prophetic voices, I found their stories to be as varied as the stories about the prophets in the Bible.

Bill Hamon's Conversion Experience
One of the prophetic voices on the forefront today is Dr. Bill Hamon. When I interviewed him, I could hear a chuckle in his voice when I asked whether or not he had prophesied at an early age. Later, as I read the preface for his first book, I knew why. His earliest religious background can best be described as "American heathen." This dramatically changed when he met the Lord as a 16-year-old. Bill earnestly sought God regarding his destiny as a Christian. In some of his early writings, he expressed his seeking like this:

When I pray, I feel that the Lord Jesus has called me to the ministry, but again, I don't know for sure. I want to know some certain way whether He has called me or not.

There is something within that makes me want to go out in the ministry and work for God; then comes that uncertainty about whether it is the Lord's will or not. But even if it were revealed to be His will, how would I ever become a minister? I didn't know how you get into the ministry.[2]

Interestingly enough, this young man who was destined to be a pioneer of personal prophecy had his first affirmation of the call to the ministry through a prophetic word. He was attending Bible school in Portland, Oregon. He had been fasting for nine days—seeking direction from the Lord—when he was given a "word" (prophecy) by a prophetic presbytery (I'll write about presbytery ministry later) of five faculty members who spoke the following message over him:

Yes, My son, even as the Spirit of the Lord burned in the heart, yea, even in the bones of My servant, Jeremiah, even so doth the fire kindle and burn within thy heart.

Fear not, My son, the hand of the Lord hath rested upon thee and the mantle of His power has come upon thee. Yea, and thy mouth shall be quick to speak the word of the Lord, and even as thou shalt speak shall the prophetic utterance come forth.[3]

It has now been more than 40 years since Bill began prophesying. During these four decades, he has laid hands on and personally prophesied over multiple thousands of people. These range from small infants to international church leaders, from farmers to politicians and professional people of all types.[4]

In thinking about the prophetic call, it is interesting to note the role of godly instruction for the person who will someday prophesy on a large scale. Bill Hamon's gift only came into manifestation after his conversion experience. Another prophetic voice I interviewed had experiences similar to mine. She would occasionally have a "foreknowing" of events (i.e., she would receive prophetic knowledge about events that had not yet taken place).

Elizabeth Alves Hears from God

Elizabeth Alves (Beth, as her friends know her) grew up in a home where they openly talked about God. Her earliest remembrance is of a time when she was three years old and an uncle had committed suicide. Quite naturally, her family was distressed about the situation. One of her relatives was tormented by the thought that her uncle went to hell because he had killed himself. (I'm not trying to relate a theological point on this issue, but it is interesting to note that what happened gave Beth's family peace.) Beth distinctly remembers sitting under a tree and having a talk with God. "God," she asked, "did my uncle go to heaven or hell?" Those words, "heaven or hell," echoed back and forth in her mind.

Just as clearly as if someone were standing beside her and speaking to her, she heard the words, "I look upon the heart. Trust Me." Her little soul was filled with peace and she knew her uncle was in heaven. She rushed in to tell her family and as soon as she shared what had happened they were flooded with a tremendous peace.

Beth and I were discussing various aspects of this subject, such as how the call of God comes and related events in our families, when she interjected, "You know, Cindy, my father was prophetic. Quite a while before airplanes were invented, he told my mother, 'Mama, someday people are going to ride in a silver bird.'"

I asked, "Beth, did you have any supernatural experiences when God touched your life in a special way and called you into ministry?"

She thought a minute and said, "Yes, I grew up in the Lutheran church and at age 12 went through confirmation. At the practice for the confirmation service, the minister was demonstrating how he would lay hands on us during the confirmation service. He had me come forward and laid hands on me to show how he would pray for us. He spoke the sevenfold spirit of God over me (related in Isa. 11:2—the spirit of wisdom, the spirit of might, and so on) and I was 'caught up in the Spirit.'" (By this, she meant the presence of God came over her so completely that she totally lost track of time.) The minister wisely let her stay a long time and when she came to herself again the confirmation practice had ended.

I don't know if something about the age of 12 is significant, but it is interesting to note that Jesus was 12 when He publicly stated in the Temple, "I must be about My Father's business" (Luke 2:49). This was also the age at which I had the series of dreams about hell. Perhaps age 12 is when children become especially sensitive to the Holy Spirit and at this age we should watch and pray for them in a special way.

John Maxwell's Calling

Years ago, a godly pastor named Reverend Maxwell would call his grandsons aside to pray over them. He would do this quietly and none of them knew he was praying for each of them in a similar way. One day, Grandpa Maxwell, as they called him, prayed for his 12-year-old grandson John. The prayer was actually a prophecy because the Holy Spirit spoke through this patriarch of the family that one day this young boy on the brink of manhood would preach the gospel. This was confirmation to the young man. He knew in his heart it was true.

The Lord, however, wasn't finished with His confirmation of young John's call. John had a junior-high Sunday School teacher named Glenn Leatherwood who took seriously his call to raise up young boys to be men of God. Each Saturday night, he would intercede for those on his class roster. After class one Sunday morning, he asked four of the boys if they would stay behind so he could pray for them. Brother Leatherwood told each boy that as he prayed, he believed that boy would preach the gospel.

Young John Maxwell did indeed grow up to be a preacher of the gospel. He has pastored the Skyline Wesleyan Church in Lemon Grove, California, near San Diego, for many years. He is a noted communicator, mentoring countless thousands of young leaders around the world through his teachings on leadership.

Reminiscing over the phone, Pastor Maxwell shared how he has always considered Brother Leatherwood's prayer his ordination into the ministry. He also went on to say, "You know, my grandpa didn't just prophesy over me. He also called my brother aside and shared with him that God would use him as a Christian businessman and make him very prosperous and that he was to use what God gave him to feed the poor, and that's just what he has done."

Dick Mills's Calling

The books of the prophets in the Old Testament are referred to as the major and minor prophets. One perspective is that prophets were often referred to as major because of the length and scope of their work. The same kind of pattern can be seen today. There are many prophetic voices in the Body of Christ and they are all crucial, wherever God calls them. Some of them, however, will be international in scope and touch a broad spectrum of the Body of Christ, and perhaps we could say they are the "major" prophetic voices of today.

One whom I personally consider to be a major prophet is Dick Mills. Dick has one of the most unusual and powerful prophetic gifts I've witnessed. He prophesies almost exclusively by giving Scripture. Through the years, he has familiarized himself with 7,700 Scripture verses from various translations. As he prophesies, he will give you a Scripture reference in a manner such as this, "And *The Living Bible* says it like this...and the *New International Version* says it like this." He almost always starts the prophecies with, "Sister (or Brother), the Lord has a good word for you."

In questioning Dick, he says, "I did not prophesy as a child or before I was born again."

One of the things I wondered was how and when Dick started prophesying. He attended the Foursquare denomination's Life Bible College in Los Angeles, California, which was started by Aimee Semple McPherson. In 1946, while at school, Dick realized he had the gift of prophecy. His first experience in prophesying came during a church service. After this initial release, the Lord continued to move in that same manner within Dick.

Dick's unique style of prophesying through various translations of Scripture came to him while fasting in 1953. During that time, the Lord put it on his heart to give precious promises to people. At first, his ministry in this manner began slowly and infrequently. As he was faithful, however, his ministry began to increase and eventually took on national and international proportions.

He is a humble man who wrote this to me in a letter about the way the Lord uses him:

> The prophecies I give to people always originate with a Scripture the Lord brings to my remembrance. I live within the realm of 1 Corinthians 14:3—edification, exhortation and comfort. I am impressed and overwhelmed by prophetic ministries functioning in the Body of Christ that are detailed and precise, and I hold them in high esteem. I feel humbled and grateful that the Lord uses me at this modest level. In a way it is awesome just to be able to give a person a word from the Lord.

If you were to receive a prophecy from Dick Mills in a service, he would probably start out something like this: First, he asks your name.

Then one of his frequent uplifting statements is: The Lord has a good word for you. And then he reels off four or five Scripture verses from various translations. These are usually written down on a pad with his name on the bottom and it says something like, "A word of the Lord from Dick Mills."

THE EFFECT OF PROPHECY

I have to tell a little anecdote about how this gift of prophecy touched my life as well as the life of Peter Wagner, a leader in the worldwide prayer movement. Several years ago, I was visiting Peter Wagner and his wife, Doris. My visit to them was right after I had taught the 120 Fellowship retreat (a class Peter teaches each week at Lake Avenue Congregational Church in Pasadena, California).

I was sitting in Peter's study. He was telling me that John Wimber, leader of the Vineyard movement, had called and said that someone named Dick Mills was going to contact Peter with a personal prophecy. At the time, Peter didn't know who Dick was and was just beginning to learn about the prophetic ministry. I said, "Oh Peter, if Dick Mills calls, you need to talk with him. He's one of the major hitters as far as prophets go."

Peter said, "Fine," and went on to talk with me about something that was on his heart. He wanted me to amplify a little book I was working on to include all aspects of intercessory prayer. I have to tell you, I was struggling.

Inside, I was having a conversation with the Lord. "Lord," I said, "I don't have a clue how to write a book. Please, Lord, can't we negotiate on this? You know I've never had a writer's class. Peter has written more than 30 books and besides, Lord, he's a seminary professor with a Ph.D.!" I think I was suffering from basic intimidation, fear and inadequacy.

At that moment, the phone rang. It was Dick Mills. Peter quickly started writing as Dick began to give him Scripture verses and to tell him how God would use him to bring three strands of the Body of Christ together for an end-time work. At the end of the conversation, Peter said, "Oh, by the way, Cindy Jacobs is here." (I first met Dick in the 1980s when he prophesied that I would one day have an international ministry.) All of a sudden, I began to have a strange feeling in the pit of my stomach. I *knew* Dick was going to share a prophecy with me, too!

When Peter got off the phone, he said to me, "Oh, by the way, Dick had a Scripture and prophecy for you too, Cindy. He said that you are here by the Lord's design and gave you the Scripture from the wedding of Cana when Mary said, 'Anything he says, do it!'" (see John 2:5).

The Lord caught two people with one phone call that day. I was certain the Lord was referring to Peter's advice to write the manuscript that became my first book, *Possessing the Gates of the Enemy*. God certainly has unique ways to get a point across! By that time, I would have had to be downright disobedient not to take Peter's counsel—and I'm glad I did.

God is calling many people to prophetic action today. Some common threads seem to run through the testimonies of those I've talked to. They will say something like, "One day I was reading the first chapter of Jeremiah and it kind of jumped out at me. The Holy Spirit began to speak to my heart that He would make me a prophet to the nations."

Frequently, people will say, "The call came when I read Jeremiah 1:5, 'Before I formed you in the womb I knew you; before you were born I sanctified you; I ordained you a prophet to the nations.'"

Just as God calls those who have a prophetic gift in a variety of ways, so the Lord uniquely trains each vessel to be used for His glory. In the next chapter, we will learn about the role of intercession and obedience in training those who have a prophetic call.

PROPHECY IN PRACTICE

1. Do you know someone who has a prophetic call?
2. Have you surrendered your life to be used of God in any way He may see fit for you?
3. Do you think it is possible for a person to hear the Voice of God today?
4. Have you ever thought about how the gift of prophecy might be used to help you draw closer to God?
5. Think back, if possible, to a time when you either received a prophecy or you had some kind of supernatural "foreknowledge" that helped you or a friend. Discuss it with someone to whom you are spiritually accountable.

Notes

1. See for example Acts 9:10-12,17; 11:27,28; 13:1,2; 16:7-10; 21:10,11; 22:14-21.
2. Bill Hamon, *Prophets and Personal Prophecy* (Shippensburg, Pa.: Destiny Image Publishers, 1987), p. 2.
3. Ibid., p. 5.
4. Ibid., p. 8.

CHAPTER TWO

"BUT I DIDN'T MEAN TO PROPHESY":
The Role of Prophetic Intercession

∎

I recently sat across from a lovely young lady who was in great distress. In a crushed tone of voice she said, "Cindy, my pastor just rebuked me for prophesying to one of the leaders of our church. He said to me, 'Susan (not her real name), if you are going to give a prophetic word you need to get it judged by me as your pastor before you give it.'" Tears filled her eyes as she blurted out, "But Cindy, I didn't mean to prophesy! All I thought I was doing was praying about a church situation at the elder's request."

Realizing she needed comforting, I put my hand on her shoulder and said, "Susan, why don't you tell me specifically what you were asked to pray for and how you prayed?"

At this, words tumbled out in a torrent. "Well, one day this elder at my evangelical church asked me to pray because there were some people causing problems and stirring things up repeatedly among the congregation. Not knowing any of the specifics, I started to pray. Suddenly, out of my mouth fell the phrase, 'And Lord, those 80-year-old ladies who are gossiping and causing problems need to be touched by You and convicted of what they are doing to the church.'"

She stopped and I prompted, "What did the elder say?"

Having a quizzical look on her face Susan breathed, "He was astonished! I had prayed specifically for what he felt was the root problem in the church. But the pastor didn't receive what I prayed. I'm not sure whether he couldn't believe these people were really the problem or he didn't understand why he wasn't told first."

I explained how people who have a prophetic gift often pray differently from other people. This is one of the first ways prophetic people start to receive what they later come to realize must have been a prophetic word. Those whom God has in the training ground of intercession often find themselves in a lot of hot water (i.e., trouble)—especially in churches that traditionally have not understood the gift of prophecy. Prophesying was new to Susan's church. The leaders in the church didn't know what to do with her and the way she prayed. Furthermore, Susan didn't know what to do with her developing gift either!

UNDERSTANDING PROPHETIC INTERCESSION

As Susan and I spoke, I realized again the need for me to write this book. Many other Susans need help! Sadly, many are so crushed that they give up, and some also leave the church! Others cause great damage to the local church because they don't know the correct way to use the gift God has given to them, or the "do's and don'ts" of prophesying—of which there are *many*. In fact, I, too, am still learning, even as I write. I will attempt to incorporate the lessons I've learned through the years, some of which I shared that day with Susan.

While I talked with Susan, I reflected on my own trials and tribulations in learning how to prophesy. It might sound strange when I say "learning how to prophesy." I simply mean, becoming skilled at effectively sharing what God seems to be saying—in a way that is in order—and bringing edification to all concerned in God's timing. Timing is crucial. We'll talk about timing quite a bit.

One reason I spent so much time with Susan was that I remembered episodes when I was first beginning to prophesy. Like Susan, I had no idea I *was* in fact prophesying. People at our church were asking me to pray for them after church. I didn't realize that what I was doing was prophetic intercession. I had no clue that such a thing as a prophetic word existed!

After a time, it became apparent that I didn't pray the same way as other people did, and the things I prayed were often accurate and fulfilled in dramatic ways. Also, I noticed a large contrast between the way I prayed and the way others prayed during times of corporate prayer. I tended to pray with more authority and with greater detail. I often was amazed at what came out of my mouth in our prayer meetings. It was sometimes painful when our pastor would ask me to pray in church, and then he would accuse me of being prideful because of the way I prayed. Of course, now I know I could have done things differently at times but, unfortunately, at that time no one knew why I prayed as I did. And I certainly had no idea what to do with this prophetic gift—sometimes it didn't seem like much of a blessing.

Things were rocky for me along the way to understanding prophetic intercession. I remember an incident in college when a group from a Christian commune had heard of the way I prayed and they decided I was demonized. They plotted with a boy I had dated to get me to the commune to "deliver me." That was a horrible night. First they told me that because I seemed to pray with some sort of foreknowledge, I had a religious demon inside me and had never been truly born again. They told me I was involved in witchcraft. I recall weeping in great anguish of soul, "If I'm not born again, what happened when I asked Jesus to come into my heart?"

Finally, after about five hours of trying to cast a religious spirit out of me, the group sat back, exhausted, and said, "You must not have any demons because none could stand the pounding we've put them through."

Needless to say, that was a scary, traumatic experience for me. I didn't know anyone I could talk to about it. I was living away from home and should have talked to my parents about it but didn't have the presence of mind to do so. I guess I just felt shamed by the whole thing.

As the years passed, I began to read some materials about prophesying. Most of it was rather vague. None of the materials discussed such things as spiritual protocol (which I describe later in this book). I spent as much time as possible in intercession, often awakening in the night and being deeply burdened for pastors and leaders. Another way I interceded prophetically was to pray while watching the news or reading the paper. It was interesting how many times I would pray concerning some treaty or government situation and the solution I prayed for would be exactly the outcome of the negotiations.

It's interesting to note that one of the Hebrew words translated "to prophesy" is *naba*, which some scholars believe is a derivative of the root *naba'*, which means "to bubble up, to gush forth, to pour forth."[1] The root of the same word is found in Akkadian (one of the languages of ancient Mesopotamia) as *nabu* meaning "to call" or "proclaim" and appears to be an older form of the Hebrew word *naba* "to prophesy."[2] The later Hebrew word reflects further the influence of divine activity upon the human personality as the prophetic message "bubbles up and gushes forth" as a mighty torrent from a prophet's lips.[3] In prophetic intercession, the Lord, through the power of the Holy Spirit, moves upon the hearts of intercessors to pray prayers far beyond their natural knowledge. It happens just as the possible root of the word *naba* suggests, "bubbling up and gushing forth, empowered by the Holy Spirit."

Susan, in the opening of this chapter, didn't realize she was going to prophesy; it bubbled up from within her. Many times when I start to prophesy, I have no idea what I am going to say before I open my mouth. I have learned that if I open my mouth, the Lord will fill it with His words. We'll talk more about how to release the prophetic gift in chapter 8.

"ALL PROPHETS ARE INTERCESSORS!"

In the beginning of my development as a prophetic voice, the "how to's" were all still very much a mystery to me. I knew the Lord seemed to be using me to pray prophetically, but I didn't have much grasp of the scriptural basis of prophetic intercession or personal prophecy. One day I was riding in a car with Margaret Moberly, who taught me quite a bit about prophesying. She said, "Cindy, not all intercessors are prophetic but all prophets are intercessors!" I let those words soak in. She quoted from Jeremiah 27:18:

> "'But if they are prophets, and if the word of the Lord is with them, let them now make intercession to the Lord of hosts, that the vessels which are left in the house of the Lord, in the house of the king of Judah, and at Jerusalem, do not go to Babylon.'"

Those words rang in my head, "If they are prophets, let them intercede!" Now, I thought surely I wasn't a prophet, but this Scripture verse gave me insight regarding the link between intercession and the prophetic. *What revelation,* I remember thinking. *I'm called to intercede prophetically!* A light bulb went on in my head. It was as though I had finally found my place, realized who I was and, at least for the moment, knew what God wanted me to do.

As the years have gone by, I have understood increasingly how interwoven intercession is with prophecy. Although as yet many prophets do not consider themselves intercessors, they spend long hours in intimacy with the Father, listening and praying. I believe someday they'll realize the strong links between intercession and the prophetic. We see it throughout the Word of God.

The first case where prayer is mentioned in the Bible is intercessory. God spoke to Abraham and told him beforehand that He was going to destroy Sodom and Gomorrah. Abraham immediately began prophetic intercession for the righteous in the city. He asked the Lord, "Would You also destroy the righteous with the wicked?" (Gen. 18:23).

Abraham's way of interceding may seem a bit presumptuous to us. Surely God in His sovereignty does not include humankind in His decision making. However, I believe the Lord invited Abraham into the process to reveal His deep love and merciful nature. The bottom line was that He didn't want Lot destroyed, so intercession needed to be made. Interestingly enough, one of the pictures given us through the interceding of Abraham in Genesis 18 conveys the meaning of the prophet as a legal defender in the court of Heaven, presenting a case before God as judge. At times when we pray, we stand in the gap as a prosecutor or legal defender, God having spoken a prophetic word to us concerning another person or a nation. We pray according to the revelation given to us in the prophecy.

Prophetic intercession is the ability to receive an immediate prayer request from God and pray about it in a divinely anointed utterance. Biblical examples can be found throughout Scripture (see Gen. 18:20-23; Exod. 32:7-14; Dan. 9:1-4,20-22; Luke 2:36-38; 22:31; John 17; Acts 9:10-17; 22:17-21).[4]

Many times, such prayer requests come in the form of prophetic words. The people praying may not realize this at the time and only later find out it was God speaking to them to pray prophetically. At times when I pray like this, it is not so much that God gives me a lengthy prophecy, but a name will come to me while I am praying. I then open my mouth to pray and trust God to fill it with the word of intercession He wants. Yet on other occasions, I will ask the Lord, "How do you want me to pray for this matter?" and He will then give me the next instruction.

TRAINING FOR THE PROPHETIC

Intercession is a training ground for the prophetic gifts. I personally believe that almost all prophetic intercessors have the ability to prophesy on a regular basis or to become prophets. As I write later on about the various kinds of prophets, we will see that they may prophesy in song, or as they counsel or in front of a congregation. Prophets all vary in nature, and so do not all use the same prophetic vehicle to prophesy.

As intercessors begin to experience regular answers to their prayers from supernatural knowledge given to them by God, many step forward to share with someone else what they are sensing. I like to mentor young prophetic believers by taking them with me as I travel and having them pray with me. They often become very excited and say, "Cindy, I knew what you were going to pray before it came out of your mouth!" The same Holy Spirit praying through me was also praying through them.

At times this kind of praying involves a progressive revelation of God's will. One day when I was interceding, I kept hearing the name George (not the actual name). I heard no other words, but yet I felt great alarm for this man. I prayed, "Father, protect him, encourage him. Don't let him do something he shouldn't do." The next day, I received a prayer request for a well-known traveling evangelist who was suffering great discouragement. He had the same name and I could then pray with even greater knowledge. I strongly sense the Lord may have averted a suicide attempt—the situation was dire right at that moment.

It is often greatly encouraging to me when God touches other people's hearts to pray for me prophetically during times of stress or discouragement. In 1993, we were trying to move to Colorado Springs, and it seemed like all hell was fighting it. Finances were tight, I was physically exhausted and wondering if we were being presumptuous in even thinking of moving to Colorado.

During that time, I received a call from Dutch Sheets, who is now my pastor. He said, "Cindy, I'm concerned for you." (He wasn't the only one; I was concerned for me, too). "Ceci (his wife) had a dream last night that you were slipping down a muddy embankment and couldn't get up. I've been praying for you." Was I glad God was warning me and having people pray. (More about prophetic dreams and visions in chapter 9.)

Another call came that same day from a prayer partner who said, "Cindy, you're going to make it. Don't give up on the move to Colorado Springs." I have to admit that Colorado was looking better all the time to me. These prophetic words and intercessions encouraged me to keep pressing forward.

Prophetic intercession often catches unaware those who are praying.

At times, a person may begin praying a simple prayer of petition when all of a sudden the tonality of the voice will change. A ring of authority comes. It is as though the intercessor has shifted gears in the Spirit as the power of the Holy Spirit energizes the prayer.

Dick Eastman tells of just such an incidence in his book *The Jericho Hour*. He was in a prayer meeting at the headquarters of Every Home for Christ, of which he is the international president. Prayer centered around the sale of the organization's building in California so they could also make a move to Colorado Springs. At first, he writes, though the prayers were sincere, nothing of particular intensity caught his attention. Then the Lord shifted the meeting into overdrive! In Dick's own words, here is what occurred:

> What happened next prompted me to look at my watch. It was 9:55 A.M. The intercessor who had been petitioning God for His intervention had completely changed the tone of his praying. He had been rehearsing in prayer certain factors God was certainly well aware of: the declining economic conditions of the city; recent articles in the local newspaper explaining how few, if any, office buildings were selling in the Los Angeles area; and the fact that our small street was lined with buildings for sale, some perhaps better and even cheaper than ours. What a faith-building prayer!
>
> But then came the change. The prayer seemed to take a quantum spiritual leap in boldness. It began with a simple phrase, "God, no matter the circumstance, You have just the right buyer for this building." Next came, "In fact, I believe You can see that buyer even now. You know his name. You can see where he is—what he's doing right now."
>
> What happened next I believe was a divinely initiated transition into the arena of prophetic prayer. The intercessor suddenly spoke directly to the would-be buyer, "I believe that even now God sees you driving along the streets near the EHC office looking for just the right building for your business." An even more startling directive followed, *"I command you to come forth now. Not tomorrow, not next week, not next month, but today."*
>
> Remarkably, an older man with a young couple walked through the front door a few minutes after 10:00 A.M. Theirs

would be the only offer on the property. The purchase was finalized exactly on time for that summer's move to Colorado Springs. And it had all begun with a prophetic prayer.[5]

One important aspect of prayer as a training ground for the prophetic is that it confirms we are actually hearing from God. Very few people who move in personal prophecy (i.e., stand in front of a person or persons and give a prophetic word on a regular basis) started out at this point. Most started as I did by praying for people and having them exclaim, "How did you know to pray that way? What you prayed is exactly my need!" (We'll touch on this more in chapter 6, "Mentoring the Prophetic Gift.")

Prophetic intercessors often receive rather strenuous training from the Lord. He requires things—to temper them—that may seem more than a little unusual to others. Rees Howells was an extraordinary intercessor whom God put through many testings to prepare him for his role in intercession for the lost and for Great Britain during World War II.

Howells called one critical time of training as his "Llandrindod experience." He shared how for five days the Lord replaced his own self-nature with God's own divine nature.

First, there was the love of money. Rees said, "Money would be no more to me than it was to John the Baptist or the Saviour." Next, He dealt with him to give up his right to a choice in making a home. "I saw I could never give my life to another person to live with that one alone. Could the Saviour have given His life and attention to one person, instead of to a lost world?"

Thirdly, the Lord touched on ambition. This meant if he were earning 12 pounds a day, and another man with a family was earning much less, the Spirit could tell him to give his job to that man. Finally, on the fifth day of this process the Lord touched on a fourth area of his life, his reputation. As he was thinking of men of the Bible who were full of the Holy Ghost, particularly John the Baptist, the Lord said to him, "Then I may live through you the kind of life I lived through him." A Nazarite clothed in camel's hair, living in a desert! Even in this, or what might be its modern equivalent, a real decision had to be made. As the Saviour was despised, he must be willing to be the same.[6]

Some people might wonder at the strictness, and at times the severity of the training, Howells received. I have found, however, that the greater the calling and responsibilities God plans to give a prophet, the more exacting, and at times lengthy, the preparation for the call. Although God may not require the same things He did of Howells, His training is stretching and demanding on those being trained, no matter what is to be their calling.

Romans 11:22 says, "Therefore consider the goodness and severity of God." We know it is a biblical principle that unto whom much is given, much is required (see Luke 12:48). It seems that others can get away with things I can't. For instance, I know people who watch movies that to me are marginal and it seems their consciences aren't bothered at all. If I were to do that, I believe the Holy Spirit within me would be deeply grieved. I would end up on my face in some dark corner of my house, repenting before God.

To persevere in the walk God has for me, it is not just important, but also *necessary* for me to spend at least one, but usually two to three hours a day, in His presence. At some point each day, I review the day and ask the Holy Spirit to show me where I have had a bad attitude or have been short with people, or where roots of selfishness or sin are present in my life. Often, I find myself calling and apologizing to someone who was the brunt of my being grumpy or distracted. This isn't integrally part of prophetic intercession but I feel it is appropriate, nevertheless. It concerns the purity of my relationship with God.

LEARNING NOT ONLY TO HEAR, BUT ALSO TO OBEY

As a person is trained to prophesy, the Lord will often work intensively in the area of obedience. There are special strategic "windows of time" to not only pray, but also to obey by doing a physical act that might be called an intercessory act or a prophetic act. At times, such acts may seem a bit unusual but can be powerful in breaking down strongholds. And still at other times, we may be more traditional in what we consider intercession. The typical view of intercession would be to gather in a prayer room or to kneel in our "prayer closets" (i.e., places where we can go regularly for quiet time with God). Let's consider a few intercessory acts in the Bible that could be considered prophetic intercession and that produced great results for the kingdom of God.

One well-known and powerful example of an intercessory act is found in Joshua 6. Prophetic instructions were given regarding how to take Jericho through an intercessory act. The Israelites' actions don't sound strange to most Christians today because we are so familiar with the story. The same God that told the Israelites to march around Jericho also told them to stand firm in the face of invading enemies, so that they sent worshipers before the army and they prevailed (see 2 Chron. 20:15-22). Another prophet, Jeremiah, was instructed to hide his girdle among some rocks where water would shrink it as a sign from the Lord (see Jer. 13:1ff.). These were all highly unusual acts.

In the late '70s and early '80s, the Lord began to train me in obedience. I once heard Dr. David Yonggi Cho say the key to his success was that he "prayed and obeyed." I didn't know his secret, but I learned in a similar fashion. One winter day as I prayed, the Lord seemed to say that I should go to a certain lighting shop to look for a fixture for my hallway. I hadn't planned to go at that time but it seemed crucial that I go *now*. My daughter, Mary, was three years old and my son, Daniel, was a baby so I had to bundle up everyone to go out.

As I drove up to the store, I could see they were having a close-out sale. At first I simply thought, *How nice, the Lord is trying to save me money.* If I had known what God wanted me to do when I got into the store, I probably would have been tempted to turn around and go home. (Have you heard John 16:12, "I still have many things to say to you, but you cannot bear them now"?)

I was able to find the light fixture I needed. As I was purchasing it, I asked the Jewish man who owned the store, "Why are you selling out?" He looked very sad and said in a quiet voice, "I am very ill and the doctors don't know what is wrong with me. They have given me handfuls of pills to take but I'm getting worse. I simply can't run my store anymore."

All of a sudden, I had one of those strange feelings. I turned the stroller with Daniel in it and grabbed Mary's arm. I had to get out of the store before... Halfway out of the store, I heard a still small Voice say to me, "Cindy, I want you to go lay hands on him and I'm going to heal him."

"Heal him, Lord? You mean You want me to walk up to him and pray for him *in the name of Jesus*? Lord, he's Jewish (as if the Lord didn't already know that). Won't he be offended or turn me down flat?"

Again the voice of the Lord, "Cindy, I want you to..."

I have to admit I interrupted that voice, "Okay, okay!" I said, "I'll do it."

Not feeling the least bit brave or anointed, I shepherded the kids back to the man and admonished them to be still. I looked at the man, who looked up in surprise.

"Have you forgotten something?" the man asked quizzically.

My heart was thundering in my chest as I murmured, "Sir, may I pray for you?" (I didn't tell him I was going to pray in the name of Jesus because I was too chicken.) I quickly laid my hands on him and blurted out, "In the name of Jesus, be healed!" You know what, he didn't hit me or anything!

Several weeks later, I went back to see the store owner. I screwed up my courage and said, "Excuse me, but I'm the lady who prayed for you a couple of weeks ago and I've been wondering how you are feeling."

I was shocked at what happened next! The store owner grabbed me by the shoulders with tears in his eyes and said, "You, you're the one who prayed?"

Uh-oh, I thought, *I'm in big trouble!*

Still tearful, he exclaimed, "I went back to my doctor and they can't find the problem anymore. I seem to be perfectly healthy now."

Needless to say, I went home floating on a cloud!

Gradually, as I obeyed these still, small voices and urges, I started to understand when the impressions were the Lord and when they were simply my own mind or flesh. The Bible exhorts us in 1 Thessalonians 5:21 to "test all things; hold fast what is good." The tests I learned to apply to know if God, my own human spirit or another spirit was speaking to me will be discussed in chapter 4, "'Is That You, God?': Learning to Hear God's Voice."

The training I received and the lessons I learned during that time have been invaluable. I recall one day in Weatherford when the Lord urged me to go to the Winn Dixie grocery store—not Kroger's nor Safeway—and stand in aisle three. A person would be there who needed to be saved.

As I drove to the store, I meditated on the passage in Acts 8:26-35 where an angel of the Lord spoke to Philip, saying, "Arise and go toward the south along the road which goes down from Jerusalem to

Gaza." The Lord gave Philip *very detailed* instructions. I believed strongly in my heart that this was a similar case.

Well, I went to aisle three in Winn Dixie and waited, and waited and waited. Finally, a lady I knew only slightly came up the aisle. She greeted me with joy, "Oh, Cindy, I need to talk with you; I'm in such a mess." I was able to give her the good news of Jesus Christ and she received it with gladness. While I drove home, I worshiped the Lord for His goodness and love for one lost sheep. The Lord would leave the 90 and 9 for the 1. I want to always be willing to do the same.

THE ROLE OF THE WATCHMAN

One important role of the prophetic intercessor is that of being a watchman for the Body of Christ (i.e., what I describe as one who is called by God to "stand guard" in prayer for a group of people—or a nation). We can see several kinds of watchmen (or women) from a study of the Word. At times, most prophetic intercessors will stand in each of these watchmen anointings. One emphasis of this chapter has been the important element of the watchman calling—that of watching over your own heart and character before God. I like what Rolland Smith says in his excellent manual, *The Watchmen Ministry*:

> The watchmen ministry starts with a view of a world many long to see and fully understand, our own hearts. It is a hidden land! Our loving God arranges circumstances in our lives so that we, for our own benefit, will discover what is in our hearts. We then are taught through these experiences to trust, not in ourselves, but in God alone.[7]

The following are a few of the possible watchmen:

The Jeremiah Watchman
This is the anointing for prophetic proclamations. In Jeremiah 1:9 the Lord told Jeremiah, "Behold, I have put My words in your mouth." The prophetic words put into his mouth were to help him fulfill his mandate as a prophet in verse 10, "See, I have this day set you over the nations and over the kingdoms, to root out and to pull down, to destroy and to throw down, to build and to plant."

These prophetic proclamations God put into Jeremiah's mouth had the power to do all of the things mentioned in Jeremiah 1:10. Prophetic proclamations are given through the inspiration of the Holy Spirit to verbally declare God's will into a situation. They might sound something like this:

"We proclaim that God's will *will not* be stopped in this country. Father, Your Word declares that every knee shall bow and every tongue shall declare that You are Lord. So we now say, 'Will of God, be done in the nation of Bhutan!' Thank You, Lord, for opening doors of utterance for the gospel into Bhutan."

Such prophetic proclamations are often stated quite forcefully. I have been with Wes Tullis of Strategic Frontiers (of Youth With a Mission) when he was interceding for a nation. This Jeremiah-type anointing comes upon Wes to declare God's will into a nation. It is a very powerful experience—one of those times when every goose bump on your body stands at attention and you are sure something has happened in the heavenlies. *Dake's Annotated Reference Bible* says:

> The Jeremiah anointing is a vanguard one. The rod of an almond tree which was shown to Jeremiah comes from the almond tree which is one of the earliest to show life in the spring. Here it symbolizes a watchman, a vigilant officer looking for invasion.[8]

The Harvest Watchman
The harvest watchman watches over the harvest fields. This calling is spoken of in Isaiah 1:8, "So the daughter of Zion is left as a booth in a vineyard, as a hut in a garden of cucumbers, as a besieged city."

> In this scripture the daughter of Zion is likened to a booth in a vineyard or a hut in a garden of cucumbers. Peculiar as this may sound to modern day ears, it was not strange at all in biblical times. They knew that temporary huts would be built in the middle of harvest fields for the watchmen of the vineyards. After the harvest booths were left to the weather to become desolate, wasted, soon destroyed, and fallen down.[9]

Harvest watchmen stand watch over what the Holy Spirit is working to bring about in the Church. For instance, many churches have a lot of visitors and some have many converts a year, but they do not hold the harvest (i.e., retain new attendees). Satan comes in to try to destroy the church and to make it look like a harvest field would look after an enemy army has trampled it under its feet.

The harvest watchman is particularly critical to have in place during times of renewal and revival. Few revivals have been maintained as far as people being converted and lives being renewed is concerned. I believe God has meant for many movements to become full-blown revivals but they were simply awakenings because the prophetic intercessory structure was not in place to watch over the harvest. Norman Grubb pinpointed this as being a problem during the Welsh revival in 1904:

> But the real problem arose as the Revival proceeded and thousands were added to the churches. As enthusiasm abated, there were bound to be many who had depended more on feelings, and not yet learned to have their faith solidly based on the word of God. The devil took advantage of this, some became cold and indifferent, and the spiritual conflict began. Those like Rees Howells, young in the Spirit though they were but at least a bit more advanced than the converts in the revival, were needed to be intercessors and teachers, to take the burden of the newborn babes, and pray and lead them on. But these young intercessors soon began to find how mighty is the enemy of souls, and that a conflict, not against flesh and blood, but against the rulers of the darkness of this world, cannot be fought with carnal weapons.
>
> Many blamed the young converts for backsliding, but we blamed ourselves, because we were not in a position to pray them through to victory. Oh, the tragedy, to be helpless in front of the enemy, when he was sifting young converts like wheat![10]

Some churches understand this concept of harvest watchmen. One such church is Community Church of Joy in Glendale, Arizona, a Lutheran church of 7,000 members, pastored by Walt Kallestad. This church believes so much in the power of the watchmen ministry that they have hired a full-time pastor of prayer, Bjorn Pedersen. They have developed intercessory prayer teams for every ministry in the church. In addition, a silent intercessor is on-site at every church function from Sunday School classes to business meetings to youth socials.

Pastor Kallestad said the Lord instructed him that he "was to put prayer in the highest possible priority in [his] own life as well as the life of Community Church of Joy." Prayer Pastor Pedersen has also developed a College of Prayer that offers 38 prayer-training courses.

Another church that has this vision is Word of Grace in Mesa, Arizona, pastored by Gary Kinnaman. Kinnaman is implementing a strategy that will provide prayer coverage for every ministry within the church and every outreach of the church. As part of the strategy, he requires all his staff to enlist in PIT crews (Personal Intercessory Teams).[11]

Harvest watchmen oversee each aspect of a church from the nursery to the senior citizens.[12] They can also be set in place to pray for those who are straying from the Lord. Although I travel so much that I think my pastor, Dutch Sheets, is going to give me a visitor's card, the Holy Spirit still alerts me to pray as a watchman for members of our church. I will begin thinking of them again and again and pray for them. When I get home, I either ask Pastor Dutch about them or call them personally to check on them.

Harvest watchmen should be able to interface with church leaders to effectively fulfill their roles. In my book *Possessing the Gates of the Enemy*, I wrote some guidelines that can be applied to watchmen in the chapters on prayer partners and corporate intercession.

Some harvest watchmen will have a scope that goes beyond that of the local church and their own areas. They will watch over and sound the alarm of the enemy's plans for the nations. For instance, they will wake up in the night and pray for the Christians in nations such as Mongolia. Others will pray for unity in the Body of Christ; the Lord will alert them to possible sources of splits and divisions in the Church nationwide or worldwide. Satan loves to divide us along denominational or theological lines and consume most of our time with nit-picking rather than focusing on the harvest. Of course, I know it is necessary to be correct theologically, but unless we are prayerful, divisions can turn into an "I'm of Paul and I'm of Apollos" kind of situation (see 1 Cor. 1:10-17).

The Warrior Watchman

The warrior watchman is one who is offensive in his stance. In the ancient Near East, one of the techniques for war was to build a movable tower or fort as part of the siege works of a city. Some translations of

Ezekiel 4:2 use the term "siege wall," which also represents a battering ram tower: "Lay siege against it, build a siege wall against it, and heap up a mound against it; set camps against it also, and place battering rams against it all around."

This tower was moved close enough to the city to peer over the city walls and harass the enemy. The watchmen would taunt the enemy verbally from this tower and report the condition of the city. Thus, these watchmen were offensive in nature rather than defensive. They would watch the enemy and report on his doings. The warrior watchman is one who actively engages in prophetic intercession against the enemy. In *Possessing the Gates of the Enemy*, I explain how intercession is twofold. One aspect is interceding to God on behalf of another person and the other half is standing in the gap against satanic attack.

Dutch Sheets tells the story of a physical attack coming against his wife, Ceci. The Lord led him into a powerful time of intercessory prayer on her behalf. She had received a doctor's diagnosis of an egg-size cyst. As Dutch sought the Lord for a strategy on how to go to war for her, he felt that he should spend an hour a day praying. This is how he described his prayer time in a recent conversation with me:

> During that hour the Lord would lead me in different ways to attack this infirmity coming against my wife. I would make declarations of her healing as well as speak the Word over her. Three or four times over the course of the month in which I warred, I had an unusual occurrence which came in the form of a vision. I saw a picture of myself holding the cyst in my hand, squeezing the life out of it. Each time I saw it, it was smaller and I'd ask Ceci, "Is the pain lessening?" Every time I asked she answered, "Yes, Dutch, it's not as bad."
>
> About four weeks into this season of intercession, the same picture came to me one last time. I saw the cyst as about the size of a quarter in my hand. I saw myself squeezing it until there was nothing in my hand and the Lord spoke to me and said, "It's done!" I knew it was taken care of. Ceci said there was just a little pain left, but I couldn't pray anymore about it after this. There was no more anointing to pray as I had no burden from the Lord. It was done.

Three or four days later, Ceci said, "Dutch, there's no more pain!"

She went back to see the doctor and he confirmed the miracle of God that came through Dutch's standing in the gap as a warrior watchman for the woman he loves.

Recently I was in Cincinnati, Ohio, leading a citywide prayer conference. It happened to be the same weekend as a rock festival that was being held in the United States, called Woodstock II. I was greatly concerned about this festival because the first Woodstock polluted a generation by unleashing a powerful spirit of rebellion and discontent. I particularly was concerned because of a prophetic intercessory word I had received two months before Woodstock II about an attack on this current upcoming generation. This was the word we released in our Generals of Intercession newsletter:

> This is the day when I am raising up the generations and restoring the inheritance of the generations for I am a tri-generational God. I am the God of Abraham, Isaac, and Jacob. I am at work linking the generations and bringing healing to the brokenness between the generations. The "Abraham" and apostolic voices are going to experience a new understanding of the Father heart of God. "And He shall turn [and reconcile] the hearts of the [estranged] fathers to the [ungodly] children, and the hearts of the [rebellious] children to [the piety of] their fathers [a reconciliation produced by repentance of the ungodly]; lest I come and smite the land with a curse [and a ban of utter destruction]" (Malachi 4:6, AMP.)
>
> There is the beginning of an outpouring upon the Isaac and Jacob generations which will have a double portion of the anointing loosed in the '60s during the Jesus People Movement. [The Isaac generation represents the older children of Generation X—those 20 and older—and the Jacob generation represents Generation Y—those 20 and younger.] This move will be different in that it will not be dysfunctional. It will cause an understanding of the Father heart of God and a cleaving to God as Father. They will not just look to Jesus as their Friend but will understand the Holiness of God and give respect and honor to their Father. The anointing of compassion will pour out with great tenderness while the fear of the Lord falls upon God's people.

Rise up, intercessors of God, for the enemy knows of this plan and is also unleashing a double portion of the strongholds poured out during the '60s—strongholds of drugs, free sex, communes with no holds barred and a denying of absolutes. The youth will become a law unto themselves if God's people do not stand against the tide of filth and ungodliness being poured out against them. A curse will be brought upon the nations of the earth if God's people do not stand against the enemy's devices.

WATCHMAN, ARISE AND SOUND THE ALARM! Cry out to God so that the enemy will not thwart the new move of God. There is still time to stand and pray and see the tide of Satan's power stopped. A standard of righteousness must be established from the "Isaacs" and "Jacobs" for God has called them to be His end time evangelists, pastors, prophets, and teachers.

This is the last and final hour of prayer when God will do marvelous works among the children and youth. They will cause the nations of the earth to marvel at His greatness. As you stand in prayer, Satan will not be able to stop the floodtide of God's power as it sweeps across the schools of the nations. His glory will explode upon the generations as He heals among and through them. They will establish His Kingdom and His Will will be done on this earth.[13]

I read this prophecy at the conference in Cincinnati, and we went to war in the heavenlies with the two-edged sword of the Spirit. This is how we warred, as closely as I can recall:

First, we humbled ourselves, declaring we had no power in or of ourselves. Second, we cleansed our own hearts of any known sin. Next, we claimed the protection of the Lord through Psalm 91. I then suggested we kneel and pray as the Lord was leading us into a time of "Korean style" prayer (praying out loud at the same time—sometimes quite loudly). I instructed that I would then lead in a prayer of agreement (at this time everyone would need to pray quietly enough to hear me in order to agree with me).

Many strategies were employed during this time of prayer. I was reminded of the story of Deborah and Barak and how God used the elements to fight against the enemy (see Judg. 5:20,21). As I thought of this, I chuckled and said something like, "What if it rained so hard that people became disillusioned and went home? It certainly wouldn't hurt to ask and then we could leave it up to the Lord."

We prayed the prayer of agreement and asked the Lord for rain. Then I went to the piano and we warred with intercessory praise. (See my chapter "Intercessory Praise" in *Possessing the Gates of the Enemy* for specific instructions.) The warring aspect of the watchman ministry was put into practice that day in an awesome way. God poured out a spirit of supplication and grace in our midst as people wept and cried out to Him for this generation and for Woodstock II.

We asked for rain, and rain it did. Lots of rain. One intercessor at the meeting shared with me that she saw rain pouring in sheets, not drops. That's exactly what happened. It poured and poured and became a huge mud bath. People left in droves. Not everyone left, but we had prayed that Satan's plan would be stopped. I believe it was thwarted, but it was a skirmish and not the whole battle. Nevertheless, I believe it was strategic.

I felt impressed to ask the Lord to give us a sign that He had heard us from heaven. My morning paper showed pictures of the mud bath and people commenting, "It simply wasn't the same as before." Amen. Hallelujah! Thank God for warring watchmen.

The Body of Christ is coming into a fresh understanding of the warring aspect of prophetic intercession. All of chapter 10 is devoted to this subject. For a more comprehensive study of the watchmen, please see *Possessing the Gates of the Enemy.* I would recommend reading my books as companion works.

To gain what you need out of this book, it is imperative for you to read chapter 5, "Redemptive Prophecy." It covers issues that are central to those who are planning to be involved in personal prophecy. Such issues will include the difference between Old and New Testament prophecy, how to release the prophetic gift in a redemptive way and the role of prophecy in the Church today.

PROPHECY IN PRACTICE

1. Do you think it might be possible for someone to have a prophetic call and not know it?
2. What is prophetic intercession and how could its use help you and/or your local church?

3. How important is it to be obedient to what God is saying to you?
4. What kind of time frame should you follow when God gives you direction?
5. Are there prophetic watchmen in your church? Can you recognize the various kinds of watchmen as they function?

Notes

1. F. Brown, S. R. Driver, and C. A. Briggs, *A Hebrew and English Lexicon of the Old Testament* (Oxford: The Clarendon Press, 1951), p. 612.
2. W. F. Albright, *From the Stone Age to Christianity* (New York: Doubleday, 1957), p. 303. Also see Brown, Driver, and Briggs, *A Hebrew and English Lexicon*, p. 612.
3. David Blomgren, *Prophetic Gatherings in the Church* (Portland, Oreg.: Bible Temple Publishing, 1979), p. 29. [Compare Hebrew *naba'*, "to bubble up, to gush forth, to pour forth," in Ps. 78:2 and 119:171 with Hebrew *naba*, "to prophesy," in 1 Sam. 10:5,6.]
4. Cindy Jacobs, *Possessing the Gates of the Enemy* (Grand Rapids: Chosen Books, 1991), p. 151.
5. Dick Eastman, *The Jericho Hour* (Altamonte Springs, Fla.: Creation House, 1994), p. 124.
6. Norman Grubb, *Rees Howells, Intercessor* (Fort Washington, Pa.: Christian Literature Crusade, 1952), pp. 40-41.
7. Rolland C. Smith, *The Watchmen Ministry* (St. Louis: Mission Omega Publishing, 1993), pp. 20-21.
8. Finis J. Dake, *Dake's Annotated Reference Bible* (Lawrenceville, Ga.: Dake Bible Sales Inc., 1992), p. 746.
9. Ibid., p. 440.
10. Grubb, *Rees Howells, Intercessor*, p. 34.
11. Cheryl Sacks, "The Bridge Builder" 2, no. 8 (August 1994): 1,4.
12. See appendix for names and addresses of ministries as resources for building this kind of prayer strategy into your own church.
13. Cindy Jacobs, *The GI News* 3, no. 2 (July/August 1992): 2.

CHAPTER THREE

CAMEL'S HAIR AND WILD LOCUSTS:
Preparation for the Prophetic Gift

■

BEWARE OF FALSE PROPHETS

It was Friday night of our big conference. We were all excited about the prospect of having as our main speaker a man whom I'll call "Reverend Simpson." He had given several "right on" prophecies to our organization. As the leadership waited on the platform, I mulled over the good reports of this prophet's ministry. Yet, for some reason, I felt vaguely uneasy. I couldn't put my finger on it, but something wasn't right. I began to talk to the Lord about how I felt. Inside my heart came the words, "Caution. This man has some severe personal problems. Watch and pray."

At this point, the speaker came into the ballroom. He looked every inch like my picture of an Old Testament prophet, except he had on a business suit rather than long flowing robes. He was tall and thin with deep-set eyes and gaunt-looking cheekbones. He had long bony fingers that looked as though they could poke a hole through you if he pointed at you. I mused to myself, *If this guy were from New Testament times he would have been a John the Baptist type—coming out of the wilderness wearing a camel's-hair shirt with wild locusts hanging out of the corner of his mouth.* Pulling my thoughts together I admonished myself for being disrespectful to our speaker. Instead of subsiding, however, the sense of something being wrong with this man increased dramatically.

This might be a good place to interject a comment about prophetic intercessors. They have God-given, built-in alarm systems that go along with their spiritual gifts.[1] It is like an early warning system that detects enemy mines and missiles before they are visible to the natural eye. From years of experience, I have learned to heed these warnings. Every time I have brushed them off as merely being a case of indigestion, I have regretted it later. In attempting to describe these warnings to you, I'd say they usually start with what I call a "check in my spirit," or a sensing that something is wrong. If I try to ignore these signals, they usually escalate to a deep restlessness, agitation and profound need to intercede. This continues until the situation is either averted, changed or minimized. Sometimes God will clearly reveal something I need to do in the physical realm to negate what is about to happen. In my opinion, most Christians receive these warnings from the Holy Spirit about various situations but they don't know what to do with the warnings. This occurs on a more regular basis with prophetic watchmen.

Now, back to Reverend Simpson. As he came up on the platform, I began to earnestly pray without uttering a sound. In addition, I quietly said, "Satan, I bind you in the name of Jesus from giving a false word to this assembly through this man." It was impossible for him to physically hear what I whispered under my breath. I was shocked by the next thing that happened. Reverend Simpson came and stood right in front of me, facing the audience. He started gesturing wildly with his hands and began stepping forward. Each step he took forced me to take a step backward until I was literally up against the wall!

If this weren't peculiar enough, he jumped off the platform looking very confused. He looked around and then called the daughter of one of our leaders to the front to "prophesy" over her. I was shocked as he apparently touched her bosom by accident, then grabbed her by her ears and pinched her so hard that she bled. By this time, I was upset and earnestly praying for this to stop, or else I was going to stop it myself. Then he gazed about the audience, muttered something about there not being any true prophets in our midst and took off out of the room! I wasn't actually in charge of the meeting or I would have addressed some of the things we had just seen, but I certainly did so in private at a follow-up meeting.

What was going on with Reverend Simpson? We had previously been blessed by his ministry. I surmise several things could have happened:

- He had some sin issues that he had been able to keep hidden up to this time.

- Pride in the power of his ministry may have entered into his life. His comment about "no true prophets in our midst" seemed to indicate he believed he was *the* "true prophet."
- There is a possibility he had some sort of emotional breakdown that allowed the "beasts in the basement" of his sin issues to become uncontrollable to him.
- In probing into the situation later, it appeared that he did not have much spiritual accountability in his life.

The above story, unfortunately, is not an isolated or unusual one. Some weird people are attracted to the prophetic movement in the Church. This is a shame because there are many more genuine, balanced prophetic leaders than there are flaky ones. Those who have severe emotional and personal problems have caused real damage to the Body of Christ, and have created a severe backlash against others who are used to prophesy. Although this damage may occur, the Bible is clear about the need to be able to receive the prophetic gifts in our midst. First Thessalonians 5:19,20 puts it this way, "Do not quench the Spirit. Do not despise prophecies." God exhorts us not to devalue prophetic revelation nor turn away from inspired instruction, exhortation or warning.

Because most Christian leaders have a deep desire to be biblical, they do not want to be guilty of quenching the Holy Spirit. However, many who have had to deal with the excesses are frustrated. Pastors have a God-given protective nature for their sheep, and flaky prophets can really mess things up in their churches. Also, many evangelical churches are beginning to have an understanding of the gift of prophecy but are not knowledgeable enough about the prophetic gift to judge what is being said. The guidelines we discuss in chapter 4 should help such leaders.

GOD'S CHARACTER TRAINING

In addition, people emerging with the gift of prophecy, like Susan in the previous chapter, are often squelched. The Holy Spirit is then quenched and grieved because of a lack of basic understanding of how prophecy should function in the Church. Yet, just as a toddler has many accidents before he or she is potty trained, the prophetic person in training will also stumble.

There is quite a difference, however, between a prophetic person in training and the wild man in our opening story who claimed to be a prophet. Often these two kinds of people are lumped into one without being discerned as two distinct situations. This results in the person who is just beginning to prophesy being crushed because of being treated wrongly as one who is not a "whole person" and "refuses to change."

This chapter will deal with the inner training by God of the prophetic person who may or may not one day be a prophet or prophetess. I personally believe many of these principles can be applied to all believers as they seek to grow in the Lord. It does stand to reason that the training of leaders who will stand before thousands will be more intense than those who are not in such a visible ministry.

Intrinsic in the nature of those in various kinds of ministries (such as the pastor, teacher and evangelist) are certain weaknesses or strongholds. Some of these problems, I believe, God allows in order to keep us totally reliant on Him. For instance, many prophetic people I know seem to have dealt with insecurity as they grew up. Although this basic flaw needs to be hammered out in the fire of God's refinery, the remembrance of it causes them to rely on the power of the Holy Spirit rather than on their own abilities. Pastors can be overly compassionate in their shepherd's role to the point that they become ineffective leaders. This allows people to get away with behavior that is destructive to the rest of the church.

As I said, the training of the prophetic person can at times seem quite severe. There are many reasons for this, some of which I'll touch on in chapter 6, "Mentoring the Prophetic Gift," and some we'll cover in this chapter. I think this training process is so important that it will take two chapters to adequately begin to touch on its significance!

It is critical to note that although someone may operate in a powerful way with the gift of prophecy, it does not necessarily mean he or she has character enough to be in a visible ministry. Paul spoke of this in 1 Corinthians 3:1,3 when he gave this strong rebuke:

> And I, brethren, could not speak to you as to spiritual people but as to carnal, as to babes in Christ. For you are still carnal.

We often do a great disservice to those who are young in the ways of God and are just beginning to develop Christlike characters. We put them into Christian service too soon without adequate mentors to help them. Young prophets often do not have the maturity to withstand the barrage of Satan against their weaknesses and strongholds. Once someone is put into a place of visible ministry, every stronghold within that person often hatches. Without proper help and understanding, the person will fall into shame. I have also seen many people who have a strong call on their lives begin to work in ministry soon after their conversions and grow rapidly into mature believers. However, they had strong leadership models working around them.

This is why it is wise, both for those God is raising up for service and for those who are training them, to allow God to deal with major character flaws while these people are less visible. I believe if this had been done with some of the major Christian leaders we have seen fall in the past few years, it would have averted tremendous hurt and pain within the Body of Christ.

Years ago when I was just beginning in ministry, I was in a season where God was dealing strongly with me concerning my arrogance and my attitude. Life was hard and it seemed as though I was getting into trouble everywhere I turned.

One day, while in a terrible mood, I was riding in a car with Margaret Moberly, who taught me a lot about ministry. That day I was working on my "B.A." degree (bad attitude degree), when Margaret suddenly turned, looked right into my eyes and said, "Cindy, one day you'll thank God for this time of your life."

Ha, I thought, *I would have to be a masochist to thank God for what I'm going through.* The rest I won't quote directly but it could be translated, "Mutter, mutter, moan, moan, God, this isn't fair!" In fact, I wasn't sure this was God at all, but rather just one big attack from the devil. The Lord in His mercy was trying to root out those terrible attitudes of mine, and the flesh dies hard. Have you ever rebuked Satan only to find out later it was really God dealing with you? Believe me, I have—and on more than one occasion.

Why does God have to deal so strongly with those who are prophetic? For one thing, they are so stubborn! (More about this later.) For another, they are more prone to pride. The prophetic gift, by nature, is often a more "flashy" gift—especially in its public form. People run around and say, "Did you hear? Prophet Big Lungs has given me this word from God." Of course, if it was from God they *should* say, "Have you heard? The Lord really touched me this morning through a prophetic word." It is my prayer that people will not remember it was Cindy Jacobs who prophesied, but that I would become more invisible in nature and simply a vessel to deliver a message.

One of the books that greatly influenced my life was *The Elijah Task* by John and Paula Sandford. The subtitle is *A Call to Prophets and Intercessors.* I have to admit that when I first purchased the book, it didn't make a bit of sense to me. After I had it for a year, however, I suddenly opened it and the words jumped off the page at me. One of the main reasons I initially didn't understand the Sandfords' counsel was because the book talks a lot about the dealings of God with intercessors and prophets. When I bought the book, I hadn't yet been through any sort of refinement by God.

Have you ever noticed how much work God can do in your life in one year—or one month—when you are yielded to Him? One of the points the Sandfords make is that God can't put new wine into old wineskins—obviously a biblical concept (see Matt. 9:17). Remember, on the Day of Pentecost the Holy Spirit prepared the 120 disciples during a 10-day prayer meeting and then filled them up with so much new wine that people thought they were drunk (see Acts 2:1ff.)!

The Sandfords go on to say, "If we could but shuck the skin of our old carnal nature merrily and quickly, all would be fun and games."[2] I'm sure those into whom the Holy Spirit poured new wine enjoyed themselves greatly, but they paid the price in prayer and preparation first.

INTEGRITY OF A PROPHET

What are some specific areas God deals with in training those who will prophesy either publicly or in hidden ways like intercession? One of the biggest areas is integrity. If the Lord is going to trust *His* words to specific people to speak, they must first be faithful in giving *their* word. For instance, in my experience, here are a few areas where God works (and in which He is working on me):

Not exaggerating. The prophet must learn to speak only what God tells him or her and go no further. In giving a prophecy, one of the temptations is to make the prophetic word more exciting, more fruitful or more dramatic than it actually was. Now, I understand different personalities perceive things in different ways. This is one reason God has given me my husband, Mike; I tend to amplify and he tends to downplay. Between the two of us, we have a good balance.

Being on time for commitments. This is an area I have to work on because I seem to be behind much of the time. I've learned not to schedule more things into a given time span than I can possibly accomplish, or not to promise to do more than I can physically do in one day. Otherwise, this is a lack of integrity and leads to frustration on everyone's part. If we are to understand God's timing in sharing what we have heard from the Lord, we must learn to order our own personal lives. I don't pretend to have accomplished this but I am working on it because integrity is of great importance.

Keeping your word. If people can't trust you to keep a promise, how can they trust you to have a prophecy from God? Sometimes at night I ask the Lord to remind me if I have forgotten any commitments or promises to anyone. I'll make little notes to myself on my side table so I won't forget again!

Proper handling of money. Prophetic leaders should pay their bills and not live beyond their means. They need to have control of their use of credit. They must not solicit funds as a prerequisite for giving a prophetic word from God. The gift of prophecy cannot be bought or sold and those who do engage in such activity fall into divination as did Balaam the seer (see Num. 22—24; cf. Acts 8:18-23). (More about this later in chapters 4 and 6.)

Speaking the pure Word from God. It is possible for the prophetic word to be "tainted" and, thus, only part of what the prophetic person is saying comes from God. We'll discuss tainting through generational sin and occultic activity in this chapter and in chapter 4.

As the years have gone by in my life and ministry, I have been puzzled by some of the areas with which I have struggled. Certain issues that I knew I had not personally been involved with would crop up and bother me, yet they seemed to pull me in a strong way. While I looked for answers, it seemed Scripture passages concerning generational sin leaped out at me in my studies. One that I meditated on often was Deuteronomy 5:9,10 (*NASB*):

> "'You shall not worship them [idols] or serve them; for I, the Lord your God, am a jealous God, visiting the iniquity of the fathers on the children, and on the third and the fourth generations of those who hate Me, but showing lovingkindness to thousands, to those who love Me and keep My commandments.'"

This passage clearly shows that the sins of the parents—and therefore the weaknesses and tendencies toward these sins—will be passed on (in Hebrew, *pagað* is "visit, appoint") to the children. This principle is no less applicable to Christians in the Church age than is the related affirmation to honor one's father and mother, as Ephesians 6:1-3 shows.

It is interesting how we can be so informed in some areas and yet not understand other godly principles. I grew up in a strong evangelical-based home. Yet, certain roots were intertwined within my heritage that affected me and also had great potential of tainting the prophetic word I would later give.

As I mentioned earlier, I seemed to "know" things from an early age. Many of these prophetic words were sent to me from the Lord. As I got older, other dark aspects came from my generations that started pulling me into more psychic powers. These came mostly from my dad's side of the family. In fact, we used to joke about ESP, and how at times we could tell what the others were thinking. I read my horoscope in the paper and didn't think a thing about it. Later on I came across Deuteronomy 4:15-19, which clearly states that this is forbidden because at the root of astrology is worship of the stars. This is witchcraft (see 2 Kings 17:16,17).

By the time I was in college, I started toying with mental control, trying to read other people's minds. Imagine all of this going on at a Christian college where I went to chapel regularly and took Bible classes! However, none of our professors talked about witchcraft or generational iniquities of the occult. Things progressed to such a state that a friend's father actually told me I would make a great medium. Why, I hardly knew what that word meant!

In their book *The Elijah Task*, John and Paula Sandford state, "One whose family has a history of occult involvement may have great difficulty, though the involvement be two or three generations removed."[3] They go on to quote Hobart Freeman from page 28 of his book, *Angels of Light?*:

> Many times clairvoyance and other psychic powers appear as a consequence of occult involvement, usually in the second and third generation. Edgar Cayce, for example, whose grandfather was a water dowser, gave evidence of occult subjection at an early age, relating various psychic and clairvoyant experiences. Strong mediums usually develop in this manner, as a result of what might be termed "psychic heredity." Personality and character defects, as a consequence of

occult sins by one's parents or grandparents, are often seen in their descendants in the form of morbid depression, violent temper, irresponsibility, immorality, chronic fear, hysteria, agnosticism and atheism, hate, persistent illness, unpredictable behavior, and many other abnormalities.[4]

GENERATIONAL SIN

In my own life, other generational strongholds were fear and worry. I had to deal with these strongholds before I could ever fully serve God. I talk about these strongholds and how God set me free in the chapter entitled "Dethroning Reigning Strongholds," which I wrote for the book *Women of Prayer: Released to the Nations* (Aglow Publications).

Quin Sherrer and Ruthanne Garlock have this to say about generational iniquity in their excellent book *A Woman's Guide to Breaking Bondages*:

> "But that's Old Testament" (Deut. 5:9-10 quoted earlier), you may say. "Doesn't the New Testament say we are new creatures in Christ when we come to know Christ in a personal way?" Yes, we are new creatures in Him, but we bring a lot of garbage with us that needs to be dumped.
>
> The iniquity of the forefathers brings a curse upon the family line. This word *iniquity* does not mean individual sinful acts; it means "perverseness" and comes from a Hebrew root meaning "to be bent or crooked." The word implies a basic attitude of rebellion, plus the consequences that iniquity produces.[5]

David says in Psalm 51:5, "Behold, I was brought forth in iniquity, and in sin my mother conceived me."

I was always curious about the dynamics of how a man of God such as David could fall into the terrible sin of adultery with Bathsheba. Knowing the effects and weaknesses produced by iniquities, I decided I would check into David's generations to see if they revealed any evidence of sexual sin on either side of his family.

Amazingly, I discovered that David is a direct descendant of Rahab the harlot (see Matt. 1:5,6). Perhaps this left a weakness that not only affected David, but also, as a result of his sexual sin, with his son Solomon who had serious problems in his relationships with many, many women. Solomon and his wives worshiped false gods—gods that, no doubt, contributed to Solomon's downfall as a king. David's son Amnon lusted after his own sister, Tamar, and committed incest with her (see 2 Sam. 13:1ff.).

Sin and Iniquity

Generational sin and iniquity were like incurable diseases in the Old Testament. Praise God for Jesus who came and bore our iniquities. Isaiah 53:6 says, "The Lord has laid on Him the iniquity of us all." Although Jesus bore our iniquities, we have to appropriate the power of the Cross in this area at times in a very specific way in order to receive freedom (see Acts 19:18,19; Eph. 4:28).

Many people are confused about iniquities because they do not know there is a difference between sin and iniquity. The Bible speaks of them a number of times as two different things (see for example Ps. 32:5, "The iniquity of my sin"). Sin is basically the cause, and iniquity includes the effect. Generational iniquity works like this: A parent can commit a sin such as occultic involvement or sexual sin and that produces a curse. The curse then causes a generational iniquity or weakness to pass down in the family line.

Here is an example that might clarify this process. A pregnant woman is X-rayed and the unborn child becomes deformed by the X ray. The unborn child didn't order the X ray and is entirely a victim but, nonetheless, is affected by the X ray. Sin, like the X ray, damages the generations. This is an awesome thought and should put the fear of the Lord in us before we enter into sin.

Just as venereal disease can produce physical deformity, so spiritual sin produces spiritual deformity in the generations. Although this book is not meant to be a complete teaching on breaking the power of the occult and witchcraft, I will mention some of the major problems people deal with generationally and how to break free of their power. Many Scripture references in the Bible speak of the evils of witchcraft, such as Deuteronomy 18:9-14 (AMP):

> When you come into the land which the Lord your God gives you, you shall not learn to follow the abominable prac-
> tices of these nations. There shall not be found among you

anyone who makes his son or daughter pass through the fire, or who uses divination, or is a soothsayer, or an augur, or a sorcerer, or a charmer, or a medium, or a wizard, or a necromancer. For all who do these things are an abomination to the Lord, and it is because of these abominable practices that the Lord your God is driving them out before you. You shall be blameless [and absolutely true] to the Lord your God. For these nations whom you shall dispossess listen to soothsayers and diviners. But as for you, the Lord your God has not allowed you to do so.

Identifying Generational Sins and Iniquities

Here are some areas to check for generational sin issues that might have produced iniquities in your life:

Occultic involvement and witchcraft. "Witchcraft is the power or practice of witches' sorcery; black magic."[6] Those who practice witchcraft may or may not claim to be satanists. Many who are witches purport to use the powers of nature for good or "white magic." One young man who was born again out of the Wicca pagan religion says, "There is no such thing as white and black magic. White magic is simply sugar-coated witchcraft but it is all from the power of Satan." Anything that draws its power from anything other than God is demonic in nature. This includes Ouija boards, astrology, tarot cards, water dowsers and "psychic healers." A helpful book about the error of psychic healing is *The Beautiful Side of Evil* by Johanna Michaelson (Harvest House Publishers).

In today's world, a resurgence of worship of the ancient gods such as Thor and Odin, goddess worship and so on is also occurring. This is nothing more than witchcraft. Peter Wagner talks about worship in the guise of renewal of culture in his book *Warfare Prayer* (Regal Books).

Secret societies. Involvement with societies such as Freemasonry, Eastern Star and the Shriners (all of which take oaths that are not biblical and are even against the Word of God) allow demonic access to the generations. Several good books are available on this subject, including *The Masonic Report* by C. F. McQuaig.

Many people innocently become involved with these organizations, drawn by the good works they do. These people leave themselves open to curses (which come from Deuteronomy 28) from idolatry and the like, which can affect their finances, cause physical infirmities and even insanity! One American minister came to me in tears while I was speaking in Argentina and said, "Cindy, I don't know what is wrong in my life. Even though I tithe, give offerings, am faithful to God and am not in any known sin, I still seem to have a curse of poverty on my finances."

As I began to pray for this minister, suddenly out of my mouth came the words, "And I break the curse of poverty that came from Freemasonry in your bloodline!" He commenced to weep and weep and praise the Lord. When he was able to speak, he chokingly sputtered, "Cindy, my great-grandfather helped bring Freemasonry into England." The curse was broken and as far as I know he is free and blessed to this day.

Robbing and defrauding God. "Will a man rob or defraud God? Yet you rob and defraud Me. But you say, In what way do we rob or defraud You? *[You have withheld your] tithes and offerings.* You are cursed with the curse, for you are robbing Me, even this whole nation" (Mal. 3:8,9, *AMP*, italics added).

Those whose families have not been tithers sometimes find that even when they begin tithing, they do not experience a financial breakthrough. Sometimes this is a result of a generational curse because their parents robbed God by neglecting to give back the portion rightfully due to Him.

Bondages. "Now after you have known God, or rather are known by God, how is it that you turn again to the weak and beggarly elements, to which you desire again to be in bondage?" (Gal. 4:9).

Bondages in the generations can pass down and become iniquities. Not all compulsions, addictions or sin habits necessarily began with our forefathers, but too often in Christian counseling this aspect is ignored. Although I believe we need to deal with today's issues and our own sin problems, it is also important to consider the sins of the fathers. I have seen people who have family histories of sexual sin or addiction become victimized again and again, even after receiving counseling, as a result of the legal right Satan has to hurt them through the generational sins of their fathers (compare Exod. 20:5; Eph. 4:26,27; Jas. 3:15). This right must be taken away through prayer, confession and repentance.

Dean Sherman gives this definition of bondages: "If we continue in a habit of sin, we can develop a bondage. A bondage means that there is a supernatural element to our problem. The enemy now has a grip on a function of our personality."[7] This is clearly what Paul is talking about in Ephesians 4:27 when he warns us not to give the devil a "foothold" through the sins mentioned in the context of Ephesians 4.

I am aware that some readers may be struggling with this concept of generational bondages, still believing these principles have no New Testament application. I can understand this. You may be familiar with the story of Simon in Acts 8. For a long time, Simon had astonished many in Samaria with his sorcery (see v. 11). Taking the Bible literally, verse 13 says that Simon was a baptized believer. The word used in this verse to indicate he was a believer is *pisteuo* ("believe"), which means to entrust one's spiritual well-being to Christ. This is the same root meaning as found in the word "believe" in Romans 10:9, "That if you confess with your mouth the Lord Jesus and believe in your heart that God has raised Him from the dead, you will be saved."

Although Simon was a Christian, Peter states the root of Simon's problem in Acts 8:23, "For I see that you are poisoned by bitterness and bound by iniquity." This former sorcerer had become a Christian but was still bound by iniquity.

Dealing with Generational Sins and Iniquities

It is crucial for all believers to be free of generational bondages and iniquities. It is absolutely critical for those who prophesy. This will become more and more apparent as we walk through this book together and delve into issues in chapter 4 concerning divination and the like. The ax must be laid to the root of all pulls of the carnal flesh as well as generational iniquities.

So how do we deal with generational sins and iniquities? I have identified the following seven steps:

1. Identify specifically the sin of your forefathers (this also includes foremothers) (see Lev. 26:40; 1 John 1:9).

2. Repent for the sin in a manner something like this (see Neh. 1:6; 9:2; Dan. 9:8,20): "Father God, I ask forgiveness for the sin of (witchcraft, lust or whatever you've specifically identified) and now repent for this sin to the third and fourth generations. I now renounce this sin and cut it off from myself and my seed and my seed's seed. By this prayer, I lay the ax to the root of this sin in my family line and break the power of the iniquity in Jesus' name. Amen."

One point of clarification. This is not praying for the dead. It is appointed unto man or woman once to die and then the judgment (see Heb. 9:27). Each person must stand before God on an individual basis. I like what Jim

Nightingale of Australia says, "It's not on behalf of their sin we are repenting, but because of their sin." When we repent in this manner, we are simply closing the door to any legal right Satan might have to afflict us or our families through the sins of our forefathers.

3. Break the power of any curses that might have come as a result of the sin. A sample prayer could be, "Father God, according to Deuteronomy 28, idolatry brings a curse. I thank You for forgiving the sin of idolatry of money. I now break the curse of poverty in Jesus' name. Thank You for setting me, as well as my generations, free in Jesus' name. I now apply the blood of the Lamb in faith to my generations."

4. Command any fruit of these generational sins to wither up and die in your life (and the lives of your children).

5. Ask the Lord to heal all negative effects of the generational iniquities in your life.

6. Identify the bondages and habits that have grown from these generational sins.

7. Take ownership of these bondages, habits and addictions. Confess them to the Lord and ask Him to work in your carnal nature to renew your mind in these areas. You may need to seek help from someone to break the bondages. James 5:16 gives us a beautiful promise concerning confessing our sins or trespasses. "Confess your trespasses to one another, and pray for one another, that you may be healed. The effective, fervent prayer of a righteous man avails much."

Prophetic people need to have the fear of the Lord operating in their lives much more than others. It is crucial that they be whole people. Whatever issues need to be dealt with, both past and present (selfishness, pride, brokenness from family of origin and so on), need to be brought under God's divine searchlight. The fire of God will purge and cleanse us as we allow the Holy Spirit to deal with bitterness and bring us to the place where we are vessels of honor in the service of the King. He will take out the parts of us that are our own flesh and cause us to be clean conduits of the flow of His power so He can bring great blessing to the Body of Christ.

Here's a prayer of consecration to ask the heavenly Father to do this work in our lives:

Lord, I now give all of myself to You. Bring to light those things that would distort my hearing Your voice. Show me any place where I am bitter and wounded. Cleanse me with Your precious blood from all unrighteousness. Do whatever is necessary to make me a whole person. Cleanse me from the iniquities in the generations of my family. Cleanse me of sin in my own past and present. I now give You permission to deal with me so I can change, be healed, restored and set free from any bondages in my life. I now pray like David in Psalm 51:10, "Create in me a clean heart, O God, and renew a steadfast spirit within me." In Jesus' name. Amen.

Now that we have learned about becoming a whole person as we listen for the Voice of God, we need to know if what we are hearing is actually from Him. The next chapter will give practical ways of knowing if what you are hearing is from God, and will help you judge the accuracy of something that has been spoken to you as a prophetic word.

PROPHECY IN PRACTICE

1. Have you ever met a "flaky" prophetic person?
2. How might the prophetic word be affected by generational iniquity?
3. Is the concept of generational iniquities new to you? Have a prayer partner pray with you to break any of their effects on your life now.
4. Are you working at becoming a whole person in every way possible?
5. What habits have become bondages in your life? Ask the Lord to help you recognize them so you can be free in every area of your life.

Notes
1. See examples in Genesis 18:20ff.; Exodus 32:7ff.; Daniel 7:1ff.; 8:1ff.; Luke 22:31; Acts 22:17ff.
2. John Sandford and Paula Sandford, *The Elijah Task* (Tulsa, Okla.: Victory House, Inc., 1977), p. 14.
3. Ibid., p. 156.
4. Ibid.

5. Quin Sherrer and Ruthanne Garlock, *A Woman's Guide to Breaking Bondages* (Ann Arbor: Servant Publications, 1994), p. 116.

6. Noah Webster, *Webster's New Twentieth Century Dictionary* (New York: Simon and Schuster, 1979), p. 2100.

7. Dean Sherman, *Spiritual Warfare for Every Christian* (Seattle: Frontline Communications, 1990), p. 107.

CHAPTER FOUR

"IS THAT YOU, GOD?":
Learning to Hear God's Voice

As we look around the world today, it doesn't take much spiritual discernment to realize that deception is running rampant. Even leaders we have looked up to for a long time are falling into serious sin and delusion. This is especially evident in the prophetic movements. Those considered major leaders are saying things that are causing the people in the church to scratch their heads and say, "Did you hear about what so-and-so prophesied? What do you think?"

MODERN-DAY DECEPTIONS

Recently, a prophecy was circulating that said on a certain date, evil would be taken out of the world. To tell you the truth, I personally prayed quite a bit about the date and the prophecy. I simply couldn't get peace about it. Each time it came up and I prayed, I seemed to feel absolutely nothing. No excitement, just concern—concern, because I knew if it didn't come to pass a huge backlash against the prophetic movement in general could occur. I think the person giving the prophecy was sincere and loves the Lord (perhaps God did a number of things in secret), but I've had to answer a lot of perplexed and upset people who felt let down because evil was not removed as they thought it would be. I'll talk about this more in chapter 6, "Mentoring the Prophetic Gift."

Another serious ripple occurred in a nation where it was prophesied that revival would come a certain year in the month of October. People waited and revival didn't come in a visible way. However, I often think of the fact that Jesus was born in a manger and His birth was an event that would impact the whole world. Yet, few people other than a group of shepherds, some wise men and a small handful of others realized the magnitude of the event or even that it had occurred!

Although these false prophecies happen, the benefits of the prophetic gifts far outweigh any problems that are caused. Houses catch fire and burn down but we still use fire. Fire used in its proper boundaries, such as in fireplaces, can bring warmth and comfort, while wildfire destroys. The danger is that some people, not being familiar with the move of the Holy Spirit, would label anything prophetic as wildfire. I hope that some of the guidelines in this chapter will help leaders and church members feel comfortable with prophetic words and moves of God while keeping satanic wildfire out of the church.

Another illustration comes from one of my real-life experiences. One day as I was driving down the highway, I looked to the right and beheld an awesome sight. Flames of fire were raging in a field and black billows of smoke were rolling across the sky. Knowing the fire could reach the town nearby, my mind raced to where I could find the closest phone to call the fire department. As I looked closer, I suddenly noticed a welcome sight. Firemen and farmers were burning the field, keeping a close watch on the fire. It was time to burn the stubble off the fields to ready them for a new harvest. The flames were under control. They were meant to help bring new life.

The farmers and the firemen were well versed in what they were doing and thus the fire was a blessing. However, a person in delusion could have set the fire, thinking to help the farmers, only to cause widespread destruction because he or she lacked the knowledge and safeguards of the experts.

Matthew 24:3,4 warns us that deception will be a sign of the latter days. Jesus' disciples approached Him and asked, "'And what will be the sign of Your coming, and of the end of the age?' And Jesus answered and said to them: 'Take heed that no one deceives you.'"

I have had people say to me, "Cindy, I could never be deceived." A wise minister once told me that if you don't think you can be deceived you already are! Much deception can take place in the area of personal prophecy. Part of this is because people are running around saying God is speaking. This doesn't leave much room for the person receiving the prophetic word to judge it on an individual level. This chapter will not only talk about how to test prophecy, but also will give safeguards against deception. For every real gift of God there is a counterfeit. A person can also be deceived into thinking that everything is counterfeit or everything is false. That is as much a deception as swallowing every prophecy hook, line and sinker!

When Mike and I were first married, I worked at a bank in California and had some rather strange people come through my teller line. I handled thousands of dollars every day and was able to find counterfeit bills upon occasion. How did I find them? By the way they felt in my hand and by the look of the bill. The texture was different or the ink seemed strange. This is one of the ways the real and counterfeit gifts can be discerned.

This chapter, as well as chapter 7, "Spiritual Protocol," will include so many do's and don'ts that you may wonder, *How will I ever remember all these guidelines?* I don't know how many of you drive a car, but at first it can be intimidating, especially when you are using a stick shift. You have to look before you pull out, put in the clutch, shift, let out the clutch, signal when you're turning and many other things. At first you think about these tasks one by one, but after you've driven awhile those things simply become second nature to you. Applying these principles about prophecy should eventually become second nature if you study and practice them.

One of the instances when these guidelines proved valuable to me was when a minister friend sent a letter to me that someone had given to him. The letter contained a prophetic word and the minister asked me to judge it. The minister is a powerful man of God but was just moving into an understanding of the prophetic.

I started to read the word, and at first it was right on target. Everything had a "green light," when all of a sudden I read a part that caused red lights to flash. The word took a turn, and an unclean element came in. It related how the man saw the Body of Christ as a naked woman on the operating table and this minister friend was going to give her a navel. At this point, I asked Mike to read the word and he had the same reaction. The part about the woman was definitely off base. We both took great exception with anything that seemed to say that God would show a male prophet a naked woman.

Later on in the evening, I called my minister friend and said, "This man has a sexual problem." I knew this was pretty strong because the prophetic word came from a recognized prophet. Nevertheless, I stuck by my conviction. My minister friend received my discernment and kept the part of the prophecy that was accurate. Months down the road, this prophet who had seen the woman was exposed as having a sexual problem. In fact, he was having women undress and then was prophesying over them, just as he had mentioned in the part of the prophecy that was in error.

A person may receive a prophetic word from God in a number of ways. A few of these ways include person to person (see Acts 21:10,11), God to an individual directly (see 10:19), through a dream or vision (see Matt. 1:20; Acts 9:10,11), by reading the Word (see Dan. 9:2-21) and by hearing the song of the Lord (a spontaneous prophetic song; see 1 Sam. 10:5; 1 Cor. 14:15; Eph. 5:19). Generally, the following guidelines will cover all of these ways, although additional fine points will be given in later chapters. As you study the points given in this book, I hope you will be able to discern in which of these ways you are receiving prophetic words.

The guidelines will be separated into two sections. The first section will cover how to test a prophecy you have received directly from the Lord, or through someone else. The second section will focus on how to respond to the prophetic word, or what to do once you know it is from God.

TESTING PROPHECY

In understanding how to test prophecy it is important to know that it is biblical. First Thessalonians 5:21 says, "Test all things; hold fast what is good." This first section will deal with how to "test all things" and the second section with how to "hold fast what is good."

1. Is what has been shared as a prophetic word scriptural?
Christians today need to know the Scriptures more than ever before. I personally believe all Christians should purchase, or have access to, a good concordance, such as Strong's, Young's or one their pastors recommend, so they can find Scripture references and read in context the verses that are given to them.

Married women have come to me on many occasions and told me that God told them their husbands were going to die so they would be free to remarry. One particularly sad instance happened at a women's meeting where I was speaking.

A young lady named Lucinda (not her real name) came to me and shared how God was going to cause a wonderful change to come into her life. When she said the words "a wonderful change," I started to feel uneasy. The feeling was strong enough to prompt me to probe a little more about what she meant. She said, "Oh, I'm going to get married."

I had noticed a wedding ring on her finger so I said with a little hesitation, "Aren't you already married?"

She looked uncomfortable and murmured in a hushed tone as she glanced around the room, "Yes, but the Lord told me I was going to marry a man I'll call Chris, one of our advisors, and he feels the same. Since I don't believe in divorce, we are just waiting on whatever God is going to do to my current husband."

When she said "Whatever God is going to do to my current husband," I started feeling extremely uneasy. Seeing my hesitancy, she went on to stutter, "You know, when he..." and her voice trailed off into thin air. She appeared shaken and whispered with tears in her eyes, "Cindy, God told me during a prayer meeting. One of our leaders said, 'The next voice you hear will be the Voice of God.' Right after she said that a voice said to me, 'And you will marry Chris.'"

At this juncture I gently said to her, "You have a really terrible marriage, don't you?"

She burst out weeping as I sensed her great pain. "Yes, oh yes, I do. My husband isn't a Christian and he's an alcoholic and I suffer so much from his abuse."

"Lucinda," I said, "do you honestly think your husband is ready to meet the Lord? Does God want your husband to burn in hell?" I waited a moment for this to sink in and then said, "Do you want him to die and go to hell without Christ?"

As I looked into her tear-stained face, I could see the deception breaking off her face. I carefully watched the tone of my voice so I would not sound condemning. I wanted to share the character of Christ as I said, "God isn't willing that any should perish. Do you honestly believe the voice you heard was the Voice of God?"

Lucinda quietly shook her head. She knew then that it hadn't been the Voice of God at all. It had been the voice of deception. Her personal pain made her an easy mark for the fiery dart of the evil one and created a vulnerability of which she wasn't aware.

I remember when a friend of mine, Pastor Bob Nichols of Calvary Cathedral in Fort Worth, Texas, said to me, "Cindy, all people need to know their 'hook in the jaw.' By this I mean, they need to know where they are vulnerable to deception."

One time I was having a terrible struggle trying to decide whether to speak at a Christian congress in Russia. If I accepted the speaking engagement, it would mean canceling several other previously booked meetings. It has always been my policy not to operate my ministry in this manner. However, the leader had said to me, "Cindy, you're the only woman speaker and we want you to speak for a main session. If you don't come, I'm not going to ask another woman."

I struggled for days. My husband kept thinking we should not cancel the previously set meetings, but I couldn't find peace one way or the other. Finally, I realized my vulnerability was the fear that I would not stand in the place of female leadership to which God has called me. After I realized this fear was a "hook in the jaw" where Satan could pull on me and deceive me, I experienced a complete release from the situation, and decided not to go.

2. Does the prophecy display the character of Christ?

Sometimes wolves in sheep's clothing manipulate Scripture for their own purposes. Just because someone is quoting chapter and verse to you doesn't make a prophecy accurate. Even if Scripture is being used, another area to check is to make sure Christ's character shines through the prophetic word. One of the most needful attributes to develop for those who prophesy is kindness. I love the verse that says, "The kindness of God leads you to repentance" (Rom. 2:4, *NASB*).

Sometimes, one of the kindest things you can do for a person is to share a corrective word. However, it is important that the word be shared in a way that the person can receive it. If the prophecy is too harsh or not shared with the love of Christ, it may so wound that the person who needs the correction may not be able to receive it. One of the greatest compliments I have ever received was from my friend Kay, who said, "You know, Cindy, I can take it when you have to share corrective things with me because I know you love me." More about this in chapter 6, "Mentoring the Prophetic Gift."

3. What is the fruit in the life of the person giving the prophecy?

This is crucial to consider. If the person is a stranger to you, you may not know the answer to this. But if it means rejecting or receiving the word, the Holy Spirit will help you discern correctly. I like the Scripture found in Luke 6:43-45:

> "For a good tree does not bear bad fruit, nor does a bad tree bear good fruit. For every tree is known by its own fruit. For

men do not gather figs from thorns, nor do they gather grapes from a bramble brush. A good man out of the good treasure of his heart brings forth good; and an evil man out of the evil treasure of his heart brings forth evil. For out of the abundance of the heart his mouth speaks."

Does he or she operate by a double standard? By this I mean, does the person say one thing but do something else in his or her personal life? On occasion, those who consistently preach strongly against sin in a harsh way are preaching to themselves. They may have deep, ungodly issues hidden in their personal lives.

Are they one person to the public and another to their families? Of course, everyone has off days, but I'm talking about doing this on a consistent basis. Do they have problems with anger? Angry people often give angry, Old Testament-type, doom-and-gloom prophecies. They don't understand the grace of God, so His grace is not extended to those to whom they prophesy.

I am not saying people will not be able to give you what could be an accurate word for your life if they have known sins or other problems. I have known this to happen. How the Lord allows such people to prophesy over you and have it be accurate can be confusing when they have personal issues that need changing. Though the word itself may be accurate, however, I believe it is possible that a negative or occultic power that is detrimental can be released because of these people's sins. These people may be flowing from divination.

Several years ago, a certain woman's hands bled, and many people were caught up with the belief that she was from God. She seemingly did some good, but was eventually found to be a charlatan. Some statues of idols bleed and cry tears; this is occultic, and though called the *stigmata*, it actually is a lying wonder (see Matt. 24:24; Mark 13:22).

4. Is anything tainting the word?

If people are not whole in certain areas or are not in touch with their biases, that can affect the way they prophesy. They may look at a person's outward appearance and it can influence what they pray or prophesy. This is what I refer to as "tainting" of the prophetic word. Remember the story about the prophet who had sexual sin in his life? This same kind of sin tainted the word given to my minister friend.

The following are some points to check to see if the word you are receiving is somehow tainted:

- Is the person critical or judgmental?

This will often "leak" into the prophetic word. Bruce Yocum, in his book *Prophecy*, says we should judge the spiritual tone and effect of the spirit of a prophecy. Prophecy that is frightening, harsh, condemning or critical seldom comes from the Holy Spirit. The Lord will often use prophecy to correct us and call us to repentance; sometimes He will even point out specific areas in our lives that are not right. But when God speaks to us, He does not condemn. Instead, He calls us to return to Him that He may forgive us and change us.

- As you examine the word given to you, is there any evidence of a religious bias?

For instance, once when I was being prayed for at a meeting, a man from a foreign country came up and rebuked me for being a woman leader. He said I should call my husband "lord" and kiss his feet. He brought both his religious bias and his cultural bias into the so-called word. Thank God for the men and women who were in the meeting. They took him aside and explained his problem to him.

Along with religious bias, I have seen those who use prophecy to promote their "pet" doctrines. They often rant and go on and on, which may stir up the spirit of the person to whom they are prophesying if that person also suffers from a religious spirit. Legalism also follows closely on the heels of people who have these biases.

5. What is the Holy Spirit giving me in the way of an inward witness?
We have a precious promise from the Lord in John 10:2-5 (*AMP*) about being able to tell if God is speaking through someone to us:

> But he who enters by the door is the shepherd of the sheep.
> The watchman opens the door for this man, and the sheep
> listen to his voice and heed it, and he calls his own sheep by
> name and brings (leads) them out. When he has brought his
> own sheep outside, he walks on before them, and the sheep

follow him because they know his voice. They will never [on any account] follow a stranger, but will run away from him because they do not know the voice of strangers or recognize their call.

When the Lord is speaking to us, an answer from within our hearts will cry, "Yes, that is God speaking to me." We will *resonate* with the word. This is what I mean by a witness in your spirit. Bruce Yocum says:

> There is a simple physical principle termed "resonance." Objects have certain characteristic frequencies at which they vibrate. If you cause one object (for instance a bell) to vibrate near another object with the same characteristic frequency (another bell of the same size and weight and shape), the second object will begin to vibrate by itself. That is something like what happens when we hear the voice of the Lord—we resonate.[1]

At times, people can present to you what they consider a personal prophecy, but inside you feel something like a scratching—a discomfort—or what I called earlier "a check in your spirit." Everything may sound scriptural and the words may sound okay. You may not be able immediately to put your finger on it but you know something isn't right.

You may be experiencing this discomfort for various reasons. For one, the word may be given through divination and not through the power of God. For another, you may have something inside of yourself that is blocking your receptivity to the prophecy.

Let's take the divination possibility first. "Divination is the practice of peering into the future or the unknown. It is Satan's copy of the gifts of knowledge and prophecy. Astrology participates in the sin of divination."[2] Deuteronomy 18:10 says, "There shall not be found among you...one who practices witchcraft,...or one who interprets omens."

The definition of the word *occult* means "to hide or become hidden from view,"[3] and divination is occultic, so it stands to reason that it might not always be easy to discern its practice when it seemingly is coming from a Christian.

Besides the inner witness of the Spirit, discerning divination in practice can be done in other ways. One is if the word doesn't bring glory to

God. A person can tell you where you live, your doctor's name and so on, but it will be divination if the word doesn't bring you closer to God. If you are impressed only by the power of the person displaying the knowledge, the source of the power might be questionable. Of course, God is able to—and does—give very detailed accounts to people about their lives. God does this to show us He is interested in everything about us. When God speaks, we will know that such accounts have a proper basis. When I am speaking to a group, it is not uncommon for the Lord to give me a proper name of a person to call out with a prophecy in a very detailed fashion.

It is possible to be accused of operating in divination when you really aren't. This happened to me when I was moving out deeply in prophecy in a church that didn't understand the operation of the gifts of the Spirit. Although it was a painful experience, it was a good opportunity for me to grow in the grace of the Lord.

As I said earlier, a second reason you may feel agitated about receiving a prophetic word is because of a block from within yourself. I'll deal with this later in the chapter in the section on responding to the prophetic word.

6. Is the prophecy from God?

According to Roxanne Brant, a prophetic word can have three possible sources:

- The Spirit of God or the Spirit of Truth;
- The Spirit of Error or Demonic Spirits;
- The Flesh.[4]

This chapter has covered a lot of material about how to know if a prophetic word is from the Spirit of God. God's prophetic word will never contradict His written Word in principle, character or exact Scripture. Brant says:

It is quite possible for a prophet to start out in the Spirit and end up in the flesh. This happened in the third century to the prophetic movement when false prophecy exploded and such deception entered into Montanus, who was a major leader at that time, that he eventually claimed he himself was the promised Paraclete. Montanus went on to purport that he would reveal to the Church the things which Jesus said that He could not in His earthly life tell His apostles, for they would not be able to hear it at that moment of time.[5]

Regarding the end times, 1 Timothy 4:1,2 says, "Now the Spirit expressly says that in latter times some will depart from the faith, giving heed to deceiving spirits and doctrines of demons, speaking lies in hypocrisy, having their own conscience seared with a hot iron."

I personally believe we are in the end times, so we need to be more careful than any previous generation not to be seduced by deceiving spirits. It is possible for people to be oppressed by demonic spirits of deception that influence the believers through their prophecies. Thus, the words they give are a mixed bag; not all are from the Spirit of God. To illustrate how this can affect a person, let me share a story.

One cold crisp day I received a phone call. The voice on the other end of the line said, "Cindy, would you come pray for a friend of mine? She's in terrible shape and has fallen into adultery."

Now, in those days I was doing more personal deliverance than I do now and I said, "Sure, I'll be right over." As I drove into the country where my friend lived I began to pray, "Lord, tell me about this situation." Almost immediately I sensed from the Lord that the troubled woman had been deceived by a demonic spirit and had become demonized herself.

When I arrived and got out of my car, I noticed the lady was still sitting in her automobile. While I walked to the car to greet her, the Holy Spirit alerted me that the spirits in her were going to cause her to run away as soon as I opened the car door! Acting on this information, I quickly opened the door, reached out and swiftly grabbed her by the arm and gave this command, "In the name of Jesus, I bind you, Satan, from operating in this woman's life. You will not cause your demonic spirits to use her hands, arms, legs or mouth." (Sometimes demonized people bite!)

After this, I gently spoke to her and said, "Do you want to come with me now?" She followed me into the house like a little lamb. When we got into the house, she said, "Cindy, I was going to run as soon as you opened the car door. I'm so glad I didn't because I really want to be free." Once the influence of the demonic powers were bound, the real person was able to express her desire for deliverance.

As we sat on the floor of my friend's living room, she urgently unfolded her sad story. She wrung her hands continually and would hardly look into my eyes. When I did look into those eyes, they were full of shame. "I can hardly bear to tell you what has happened to me," she murmured quietly, "but here goes."

Evidently she had attended a revival meeting at her local church in a small western town. The handsome young evangelist conducting the meetings started flattering her. She was a married woman but was vulnerable to his attentions. He was also the brother of a famous televangelist. This contributed to her being star struck. Eventually he talked her into going to bed with him. This went on repeatedly during the meetings. Each time they had sexual relations he had her pray with him for God to forgive them of adultery. Sadly, he was seduced into believing this would make everything all right with God!

As I prayed with her, tears started streaming down her face. She was completely set free from deception and went back to her husband to begin their relationship again.

Besides being influenced by demonic spirits, it is also possible to be deceived simply by the desires of your own flesh. Sometimes people "cast out the flesh and crucify the demons." In other words, they keep blaming things on demonic spirits that are solely the results of their own carnal natures.

Roxanne Brant says, "Often, we find a mixture of the flesh operating through a person at the same time that God's Spirit uses that person. It is important for Christians to know that this can happen."[6] This kind of dichotomy was the case with Peter when he professed Jesus to be "the Son of the living God" (Matt. 16:16), only immediately to contradict Jesus, and later to deny Him three times (see 16:22; 26:75).

Often dire consequences occur when we come under the influence of someone operating strongly in the flesh. Jane Hansen, head of Women's Aglow Fellowship International, tells the story in her book, *Inside a Woman* (Aglow Publications), of how she was divorced at an early age.

Jane shares how a wrong prophecy pushed her into making a grave mistake in her life. When she was 18, one of the ministers who came to speak at her dad's church came to her and said that God had told him they were to be married. This frightened her terribly. Rather than marry the one who gave her the "prophecy," she married another young man in reaction to what had been told her as being from God. The relationship ended in pain and tragedy. Unfortunately, I have heard variations of this story again and again from both men and women.

RESPONDING TO THE PROPHETIC WORD

Once you are fairly certain that the prophetic word you have been given is from God, you need to know how to interpret the word accurately (i.e., discern what God is trying to say through the prophecy). Many people have received prophecies that were accurate, but these people have gotten into a lot of trouble through misinterpretation or misapplication of the prophetic words. Here are some steps I would suggest you might want to follow.

1. Try, if possible, to tape-record the prophetic word as the person gives it (or write it down). I personally try to tape most of the prophecies I give because a recording offers much more accountability. I also find that it prevents my being misquoted or part of the prophecy being taken out of context.

One time I was prophesying over a young couple at our home-cell meeting. The couple had been struggling financially for quite some time. The prophecy said that God was going to give them a house if the husband would be diligent in his work and do his part, and if he would be obedient to God in every area of his life. I heard through the grapevine later that this couple had bought a trailer on credit. Still later, I heard that the trailer had been repossessed and that the couple was mad at me and accusing me of being a false prophetess! Neither of them ever went out to get a job, however; they expected the money to fall from heaven. They were in serious presumption and took the prophecy about the house totally out of context. Not once did they try to contact me to clarify the word. I, unfortunately, found out about the misinterpretation too late to be able to help them.

I believe that all prophecy is conditional upon our obeying God's laws even if the word itself does not specifically say it is conditional.

2. Write the prophecy down and share it with someone you respect who is an "elder" in the Spirit (i.e., more spiritually mature than you) and knows something about testing prophecy. Are any conditions to the prophetic word being fulfilled? More about this in chapter 7, "Spiritual Protocol."

3. Be careful not to interpret the word in the light of your own wants and desires. I have had many singles come to me saying God has promised them certain mates because they were told so in prophecies. When I asked them what the prophecies said, they came up with something like, "God said He would give me the desires of my heart and so-

and-so is the desire of my heart." As I wrote earlier in this chapter, that may be the desire of their flesh but God may not have anything to do with it at all.

A couple I know stopped me one time at a meeting and said, "We're getting ready to move to (some faraway place)." I was rather stunned because I strongly doubted it was God's will for their lives. They looked puzzled and said, "Why, Cindy, don't you remember giving us the word that change is coming?" When the word "Change is coming" is given, it is important to let God bring further specific confirmation about what that change is and what it entails.

I remember hearing a sad joke about a couple who went forward on a vague prophecy without getting further specific confirmation from the Lord. This couple had been looking at a map one day and decided God was calling them to a very remote island, far away in the south seas. They didn't do any research on the island nor did they ask their pastor to pray with them about their decision.

Time passed and the couple sold all their furniture and their home. At each step of the way they kept saying, "Lord, are we in presumption?" Yet, they never went to anyone in spiritual authority over them to test what they thought they had heard from the Lord. The day came to leave and they got on the plane, saying the same thing, "Lord, is this presumption?" They still had not done any physical research about the island.

Finally, they arrived after a long, difficult trip. As they got off the plane, one thing became instantly apparent. They were in the wrong place at the wrong time. The nation was in civil war and soldiers with heavy artillery were shooting at their plane. The last thought each of them had as they were dying was, *Lord, were we in presumption?* In heaven, they thought, *Never mind, Lord, we're with You now.*

4. What is the timing of the prophetic word given to you? Of course, this can be difficult to ascertain, but remember, if you follow proper checks and balances, the timing of a word will become clear to you. Unfortunately, people run ahead of God and suffer terrible financial consequences or family problems because they simply don't wait for the proper time. Sadly, whole families suffer because parents think they have "heard from God." Time and time again I have prayed with children whose godly parents moved in presumption and then the children were angry at God for the whole mess.

Most people probably miss the timing of God in a particular area of their lives at one time or another. I know I certainly have. However, I've tried to learn from my blunders. I am aware that everyone is going to make mistakes. I just pray that mine will be small instead of big ones.

The following questions will help you stay out of presumption and follow the timing of God:

- Is this consistent with everything God has been saying about my life?
- How will this affect my current responsibilities? For example, will I be able to take care of my family financially? What kind of stress will this put on my family? Are they willing to sacrifice what will be required if I make these changes in my life?
- Have I reached a maturity level in my life that will enable me to perform with integrity the new tasks and/or changes, or will I flake out because I am not properly prepared?
- Do brothers and sisters in the Lord witness to this word, especially those in authority over me?

5. Believe God to fulfill the prophecy in His own time and way. Some people say that every prophecy should be put on a shelf. I agree this needs to be done with some prophecies, but not all of them. Certain prophecies need to be prayerfully warred over so that satanic opposition will not keep them from being fulfilled. Paul knew this principle and exhorted Timothy in 1 Timothy 1:18 (italics added), "This charge I commit to you, son Timothy, according to the prophecies *previously made concerning you, that by them you may wage the good warfare.*"

A CONFIRMING GOD

Many people have had prophecies concerning their children while the children are still in rebellion. The parents have to pray diligently about these prophecies because Satan wants to destroy their heritage. The words are to encourage the parents to keep on warring, praying and believing.

Others will try to lead you to believe that prophecies should only concern what you already know. In other words, they should be confirmation only. It's true, prophecy does confirm; however, that is only part of what prophecy accomplishes. I have had prophecies given to me at times that were so huge they boggled my mind. I had never ever thought of doing the things the person was prophesying. One that comes to mind was given to me by Bill Hamon in a meeting in 1984.

My husband, Mike, and I were attending a prophetic conference in Phoenix, Arizona, when a man made a beeline for us. He introduced himself as Bill Hamon and said, "God has a word for you." He proceeded to hold up my hand and pronounce, "You will be the wrist joint that holds together the hand and the rest of the Body of Christ in intercessory prayer. The fingers are the major Christian leaders." He went on to name five people who were Christian household names, none of which I had come anywhere close to meeting.

When he finished, I simply stood there, stunned at what I had just heard. A thousand thoughts were whipping through my brain. *How could that happen? I don't know any of those people. What a strange word...a wrist joint!* Little did I know that the very next year the Lord would give me the mandate to gather the "generals of intercession" to pray for the nations. Today, the people named in that prophecy are people with whom I teach and pray at conferences throughout the world.

A good thing to remember is this: *God never minds confirming His word to us.* Matthew 18:16 says, "By the mouth of two or three witnesses every word may be established." If you are unsure whether something is from God, ask Him for further confirmation. I have had Him graciously confirm prophecies to me again and again until I was sure they were from Him. He will confirm the word in many ways for you.

Remember, it rarely hurts to wait. If I am feeling pressured, I usually dig in my heels and spend time praying and seeking the Lord, waiting until I am really sure. Here is a good rule of thumb: Satan drives but the Holy Spirit guides. If Satan cannot get you to disregard God's word to you, he will try to ruin you through doing it too soon.

It is crucial to understand the difference between Old and New Testament prophecy to properly discharge a prophetic word. We'll talk about this in the next chapter, entitled "Redemptive Prophecy."

PROPHECY IN PRACTICE

1. Do you know anyone who has come into serious deception? Can you discern the steps that led to that person's full-blown deception?

2. Examine your life and see if you have any blind spots or serious spiritual weaknesses. Ask a friend to pray with you to determine if you might need to deal with areas that could lead to deception.
3. Have you ever been give a personal prophecy? How do you test the word?
4. Has there ever been a time when a personal prophecy was a great blessing in your life?
5. Do you think you might not have received the fullest blessing from a prophecy because you didn't know how to respond to what was given to you?

Notes

1. Bruce Yocum, *Prophecy* (Ann Arbor: Servant Publications, 1976), p. 115.
2. John Sandford and Paula Sandford, *Healing the Wounded Spirit* (Tulsa, Okla.: Victory House, Inc., 1985), p. 293.
3. Noah Webster, *Webster's New Twentieth Century Dictionary* (New York: Simon and Schuster, 1979), p. 1237.
4. Roxanne Brant, *How to Test Prophecy, Preaching and Guidance* (O'Brien, Fla.: Roxanne Brant Ministries, 1981), p. 26
5. Ibid., p. 30.
6. Ibid., p. 28.

CHAPTER FIVE

REDEMPTIVE PROPHECY

■

Several years ago, I was asked by my good friend Peter Wagner to teach a retreat for his Sunday School class, the 120 Fellowship. He specifically requested that I share on the subject of prophecy. Around this time, many people had a great interest in the subject, but it was also extremely controversial in some circles.

During the weekend retreat, I prayed for all those present and asked the Lord to release the spirit of prophecy in our midst. I have found that when I pray this kind of prayer, the Lord stirs up the ability to prophesy in a corporate way and God is glorified through the resulting testimonies (see Rev. 19:10).

This Sunday School group was fairly familiar with praying for each other for healing, at which times they would sometimes receive information from the Lord in a supernatural way about a person's ailments. Knowing this, I thought they could take this understanding and ask the Holy Spirit to give them facts about each other that would go far beyond their natural knowledge.

I also prayed and asked the Holy Spirit to bring to their minds thoughts that would be great blessings to those for whom they were praying—thoughts that would confirm that God was intimately aware of their problems, needs and concerns. After I had prayed, they gathered in groups of two or three to pray.

What happened was amazing! As the class members believed that God would give them special insight for the persons they were praying for and trusted God for specific details, they were touched by how the Holy Spirit prayed through them. In fact, I couldn't say who was more blessed, the person being prayed for or the person who received and then prayed with such accurate details!

As we shared testimonies after the prayer time, I asked both the person who received a blessing by being prayed for *and* the person who prayed to testify together. At times, they were both so eager to share that their words bumped into each other in the excitement of what God had done. One said, "I hadn't told anyone in the class about my financial troubles but Sally (or Sue or Jim or whoever) prayed exactly for my need." Another would share, "I've been trying to make a decision and so-and-so prayed that God would give me guidance at this time in my life."

A very important thing happened for the Sunday School members that day. *They realized God intimately knew them.* It was redemptive, life-bringing and freeing. The details prayed were just what they needed to hear.

PRAYING PROPHETICALLY FOR ONE ANOTHER

Peter Wagner, in his book *Churches That Pray,* has this comment, "Many of us are now beginning to experience two-way prayer and are hearing the voice of God. As we grow in this area, we can expect much of our rhetoric prayer to be changed to exciting action prayer."[1]

The next day at the retreat I taught again on prophecy and then announced that I was going to prophesy. I purposely did not prophesy the first day because I didn't want to intimidate the group members before they had a chance to try their wings through prophetic prayers. Peter Wagner talks about that day in *Churches That Pray:*

> Cindy not only taught us prophecy, but she announced to us the second day that she was going to prophesy. This was something different and slightly risky to us Congregationalists, most of whom may have heard about personal prophecy but had never been up close to it in this way. As I observed Cindy, I noticed she was following all the rules Bill Hamon [a respected prophet and author of the book *Prophets and Personal Prophecy*] had spelled out.
>
> The resulting ministry was truly remarkable, and to this day many attendees date important changes in their lives to that retreat. We transcribed and published the prophecies in our *Body Life* newsletter, and in subsequent newsletters many

class members shared testimonies of healing in their lives. One prophecy that Doris and I will long remember was the healing of some chronic addictions in our own nephew, Jon Mueller.[2]

I quoted this last section to focus on the prophecy given to Jon Mueller. At that time, I had never met Jon, nor did I know he was Peter and Doris's nephew nor anything about him. I didn't know he was hooked on snuff (a form of chewing tobacco) and addicted to alcohol. One day when I was batting around ideas for this chapter, I asked Jon if he would mind if I used his story in this book and he quickly agreed.

In interviewing Jon, he started his story this way:

Cindy, I was addicted to snuff and alcohol and I had been hiding it from everybody, living a double life. Although I could not stand myself for it, I was too ashamed to tell anyone. That was why I had my snuff rolled up in my sock where nobody could see it. I also had been hiding my problem with drinking.

When you called me to the front to share the prophecy with me, I didn't know what was going to happen, but I loved God and wanted a change in my life. Interestingly enough, you didn't directly address my addictions. Instead, you began to speak about the destiny of God on my life. How God had powerful plans to use me for His kingdom.

The power of God through the prophecy was so strong that Jon was completely delivered from snuff and alcohol and hasn't needed them since. Jon heard the Voice of God speak to him that day and it healed deep issues of rejection and pain, which were the reasons for his addictions. God knew about Jon, cared personally and had a destiny for his life!

REDEMPTIVE PROPHECY

That kind of prophecy is what I call redemptive prophecy. Redemptive prophecy is that which speaks to the destiny of God for an individual in a life-bringing, redemptive way. Although as I looked at Jon I was sensing some things about him that were bondages, at that point, God wanted Jon to know how valuable and precious he was. This brought great comfort and joy to Jon and made him want to reject the bondages in his life. He started agreeing with the Lord, hope rose up, and this caused him to be set free from the addictions holding him captive.

When I have a prophecy for someone, the Holy Spirit might bring to my mind things that need correcting. I have found, however, that He usually wants me to go away and pray about those things rather than to openly rebuke the person. In my opinion, it is only on rare occasions that the Lord would have a person rebuked through a prophetic word in a public arena. If the person has been privately warned again and again and is in extreme rebellion, it is possible that the only way the person can be reached is through a strong prophecy that gives a huge warning or a stop sign.

Redemptive Conviction

A biblical example of a redemptive prophecy would be the story of David, and Nathan the prophet, in 2 Samuel 12:1-4. After David's sin with Bathsheba and the murder of Uriah, Nathan went to David and prophesied to the righteous leader's heart through a prophetic parable. He spoke to the protective nature of David for his people to awaken the standard of righteousness in him and to break the deception into which this great leader had fallen. As far as Scripture indicates, Nathan went to David one-on-one to give the strong correction, instead of denouncing him in the streets.

Nathan told a story to David about a poor man who had one little lamb and a rich man who had exceedingly many flocks and herds. He drew a word picture of how the rich man had stolen the only lamb of the poor man. This caused David to be extremely angry at the rich man in the story and he cried out, "As the Lord lives, the man who has done this shall surely die! And he shall restore fourfold for the lamb, because he did this thing and because he had no pity" (vv. 5,6).

After this, the prophet Nathan issued a strong judgment and David was deeply convicted of his sin. Why was the conviction so strong? One reason may be because it was redemptive even though it included judgment. The prophecy spoke to the good things in David's life, his sense of justice and right and wrong. It spoke to his destiny in God as a ruler. This kind of redemptive prophecy or correction is an important strategy in learning to prophesy and will be discussed more in subsequent chapters.

Redemptive Proclamation

Another example of a redemptive prophetic word being given is through the angel Gabriel to Mary, the future mother of Jesus. Startled as she must have been by the angelic announcement "And behold, you will conceive in your womb and bring forth a Son, and shall call His name Jesus" (Luke 1:31), things resonated within Mary that told her this proclamation was true.

I have been told that when each girl of Mary's time reached puberty it was proclaimed, "May you be the one!" Which one were they talking about? Why, the mother of the Messiah, of course. It is possible that Mary's thoughts shifted quickly to the prophecies about the Messiah being from the house and lineage of David. She was a descendant of David as was her espoused husband, Joseph.

To further confirm that what Gabriel said was from God, he gave her some interesting news, "Elizabeth your relative has also conceived a son in her old age; and this is now the sixth month for her who was called barren" (v. 36). Remember, I said God never minds confirming His word? The questions Mary asked the angel were answered in a way that resonated through her and out of her heart burst the cry, "Behold the maidservant of the Lord! Let it be to me according to your word" (v. 38).

The Lord in His merciful redemptive way knew that what little Mary would deal with was monumental in her culture (I say "little Mary" because girls were usually betrothed soon after puberty, around age 14 or so). One consequence for conception out of wedlock was death by stoning. Mary's heavenly Father, however, had a hiding place for her that would protect, strengthen and confirm what the angel said—her cousin Elizabeth's house.

Do you recall how Gabriel told Mary that her previously barren cousin was with child? If I were Mary, I would have desperately wanted to see Elizabeth and find out if she were pregnant so I wouldn't think I had been having angelic hallucinations!

I do not think God wanted Mary to have to wait one second longer than necessary for this confirmation. The moment she greeted Elizabeth, an exciting thing happened—the baby leaped in Elizabeth's womb and *she* began to prophesy with a loud voice:

> "Blessed are you among women, and blessed is the fruit of
> your womb! But why is this granted to me, that the mother

of my Lord should come to me? For indeed, as soon as the voice of your greeting sounded in my ears, the babe leaped in my womb for joy. *Blessed is she who believed, for there will be a fulfillment of those things which were told her from the Lord*" (vv. 42-45, italics added).

Isn't it interesting that the prophet John the Baptist prophesied from inside the womb about the coming of the Lord in a leap for joy? What a case for the argument that babies can experience emotions in the womb!

You know, Mary must have had a lot of doubts about what had occurred in her meeting with the angel, but God did not rebuke her for wondering. He knows our frames and weaknesses and is tender and redemptive as He tells us of things to come. What a great example of the father-heart of God and the tenderness with which we should prophesy to the Lord's children.

Just as the Lord dealt with Mary with love and kindness, so He expects those who prophesy to manifest His love toward those to whom they are speaking. First Corinthians 13:2 (*AMP*) says it this way:

> And if I have prophetic powers (the gift of interpreting the divine will and purpose), and understand all the secret truths and mysteries and possess all knowledge, and if I have [sufficient] faith so that I can remove mountains, but have not love (God's love in me) I am nothing (a useless nobody).

Pretty strong? Sometimes I read through this love chapter and repent for any way I have not shown Christlike love. (Maybe I need to do that more than I do. Perhaps we all should.) We need to keep 1 Corinthians 13 in mind as we prophesy to people. If I have a corrective word to give to someone, I will at times walk the floor, praying about it for a couple of days or more, seeking the Lord for the right timing and way to give the word. One of the plumb lines of my prophetic life has to do with my attitude toward the person to whom I am giving a corrective word. If I have any animosity, bitterness or anger in my heart toward the person, or if I relish being the one to give the corrective word because that person has wounded me in any way, I am not the one to give the word. Either I have to cleanse my heart before I give the word or God will use another purer vessel to do His work. This will be covered more extensively in the next chapter, "Mentoring the Prophetic Gift."

OLD AND NEW TESTAMENT PROPHECY

As most of you who are reading this probably know, the Holy Spirit was not given to each person in the Old Testament (see for example Num. 11:25). The prophets were specially appointed and anointed spokespersons for God. When people were true prophets, their prophesying was consistently accurate (see Deut. 18:21,22), their prophesying and teaching led people to worship the Lord alone (see vv. 15-20; cf. 13:2,3), and they bore good fruit in their lives and ministries (see the contrasts in Jer. 23:10,11,14). This does not mean that true prophets never prophesied inaccurately. Scripture makes it clear that on occasion true prophets knowingly or unknowingly prophesied inaccurately, though they were not put to death or branded false prophets for such inaccuracies. (See for example 2 Sam. 7:3ff.; 1 Kings 22:15.) Jeremiah seemed uncertain that he had heard the word of the Lord accurately until it was confirmed by corresponding events: "Then I *knew* that this was the word of the Lord" (Jer. 32:8, italics added). The inference was that until that moment, Jeremiah was not certain that what he had heard was indeed a true word from the Lord.

What separated false prophets from true prophets was more than just consistency in prophetic accuracy. False prophets were, by contrast, presumptuous and proud in attitude (see Deut. 18:20; 1 Kings 13:18; 22:24; Jer. 23; Ezek. 13); they bore bad fruit in their lives and ministries (see Jer. 23:10,11,14); they were consistently inaccurate in their prohecies (see Deut. 18:22; Jer. 23:10-32; Ezek. 13:10-19); and in cases where they did manage to prophesy accurately, their prophesying and teaching led people away from worshiping and obeying the Lord alone (see Deut. 13:2; 18:20).

It was critical for true prophets to give the word of God because this was the main way God spoke to His people at that time. A strong admonition was given to Ezekiel to speak the word God gave him:

> "When I say to the wicked, 'You shall surely die,' and you give him no warning, nor speak to warn the wicked from his wicked way, to save his life, that some wicked man shall die in his iniquity; but his blood I will require at your hand. Yet, if you warn the wicked, and he does not turn form his wickedness, nor from his wicked way, he shall die in his iniquity; but you have delivered your soul" (Ezek. 3:18,19).

I have talked with some young emerging prophets and prophetesses who are very confused on this issue. It causes them to miss God's timing as they push their way in where they become out of order. They then appear wild-eyed and weirdly mystical because they thought no one else could speak God's word except them. It is true that we are personally responsible before God to give a prophecy when He asks us to. If in our disobedience we do not give the prophecy and the person does not hear it, the blood of that person is upon the prophet's or prophetesses' hand (see Ezek. 33:6), but consider this—the Holy Spirit often prompts more than one prophet with the same word for a person, as insurance that His word will not fail to be given. If one person is not obedient, He will use another. Unlike Old Testament times, many people now have the power of the Holy Spirit, not just a select few.

I have always held the opinion that Old Testament prophets were so divinely inspired that everything they said was always 100 percent accurate, or they were considered false prophets and were stoned to death. My good friend John Sandford, however, urged me to study further. As was stated earlier, recorded instances of Old Testament prophets reveal that they were neither put to death nor branded false prophets for inaccuracies. This was puzzling to me. It also led me to reread passages such as Deuteronomy 18:20-22 (italics added):

> "'But the prophet who *presumes* to speak a word in My name, which I have not commanded him to speak, or who speaks in the name of other gods, that prophet shall die.' And if you say in your heart, 'How shall we know the word which the Lord has not spoken?'—when a prophet speaks in the name of the Lord, if the thing does not happen or come to pass, that is the thing which the Lord has not spoken; the prophet has spoken it *presumptuously;* you shall not be afraid of him."

According to Gary Greig, associate professor of Hebrew and Old Testament at Regent University, Virginia Beach, Virginia, the word "presumes" in the Hebrew of Deuteronomy 18:20 carries the connotation of being proud and insolent in attitude. Gary also gives the following points as the difference between true and false prophets in the Old Testament:

The difference between the two is *not* that the true prophets were 100 percent accurate, while false prophets made mistakes. False prophets bore bad fruit and seemed to have been consistently inaccurate.

- *False prophets* may have been *recognized in the past* to be *true prophets* of the Lord—they may have had a reputation of hearing from the Lord and prophesying accurately in the past (see for example 1 Kings 13:11-20);
- *False prophets* were *presumptuous, proud and insolent* in attitude (see Deut. 18:20; 1 Kings 13:22; Jer. 23; Ezek. 13);
- *False prophets* bore *bad fruit*—their motives and actions were evil and they encouraged evil and disobedience to the Lord (see Jer. 23:10,11);
- *False prophets'* teaching and prophesying led people *away from the Lord* (see Deut. 13:2; 18:20);
- *False prophets* seem to have been *consistently inaccurate* in their prophesying according to Jeremiah 23:10-22 and Ezekiel 13:10-19. When false prophets were accurate, their prophesying and teaching led people away from worshiping and obeying the Lord alone (see Deut. 13:2; 18:20).

True prophets, according to Gary, by contrast to false prophets, bore good fruit, were godly, humble, submitted to the Lord and encouraged godliness. Their teaching and prophesying led people to the Lord and they were more consistently accurate than false prophets (which is the whole point of the story of Micaiah in 1 Kings 22:25-28; see also Deut. 18:18-22; 1 Sam. 3:19).

In Deuteronomy 13:1-3,5 we read:

> "If there arises among you a prophet or a dreamer of dreams, and he gives you a sign or a wonder, and the sign or the wonder comes to pass, of which he spoke to you, saying, 'Let us go after other gods'—which you have not known—'and let us serve them,' you shall not listen to the words of that prophet or that dreamer of dreams, for the Lord your God is testing you to know whether you love the Lord your God with all your heart and with all your soul. But that prophet or that dreamer of dreams shall be put to death, because he has spoken in order to turn you away from the Lord your God, who brought you out of the land of Egypt and redeemed you from the house of bondage, to entice you from the way in which the Lord your God commanded you to walk. So you shall put away the evil from your midst."

I realize this is not what many, including myself, have been taught for years about Old Testament prophets, but I encourage you to pray about it, search the Scriptures and consider it.

Here are some thoughts that emerged after I studied this issue further:

1. The teaching that all Old Testament prophets were always 100 percent accurate, or that they were false, has created a sense that they were "better" or of a higher caliber than today's prophets.

As I meditated upon this, I pondered, *That teaching seems to infer that the Old Testament prophets had more power of the Holy Spirit poured upon them than the Church received on the Day of Pentecost.* The Old Testament prophets, however, didn't have the revelation we have had since Jesus came to earth, neither did they have the insights of the New Testament. Shouldn't the prophecies we receive today be greater in measure than the prophecies of the Old Testament? In principle, God seems to always save the new wine, or the best, for the last. Wouldn't it be the same with prophecy?

I am not saying that today's prophecies, both those that have been given and those yet to come, are greater than those given in Scripture. The Old Testament prophets, however, were human—they made mistakes, but were not always stoned for doing so. If Old Testament prophets who gave inaccurate words were stoned, why wasn't Nathan stoned when he prophesied inaccurately to David? Why wasn't Micaiah stoned when he lied before giving God's true word (see 1 Kings 22:15)?

2. This teaching has led to the erroneous thinking that all New Testament prophets have to be 100 percent accurate or they or not true prophets or prophetesses of God. Many prophetic people have suffered harsh criticism and have been publicly denounced because of this teaching. It is true that they will consistently be accurate in their prophecies and bear the godly fruit of the Spirit in their daily lives.

In the Old Testament, prophets were the main people who heard from God—people such as Moses, Daniel, David and Deborah. Therefore, if they did not discharge what God was saying, the people would not hear. Today, however, if a person does not hear the Holy Spirit, God has many more avenues through which to speak to His people. God's prophetic word to His people doesn't depend on just a small group of prophets anymore. Although God certainly does use prophets today in the Church and the Ezekiel passage is still applicable, God will use many to prophesy to His people. Of course, if prophets are in disobedience or rebellious to do what God asks of them, they will certainly have to answer to the Lord.

On the Day of Pentecost, the Holy Spirit was poured out on all flesh. Peter illuminated what had occurred on that day in his sermon in Acts 2:17,18:

> "'And it shall come to pass in the last days, says God, that I will pour out of My Spirit on all flesh; your sons and your daughters shall prophesy....And on My menservants and on My maidservants I will pour out My Spirit in those days; and they shall prophesy.'"

The ability to hear from God on an individual basis and perhaps even to prophesy is a powerful concept. Prophesying is strongly encouraged in the Bible. First Corinthians 14:1 says, "Pursue love, and desire spiritual gifts, but especially that you may prophesy." This is again emphasized in verse 39 of the same chapter, "Desire earnestly to prophesy."

This passage seems clearly to be saying that all believers will have the ability to prophesy. This does not mean they all *will* necessarily prophesy but, unlike the Old Testament dispensation, they have the power of the Holy Spirit in them to do so.

I was discussing this concept with my good friend and author Gary Kinnaman, pastor of Word of Grace Church in Mesa, Arizona. (One of my greatest joys is to have a dialogue with my pastor friends on subjects I'm writing about or teaching on to help keep me straight.) Gary commented to me, "Cindy, I think one of the most significant signs of Pentecost was the power for all to prophesy." He went on to expound, "Prophecy is not just to give a word of revelation, but also the power to see into and utilize the spiritual dimension." I certainly agree and also feel it is one of the most *overlooked* aspects of Pentecost.

When I was growing up in my family's church, the only kind of prophecy I heard about was end-time prophecy; nothing is wrong with that. But I was never introduced to the *concept* of personal prophecy spoken of as a fulfillment of the outpouring of the Holy Spirit in the last days. According to the signs given us in the Bible, however, we certainly are in the end-time or latter days.

We read that New Testament prophets only prophesy "in part" (1 Cor. 13:9). Although many accurate prophets filter little of what they are hearing from the Holy Spirit through their own personal emotions, thoughts and opinions, I do not believe anyone is 100 percent accurate. I know I strive to be extremely accurate and not add the interpretations of

Cindy Jacobs to what God is saying to me by the Holy Spirit, but at times it has been done in part. All of us see through a glass dimly (see v. 12).

Moses made a powerful statement in Numbers 11:29 when he said, "Oh, that all the Lord's people were prophets and that the Lord would put His Spirit upon them!" This might even have been a yearning of things to come from the Holy Spirit. He longed for the day when many would prophesy.

NEW TESTAMENT PROPHECY

What exactly is New Testament prophecy? I've found several definitions coming from varying viewpoints. Wayne Grudem defines it this way:

> Not as "predicting the future," or "proclaiming a word from the Lord," or "powerful preaching"—but rather as "telling something that God has spontaneously brought to mind.[3]
>
> Prophecy is the reception and subsequent transmission of spontaneous, divinely originating revelation, [in order to]...see facts in relation to God's purposes, and to report that information in such a way that the church might be built up, encouraged and consoled (1 Cor. 14:3).[4]

For those who have grown up hearing that prophecy was simply preaching, modern-day prophecy may be a new idea. Many evangelical leaders, however, are beginning to realize that prophesying is indeed for today. On the other hand, charismatics and Pentecostals might be totally put off by Grudem's definition because he doesn't believe that someone who prophesies is "proclaiming a word from the Lord." Defining prophesying as simply "telling something God has spontaneously brought to mind" would be highly offensive, especially to those whose lives have been dramatically touched through a prophetic word that they knew was straight from the heart of God to them personally. Donald Bridge, a charismatic writer, says it like this:

> If prophecy is assumed to be directly inspired by God, authoritative and infallible, then clearly there can be no prophecy today. The Bible is complete....However, there is

no need to force all prophecy into such a definition....What authority does prophecy carry? The same authority as that of any other Christian activity in the church, like leadership, counseling, teaching....If it is true, it will prove to be true. Spiritual people will respond warmly to it. Wise and proven leaders will approve and confirm it. The enlightened conscience will embrace it.[5]

Donald Gee, a Pentecostal Assembly of God leader, says, "We hear to a point of weariness the phrase, 'I the Lord say unto you'...it is not essential. The message can be given in less elevated language."[6]

Although I certainly agree with Donald Gee, and Grudem's definition fits many personal prophecies given today, I personally have had times when what I received from the Lord was so strong, clear, detailed and intimate that I felt I was under the inspiration of the Holy Spirit giving the prophecy. There have been times when I have used the first person and believed I could confirm it as something the Lord had spoken to me. When this happens to me, it seems there is a coupling with the gift of faith for the thing prophesied to come about.

For instance, when I was in Brasilia, Brazil, I prophesied that the power from the Marches for Jesus in Brazil would bring down the carnival celebrations. The pastors from the various denominations who heard the prophecy took it to heart and passed it around Brazil. They believed it was a prophetic word from God and prayed that God's power through the Marches for Jesus would break down the strongholds of the carnival. (For those of you who don't know, Brazil has many festivals called "carnivals" that are demonic and wicked.) I have a faxed letter from the head of March for Jesus in Brazil telling me how accurate the prophecy was and that five carnivals have already been closed down by Brazilian mayors who declared them to be too immoral.

There are other times when I simply do not believe I can say something is a word from the Lord, but rather it is something I am sensing or it is an impression. I try to be careful to preface just regular counsel I am giving as being something I feel rather than something I think the Holy Spirit is giving to me. Unfortunately, I have had people run off saying I prophesied something that was merely advice given by me personally.

In applying prophecy in the Church today, Grudem says, "There is a danger that prophecy will be overvalued, and there is the opposite danger that it will be rejected altogether."[7]

I have attended meetings where a prophecy rang out from the midst of the congregation and we knew we had heard a direct prophetic message (or word) from God. The power of God came into our midst, the air became heavy with the anointing of God and our lives were dramatically changed.

So what am I saying? I believe that many prophecies are exactly what Grudem says: "Telling what God has spontaneously brought to mind." Many times in certain kinds of churches people may quietly share during the worship service, "I am sensing God is telling us He loves us," or "The Lord is pleased with our worship." Just to define it, I call this the simple gift of prophecy. No forthtelling (i.e., divinely received information of things to come), revelation or directional words have been given.

On the other hand, those who are proven prophets prophesy in quite another manner. For such prophets, their prophetic words have much more of a supernatural element of revelation. Their prophecies will often embody a mix of several other spiritual gifts such as exhortation, forthtelling, discernment of spirits, miraculous power to heal and set captives free, and revelation far beyond their natural knowledge of a situation. The knowledge they receive supernaturally from the Lord is often quite specific.

For instance, one time in Canada, I was prophesying at a spiritual warfare conference. In charismatic terms, the kind of ministry I was doing is called "flowing in word of knowledge," which means a supernatural word God gives you directly. I know some discrepancy exists regarding whether or not it is accurate to call this a "word of knowledge"; but what I am referring to is generally understood as prophetic knowledge that brings revelation that the person ministering could not have known, and that greatly edifies the listeners.

I am aware that the way I use the word "revelation" may be disturbing to some sectors of the Church. The word "revelation" is used here not to refer in the technical sense to the words of Scripture. "Revelation" is used here in the broader sense of the word in such passages as Matthew 11:27; Romans 1:18; 1 Corinthians 14:30; Ephesians 1:17 and Philippians 3:15 to refer to communication and prophetic words from God that are not equal in authority to Scripture. I would like to refer again to Grudem's excellent book *The Gift of Prophecy in the New Testament and Today.* He draws on the word "revelation" from 1 Corinthians 14:30 where the Greek term is the verb *apokalypto.* This is what he has to say:

As I shall argue in chapter 5, below, this term "reveal" (apokalypto), along with evidence in 1 Cor. 14:32-33, indicates that it is a specific revelatory activity of the Holy Spirit which gives rise to any prophecy by a New Testament prophet. Paul pictures some kind of process whereby the prophet is spontaneously made aware of something about which he feels God has caused him to think.[8]

Grudem goes on to say that this does not necessarily imply that the prophet was speaking with divine authority and that neither should we be thought to have authority equal to Scripture itself in our lives.

Although New Testament prophecy never has authority equal to Scripture in our lives, it can carry with it revelation for the hour (or present time) about which the Holy Spirit wants the Church to know. We see this pattern all through the book of Acts.[9]

Back to that night in Canada. As I was ministering, the Lord was bringing thoughts to my mind that I then passed on to the people. This went far beyond the simple gift of prophecy. I have learned that when I am speaking, if I am walking in a close intimacy with the Lord and have spent time preparing and listening to Him, my thinking becomes "sanctified" to a degree. I can trust the Lord to fill my thoughts with words that will bring great blessings to the people.

This particular evening, I felt I kept hearing the name Albert again and again. The unusual part was that I sensed Albert was the relative of some people attending the conference. The relatives were not sure whether or not Albert was in heaven, and the Lord wanted to put them at rest. The prophecy went something like this: There is someone here whose dad was named Albert, and you are not sure if he went to heaven when he died. The Lord wants to comfort you with the knowledge that your dad is with Him. The reason I hesitated so much was that my own dad's name was Albert and he had been with the Lord for some time. (Thank God I have no doubt where he is—he was a godly man.)

Finally, the name and message was ringing in my spirit and so I leaped out in faith and gave the prophecy. (It really does take faith to prophesy some of the things you hear from the Lord when ministering in a public arena, because some prophecies can seem unusual and fear can come into your heart.) But Romans 12:6 says, "Having then gifts differing according to the grace that is given to us, let us use them: if prophecy, let us prophesy in proportion to our faith." For those whose gift is prophecy, let them prophesy!

So I said, "There is someone here who had a relative named Albert and the Lord wants you to know that he is in heaven." As I was moving very quickly, I did not stop to find out for whom the word was given.

Later on, after the meeting ended, a lady came up to me with a glowing face and said, "Cindy, I was here tonight with my sister and we were so blessed by the word you gave about Albert. Albert was our dad and we never knew whether or not he was a Christian when he died. Tonight we have been given great reassurance and peace."

Needless to say, I was so glad I had been brave enough to leap out in faith even though the word was rather unusual and the name the same as my own dad's.

One thing I have wanted to do in this book is to make it practical. I have wanted to answer questions people want to ask such as, "How did you start prophesying?" and "How do you know it's God?" and "Did you feel scared when you first started out?" Scattered throughout this book will be answers to these questions (given to the best of my ability). I had to learn the hard way about prophesying and received a lot of serious emotional pain and hurt because I did not know the "how to's." The chapters on "Spiritual Protocol" (chap. 7) and "Mentoring the Prophetic Gift" (chap. 6) will include some of those things I learned the "hard way."

To understand New Testament prophecy, it is important to clarify the role of prophecy in the Church today. Because the Holy Spirit inspired the writer of Corinthians to write "desire earnestly to prophesy," learning the purposes of prophesying for the Body of Christ is crucial in obeying Scripture. The main text used in Corinthians for the purpose of prophecy in the Church is found in 1 Corinthians 14:3, "But he who prophesies speaks edification and exhortation and comfort to men."

Drawing again from Grudem, he writes:

> Why then is prophecy so important a gift? The answer is found not in the function of prophecy but in the fact that prophecy is based in a divine "revelation." Because of this revelation, the prophet would be able to speak to the specific needs of the moment when the congregation assembled. In many cases the things revealed might include the secrets of people's hearts (cf. 1 Cor. 14:25), their worries or fears (which

need appropriate words of comfort and encouragement), or their refusal or hesitancy to do God's will (which need appropriate words of exhortation).[10]

The principles given here for the corporate use of the gift of prophecy can also apply to individual situations. Sometimes a prophecy may come during a church worship service, but other times it may come one to one as Agabus prophesied to Paul in Acts 21:11 about being delivered into the hands of the Gentiles. (Later, I'll discuss the first part of Agabus's prophecy that was seemingly inaccurate.)

THE THREE FUNCTIONS OF PROPHECY

Let's look at the three functions of prophecy listed in 1 Corinthians 14:3.

Edification
Another word for edification is "up-building" (or the Greek word *oikodome*). Although it is true that many other functions of the church result in the up-building of the Body, a *kairos* (a word meaning "time, season" and used to refer to strategic times of visitation) prophecy has the ability to become catalytic even to the point of directional change for the whole church. Something similar might be, "Many new things are coming about in this Body. Get ready for change, be flexible. In the past, it has been a time for building this local Body, but now it is also a season to send missionaries from this church, to invest in sending those who will be church planters."

As I will discuss in the next chapter on spiritual protocol, this kind of prophecy should be given to the church leadership first before it is submitted to the Body as a whole. Even if the person giving the word has been received as a prophet in the church, it should usually first be given in a closed session and judged by the pastors or leaders of the assembly.

Directing the church is primarily the responsibility of the pastors and elders of the church. They are to "watch over" the souls of the sheep as undershepherds. As such, they understand about the condition of the church as a whole, the timing of the word and its effects on the church in general. Allowing them to judge the word before it is given, gives them the grace of putting the prophecy into the overall picture of what God is doing and saying to the congregation. A directional prophecy given out of God's timing can cause young sheep to run off ahead of God or to get mad at the leadership for not responding immediately. Those who have the authority in the church must also be honored by giving them the grace to process the word before it is given to the congregation as a whole.

The *New International Version* translation uses the word "strengthening" instead of edifying. And *oikodomeo* literally means "to build a house." Thus, the significance of prophecy for Paul was to contribute toward building up the household of believers by communicating the word of God into the fellowship.[11]

Sometimes someone gives a supposed prophecy and it acts as if a wet blanket were put on the congregation. It does not build up; in fact, it does just the opposite—it looses a heaviness onto the church. This would not be a prophetic word given by the Spirit of God. Even a convicting word will be up-building, although people may weep when they hear the word.

Several jokes are floating around about prophecies given in the church that are not edifying. I remember hearing one about a lady who came to a service, stood up and spoke in a very dramatic voice, "And God says, because you have disobeyed Me, I am going to write Michelob over this church." (For those of you who are from countries other than the United States, Michelob is a brand of beer.) The woman meant to say, "I will write Ichabod [meaning, 'the glory has departed'] over the church." Perhaps the Lord in His sense of humor would not let her pronounce such a thing over that congregation.

On occasion, the enemy will try to sneak its way into services through prophecies (see Matt. 7:15,22,23; 1 Tim. 4:1,2). A leader told me of a prophecy he had heard about where one of the worship leaders started saying, "I hate it when you praise the Lord [speaking from the demonic], for I cannot do my work in your midst." If I were the pastor of that church, I would be a little concerned about having someone lead worship through whom the enemy could speak so freely. Satan never edifies, but he does try to nullify the work of God.

Encouragement

The Greek word for "encouragement" in 1 Corinthians 14:3 is *paraklesi[s]*, which comes from the same root as the special term "Paraclete," which, in John's Gospel is the term used by Jesus for the Holy Spirit. How wonderful it is to be encouraged through a prophetic word that reminds us we are not alone, that God has everything in control and that all the promises of the Bible will always be there for us to believe.

I particularly remember the time several years ago when I was diagnosed as having a grapefruit-size tumor. Needless to say, I was very discouraged. The doctors were not sure whether it was cancerous. Right before this happened, however, I had been given an unusual Scripture verse of encouragement but I had not been able to relate it to anything in my life at that time. In fact, it had rather disturbed me. The verse was Revelation 2:10, "Do not fear any of those things which you are about to suffer. Indeed, the devil is about to throw some of you into prison, that you may be tested, and you will have tribulation ten days. Be faithful until death, and I will give you the crown of life."

The part that really bothered me was "be faithful until death." I did not know if the Lord was trying to tell me I would be tested 10 days and then the "be faithful until..." (I didn't prefer to think about the rest.) Then I read where it said the devil was about to do his work and so I stood firm on the Word of God and prayed for a healing.

I asked the doctor if I could postpone surgery for a while so I could receive prayer. He was a Hindu, so a rather strange look came on his face—but he agreed. My husband, among others, anointed me with oil and later I went back to the doctor. After a careful examination the doctor looked at me and said, "I cannot explain it, but the tumor is totally gone. Not only is it totally gone," he said, "but there is no sign of stress on the other organs, as there would be if there had been a tumor." Later on, when I counted up the days, it was exactly 10 days from the beginning of the time I first went to the doctor to the time I had confirmation of my healing.

This might be a good time to interject about prophetic words concerning healing for those who have a terminal illness or some serious medical condition. It is important to receive a word of the Lord regarding *how* He wants to heal you. Notice that I went to a medical doctor and waited for a specific time to see whether or not I would be supernaturally healed. If at the end of the 10 days the doctor had recommended surgery, I would have had the surgery.

Over the years, I have heard one sad story after another about how people found tumors or lumps and did not go to the doctor until the condition was well advanced. By then, they were beyond medical help and died. Although there have been times when the Lord has given me a *rhema* word (living word), that He was going to supernaturally heal me (and He did), there have been other times when He had me go to a doctor and healed me through the doctor.

One of the saddest stories I have heard was of a young mother who was attending Bible school. She had cancer and did not tell anyone nor did she seek medical attention. Her tragic death affected the whole school and will most likely affect her children for the rest of their lives.

Of course, I am not trying to push my beliefs onto you, but I am asking you to consider them. Nor am I trying to destroy anyone's faith. In truth, I believe strongly in supernatural healing through the power of prayer, but I think that every good gift comes from the Father (see Jas. 1:17) and that God also uses medicine and doctors (see 2 Kings 20:4-7; 1 Tim. 5:23). Could this be one of the reasons Luke, the physician, was included in the Bible?

Prophecies concerning healing can sometimes be presumptive rather than redemptive. As a youth, I was witnessing at The Green Gate, a Christian club, when a drunk man staggered in to try to get some food. He looked at me in a bleary-eyed way and said, "Jesus, oh, I once knew Jesus. In fact, I was a healer for Him. One day I told a man not to take his three-year-old daughter to the doctor because God was going to heal her—and she died!" With a deep sigh of grief he moaned, "I'll never forgive myself for that little girl's death." After talking for several hours he was finally able to receive God's forgiveness and cried like a little baby as he was reunited with His Lord.

Comfort

The word for "comfort" used in 1 Corinthians 14:3 is *paramuthia*, which, according to Clifford Hill, literally means to exercise a gentle influence by speaking words of comfort, consolation or encouragement. The emphasis here is upon gentleness. Paul has in mind the still small Voice of the Spirit speaking quietly into the ear of the Church, particularly during times of stress or persecution.[12]

Recently, it seemed our local Body (i.e., local church) was under a lot of attack and discouragement from the enemy. The Lord spoke a word of comfort to us that broke apart the despair. It went like this:

> There is a subtle deception coming upon this Body, trying to make them feel that I do not care about their every need. It

has come through trying circumstances and problems that wear My children down and make them doubt Me. For there are things that have happened to you that you cannot explain. Things that have not been as you planned. But I say to you, My children, even if you have missed My voice through your own foolish plans, am I not greater than your mistakes? Can't I take these things and turn them for good? For if you make a mistake and Plan A doesn't work then I have Plan B and if Plan B falls apart I have Plan C. Haven't I said I will never leave you nor forsake you? Is there anything in your life too big for Me to handle? For I am your provider and a good Father. I am not here to berate you for your mistakes but to give you another chance, for I am the God of the second chance. I am the lily of the valley, I am the cleft in the rock, I am the good shepherd and I see the end from the beginning. There is nothing you have need of that I cannot take care of, for I am an extravagant God. So trust Me; know that I am with you. I will never leave you nor forsake you.

At the end of the prophecy, the church began to praise God. Tears streamed down from many faces. The Lord had comforted Zion with His word and presence and our lives were changed by His love.

Realizing what a blessing the prophetic word can be in an individual life or in a congregation, it is important to know how to mentor those whom God wants to use to prophesy. We'll cover this in the next chapter, "Mentoring the Prophetic Gift."

PROPHECY IN PRACTICE

1. Did you know there was difference between Old and New Testament prophecy?
2. List several differences between the two and give examples.
3. How would you generally begin to give a New Testament prophecy (i.e., what words would you use to start the prophecy)?
4. What should your attitude be toward the person to whom you are giving a prophecy?
5. Name some reasons people might give harsh, critical prophecies.

Notes

1. Peter Wagner, *Churches That Pray* (Ventura, Calif.: Regal Books, 1993), p. 77.
2. Ibid., p. 73.
3. Wayne Grudem, "Why Christians Still Prophesy," *Christianity Today*, Sept. 16, 1988, 29-31.
4. Wayne Grudem, *The Gift of Prophecy in the New Testament and Today* (Westchester, Ill.: Crossway Books, 1988), p. 120.
5. Donald Bridge, *Signs and Wonders Today* (Downers Grove, Ill.: InterVarsity Press, 1985), pp. 202-204.
6. Donald Gee, *Spiritual Gifts in the Work of Ministry Today* (Springfield, Mo.: Gospel Publishing House, 1963), p. 48.
7. Grudem, *The Gift of Prophecy in the New Testament and Today*, pp. 113-114.
8. Ibid., pp. 81-82.
9. See Acts 9:10-12,17; 11:27,28; 13:1,2; 16:7-10; 21:10,11; 22:14-16,17-21.
10. Grudem, *The Gift of Prophecy in the New Testament and Today*, p. 152.
11. Clifford Hill, *Prophecy Past and Present* (Ann Arbor: Vine Books, 1989), p. 212.
12. Ibid., p. 213.

CHAPTER SIX

MENTORING THE PROPHETIC GIFT

■

Years ago, as a young person whose prophetic gift was beginning to emerge, I had a propensity to stick my foot into my mouth. (And other people's mouths, too, for that matter.) It seemed as though I was in trouble more than I was out of it. I couldn't understand what I was doing wrong. Among my problems were bad timing of the prophecies I shared, harshness, and pride that "I was *the* one hearing from God." One of my friends described me in this part of my development as "raw faith looking for a place to happen." This was actually pretty nice compared to what she could have said.

During one particular prayer meeting, I was in rare form. A daughter of a friend of mine was visiting and I discerned she had a drug problem. Without finding out anything about her situation, I pointed my finger at her and said with a loud voice full of drama, "You have a demon of drugs!" Ouch! The girl completely freaked out. Her mother had worked with her for weeks to try to get her to attend church and I blew the whole thing. To tell you the truth, I feel rather embarrassed now just thinking about my behavior.

WANTED: MENTOR PROPHETS

Needless to say, the Lord started putting some pressure on me to change, but I just wasn't understanding what He was trying to tell me. Little did I know that God in His mercy was trying to get me to a place where I would cry out for help. Finally, one day I lay flat on my face in my laundry room (of all the dignified places) and pleaded with God to send someone to teach and to train me. My prayer went something like this, "Lord, I don't know what is going on, but I am getting into trouble almost everywhere I turn and all I am trying to do is help people! Please send me a person who can explain to me what's happening. Where does one go to find a teacher for a young person like me?"

I'm sure the Lord sighed from heaven and said, "Finally, she realizes she can't do it all by herself." Frankly, I didn't know enough in those early days to realize I was an emerging prophetic voice. I desperately needed mentoring but I hardly knew there was such a thing as a mentor.

Through the years, the Lord did, indeed, answer my prayer by sending people along my path to help me. In fact, He has sent many mentors. I've always joked and said, "I guess I was such a hard case that just one wasn't enough." Many leaders have influenced my life at various stages. Some were real enough to say, "You've gone beyond my level of expertise," and would pray with me for God to send another person to help me. As I look back on my life, most of what I've learned I learned the hard way—by doing it wrong and suffering the consequences.

After one particularly hard lesson, I made a vow to the Lord that if He would teach me, I would train up young leaders and help them. I don't want anyone to suffer the things I have gone through if it isn't necessary. As a woman, I had some real challenges and I didn't have many people ahead of me who were able to help. My friends Jane Hansen, Beth Alves and Margaret Moberly have been absolute gifts from God in my life. Peter Wagner has been my mentor for the past few years and has taught me about writing, evangelicalism and lecturing at seminaries. (I'm still very much in process in these areas, incidentally.)

Mentor Relationships

Some mentoring relationships will last for only a season and some will last for a lifetime. The Lord brought Ruth and Naomi together for a lifelong relationship. Esther and Mordecai were relatives whom God called for His purposes for a nation. My first mentor, Vinita Copeland, who is now with the Lord, taught me a lot about intercessory prayer as well as casting out demons. She also mentored my friend Beth Alves. We always tease that Beth is the child and I am the grandchild of our mentor. The next intense learning situation was through an organization in which I sat on the board of directors with other women leaders.

Through the years of being mentored, I've had some good experiences as well as some bad experiences. I have had experiences of deep valleys, including some with people who didn't understand the gift of prophecy and consequently hurt me as they tried to bring correction.

One day, a prophet was sharing with me that I needed to change an area of my life regarding my style of prophetic ministry as a prophetic voice. After listening for a while, I said to him, "Where does one go to learn the kind of practical things you are sharing with me now? Has anyone written a manual?" Little did I know that I would one day write something along these lines myself.

In my early days as a minister, I was hungry to learn. I didn't want to blow people up or hurt them or scare them. Why, I hardly knew what I was doing! That's why I so relate to Susan in chapter 2. One way I learned was through reading books. I gleaned so much about being a Christian leader from biographies—Rees Howells, Amy Carmichael who worked with the temple children in India, Henrietta Mears who started Gospel Light Publications, and Catherine Booth of the Salvation Army.

In fact, after reading the story of Catherine Booth's life, entitled *Mother of an Army*, written by Charles Ludwig (Bethany House Publishers), the Lord spoke to me saying that He was going to use me to help raise up a prayer army all over the world. No wonder the pages of the book were wet with my tears. What a story of perseverance in the face of impossible odds! I remember begging God, "Use me, Lord. I want to do something for the kingdom of God that will impact the whole world. I want to leave behind an eternal legacy." Something of the spirit of Catherine Booth rubbed off on me through that book.

God's Provision

You might just be starting off in ministry and wondering how you will ever make it and learn everything you need to know. I believe I can boldly assure you that God will have someone to mentor you or, if you live in a place where there aren't any mentors, He will find a way to train you. God doesn't have favorites. If you are faithful and persevere, He will see that you receive all the training you need. For some of you, this book will be a starting place.

Is it biblical to look at the lives of those who have gone before us? Hebrews 13:7 seems to indicate as much: "Remember those who rule over you, who have spoken the word of God to you, whose faith follow, considering the outcome of their conduct." Paul admonished the Corinthians to follow him and the example he set in Christ (see 1 Cor. 4:15,16).

Moreover, we are to look to our leaders and superiors in authority, consider carefully their manner of living and imitate their faith.

Overall, in looking back, my greatest mentors were my parents. My dad was a Baptist church planter with the Home Mission Board and my mom did everything to help start the churches. I learned much from their examples. The greatest thing I learned was to be a person of integrity. I don't remember ever catching my parents in a lie. They kept their word both to me and to others.

One way my dad mentored me was through oral dialogue. I would come to him with a question and he would patiently go through the Scriptures. At times, I would have to say, "Dad, I only have three minutes. I need a simple yes or no!" He was always challenging me to think for myself concerning truth. One day I said to him, "Dad, what would you do if you found you didn't have the truth?"

He looked at me intently and softly said, "I would go where the truth was."

I saw him change and mature as the years went on. Although he died of a heart attack at age 49, I already had a lifetime of wealth stored up in my heart about the ways of God from having sat at his feet.

Robert Clinton of Fuller Theological Seminary gives this definition of mentoring:

> Mentoring refers to the process where a person with a serving, giving, encouraging attitude, the mentor, sees leadership potential in a still-to-be developed person, the protégé, and is able to promote or otherwise significantly influence the protégé along in the realization of potential.[1]

He goes on to state:

> A mentor is someone who helps a protégé in some very practical ways; by giving timely advice that encourages the protégé; by risking his or her own reputation in backing the protégé; by bridging between the protégé and needed resources; by modeling and setting expectations that challenge the protégé; by giving tracts, letters, books or other literary information that open perspectives for the protégé; by giving financially, sometimes sacrificially, to further the protégé's ministry; by co-ministering in order to increase the

credibility, status, and prestige of the protégé; and by having the freedom to allow and even promote the protégé beyond the mentor's own level of leadership.[2]

BEING A MENTOR

This chapter will discuss both how to mentor and how to receive mentoring. First, let's look at how to be a mentor. When God calls you to be a leader, whether you like it or not, you will become a mentor to those who listen to you, are affiliated with you and who watch you. This may be uncomfortable to some, but it simply goes with the territory; it is part of the responsibility of a leader. Among those in leadership, some will have a special calling to mentor and raise up young leadership behind them.

As I have traveled around the world and observed many cities, I have come to the opinion that many generations are fatherless and motherless. In other words, these generations are basically dysfunctional from a lack of spiritual parenting. Most of their patterning has come from observing very visible but distant leaders, without receiving very much—if any—accountability. It is very sad to sit and listen to pastors in their 30s and 40s say, "Where are the fathers in the gospel for my city? Isn't there anyone from whom I can learn?"

Unfortunately, many young promising leaders have suffered abandonment from the very leaders who could have been their mentors. Pastors of the churches where they were youth pastors or associate pastors rejected them for various reasons as their gifts matured. Oftentimes, rejection came from jealousy and a fear of losing position. Other times, the more mature leaders presumed the younger leaders knew things they themselves didn't know and judged them harshly, rather than entreating them with gentle correction. In such cases, the younger ones often turned and ran. Many new churches have been started from just such beginnings.

I believe I can safely say in a prophetic way that God is looking for fathers and mothers in the faith. He is looking for those who will be willing to pay the price to learn how to mentor and parent the new generation of powerful leaders God is raising across the world.

The Elijah Principle

In essence, God is searching for Elijahs to fulfill Malachi 4:5,6, "Behold, I will send you Elijah the prophet before the coming...day of the Lord. And he will turn the hearts of the fathers to the children, and the hearts of the children to their fathers, lest I come and strike the earth with a curse."

Although I am aware this Scripture verse can have several prophetic meanings, I believe we can apply it to a "spirit of Elijah," or those who have the mentoring spirit who will raise up end-time Elishas—those to be mentored. The spirit of Elijah will bring healing between the generations. God is a trigenerational God, the God of Abraham, Isaac and Jacob (see Acts 3:12,13). Because of a lack of mentoring, a great woundedness exists between the generations. When no training occurs by the Abrahams, and the Abrahams are jealous of the new work of God, dysfunction exists within the Church.

Of course, we could also say that when the Isaac generation has no respect for the Abraham generation (i.e., no honoring of those who have gone before them), no blessing can be placed on the Isaacs. It doesn't go well with the Isaacs because they have not honored their fathers in the gospel. If these things I've described happen, what chance does the Jacob generation have of being whole?

I have actually seen older prophets be so jealous of emerging prophetic voices that they essentially either ran them off from the church or shut down any ability for the young ones to speak into the life of the church. In some churches, "dueling prophecies" have occurred with each prophet saying his or hers was "the only prophecy from God." This distresses me each time I hear about such situations.

At other times, I go places to minister and I notice young leaders who are obviously prophetic but are shut up inside themselves. They are so smashed when they share something they think is from God that they make a vow never to try again. My, how I understand that feeling! Many times I was so crushed, I said to the Lord, "Just don't ever ask me to prophesy again! It hurts too much."

Frank Damazio gives a fascinating explanation of the term "father" in his insightful book *The Making of a Leader*. He quotes from 1 Corinthians 4:15: "For though you might have ten thousand instructors in Christ, yet you do not have many fathers," and states:

> In the original Greek language, the word for instructor meant "A boy leader, tutor, guide, guardian or servant whose office it was to take the children to school." The word carried with it the idea of severity; an instructor was a stern censor and enforcer of proper morals for the young men. This

Pauline verse uses the word "instructor" to present a strong contrast. Paul wrote to the Corinthian Christians that they had many tutors or instructors (those who freely offered them strict teaching and rigid rules) but not many fathers. The word instructor denotes a student-teacher relationship of instruction, whereas the word father denotes a father-son relationship of love. The Book of Proverbs was built on this concept of the father-son relationship. The father's wisdom, knowledge and understanding of life is transmitted to the son in a loving father-son relationship.

As in Paul's day, so it is true in our day, that the Church has ten thousand instructors, but not nearly as many fathers. The Church has many scholars and professional ministers, but not nearly as many spiritual fathers. Many scholars and professional ministers in the Church today can deliver eloquent, impressive sermons that touch our minds and thoughts. But where are the fathers? Some religious colleges and seminaries today seem bent on mass-producing teachers. But who is attempting to produce spiritual fathers? Will the Church allow a leadership of orators, educators, and instructors to forever rob her of the spiritual blessings which only spiritual fathers can bring her?[3]

Young leaders need heroes and heroines of the faith—those who have gone before them and blazed a trail. The mentoring in their lives makes a mark on the next generation.

I'll never forget going out to dinner one night with Freda Lindsay, then the chairperson of the board of directors of Christ for the Nations Institute. After her husband died in 1973, she took command of the Bible college and built it into an international organization. Many of the Bible school students call her "Mom Lindsay." Her faith in God is an inspiration to me. That night after we ate, she turned and looked me straight in the eye. "Cindy," she said, "do great things for God. Burn with the fire of the Holy Spirit."

With a lump in my throat I looked back at her through the mist in my eyes and answered, "Mrs. Lindsay, if I do half what you have done in your life I will consider I have done great things for God." I've been with her a number of times since and each time she exhorts me in some special way. She probably doesn't realize how that statement spurred me on to attempt courageous deeds for God's kingdom. Sometimes just such a seemingly small statement can a have major effect.

Another heroine of the faith who lived before my time but has, nevertheless, reached out to me is Henrietta Mears, whom I mentioned earlier. She understood mentoring as few have. Miss Mears established what is now Gospel Light Publications and GLINT (Gospel Literature International), and was largely instrumental in many organizations such as Campus Crusade for Christ. Billy Graham said of Miss Mears while she was still alive, "She is certainly one of the greatest Christians I have ever known!"[4]

> "What you are is God's gift to you. What you can become is your gift to Him. You teach a little by what you say. You teach the most by what you are." With statements like these, Dr. Henrietta C. Mears inspired and challenged countless people to do great things for the Lord. And the young people she inspired? They grew to be some of the most influential Christians of our time—Billy Graham, Bill Bright and Richard Halverson, to name just a few of the over 400 who went into Christian service.[5]

C. Peter Wagner has mentored many leaders from his position with the School of World Mission at Fuller Theological Seminary. As I mentioned earlier, he is a mentor to me. He is one of the heroes of the faith.

God is faithful to meet our needs. I missed my dad so much after he died and then the Lord sent Peter to be my spiritual dad. In fact, his whole family is close to mine and we have also spent vacations together. As I read J. Robert Clinton's definition of mentoring, I realized Peter has provided such mentoring for me. He has sent me articles, had me teach with him and lent me his credibility. (Brave man that he is!) I, on the other hand, often pray that the Lord will find me faithful with this great blessing.

Because I am like a daughter, Peter has gained many spiritual grandchildren because I regularly pass along the points he has given me in various areas of my life. The lessons learned through mentoring are not to be kept, but to be freely given away. Often leaders blossom for just one generation in their ministries because they do not take the time to mentor. Although these leaders are highly gifted, they are not willing to share the insights of the great ministries God has given to them and thus these truths essentially die with them.

People aren't willing to mentor young leaders for many reasons, especially those who are just learning to prophesy. One big reason is that young prophets are often stubborn, obstinate and unteachable. I'll go into this in greater detail later in the section on children.

Another reason leaders fail to train others is that they are often ignorant of how to mentor. Mentoring is a real art, but tips can be gleaned from such books as Clinton's *The Making of a Leader*. Other leaders are simply ignorant that they need to mentor. I believe that one of the hallmarks of good leaders is their ability to replicate themselves in the anointing God has given them. Many young Timothys and Esthers are yearning to be instructed.

An interesting part of mentoring is that physical age is not the qualifying factor regarding whom to train. It is common for people who are 10 or 20 years older than I am to consider me as their teacher. I even receive Mother's Day cards from some of them, thanking me for being there for them when they needed counsel or advice.

Part of the grace of being a good mentor may require you to recognize when your student has gone beyond you and is now your superior in spiritual authority. Clinton discusses this factor in the relationship Paul had with Barnabas. During Paul's first trip to Jerusalem as a Christian, Barnabas was Paul's mentor, but it appears that Paul was the leader in their later trip to Cyprus and had, in fact, become the leader.

This kind of maturity was shown by Pastor Bob Stennett of our church, Springs Harvest Fellowship, in Colorado Springs. Pastor Bob started the church in 1986 as Mountain Shadows Christian Church and served as the senior pastor for several years. In 1992, the Lord showed him that he was to allow Dutch Sheets to become the senior pastor while he became the associate pastor. Although Bob was not mentoring Dutch, Bob was an example to Dutch as Bob mentored other people. Today, Bob models a spirit of humility that continues to speak to leaders. The modeling of humility Bob walks in still speaks to leaders today.

The Servant-Leader

The mark of a good mentor is that of a servant-leader. Most mentors have been mentored by other leaders. This is what I would call the "Elijah-Elisha principle." One way to become a servant leader is through serving others. In my early days of ministry, I was thrilled just to ride in the cars of some of the outstanding leaders of my day. They'd say, "Cindy, do you want to go with me to such and such a city?" I would come home and jump up and down, I was so excited to be able to go out and learn. When I would go with these leaders, I'd watch them like a hawk to see how they did things. Not only did I watch the leaders, but I would also gauge the response of the people, noting what methods seemed to minister effectively and what methods fell flat.

Other times, I would go and clean these leaders' houses. At times, they'd let me ask them questions and I always seemed to have a list of them in my mind. "Why did you do that in that manner?" "How should I answer someone who asks me this about the anointing?" "Do you see anything in me that needs tempering?" (A really loaded question, I might add.)

One thing I have found to be true is that you don't skip steps in dealing with the Spirit. Some lessons are foundational, such as being a servant, and if you try to skip them, you will just have them arise in your life in another way. Some people say that those who miss the lesson God wanted them to learn have to "go around the mountain one more time." Some people go around the mountain so many times because of their pride and inability to become a servant that they have formed a well-beaten path. God is just as tenacious as we are stubborn!

Being a mentor to another person is an awesome thing. I often look at my own weaknesses and think, *How could I mentor someone else?* Almost everyone, however, has something to give to a person who is younger in the Spirit. Of course, mentors should have their lives fundamentally in order and be living sanctified lives—but if they wait until they are perfect, they will never mentor anyone.

It never hurts to ask the Lord, "Do You want me to mentor?" If the answer seems to be yes, the next step might be to seek the person with whom He wants you to work. For myself, most of those I have mentored have not been those I have sought out, but those who have come to me rather spontaneously. Long ago, I gave myself to the Lord for any such work He wants me to do. I am mentoring several people because the Lord spoke to me through a word of knowledge that I was to teach them and to do everything I could to help them advance in the kingdom of God.

One person I have had the honor of mentoring is the prayer leader for Generals of Intercession, Chuck Pierce. A few years ago I spoke at Chuck's church, Believers' Fellowship, in Denton, Texas. Afterward, Mike and I went out to eat with the elders. At the table, I suddenly turned to Chuck and said, "I'm going to introduce you to so-and-so and so-and-so because you need to meet them." In addition, in my heart, the

Lord said quietly, "He has a powerful prophetic gift. I want you to work with him and help him develop it."

As I listened to Chuck, I could tell he had great insight but was communicating with so much typology (or symbolism) that it was hard for the average Christian to understand his teaching. Since that time, Chuck has become affiliated with our organization and has helped us greatly in the area of administration. I have worked with him to help him share in an understandable way the prophetic words God is speaking. He is now a favorite to speak at conferences because his message is clear and sharp.

When God gives you a person to mentor, He also bestows a special grace for the task. This is necessary because without grace, you will be tempted at times to throw up your hands and give up. At other times, just as natural children do, the disciples (or spiritual children, as some prefer to call them) will blatantly refuse your advice and fall flat on their faces. They may embarrass themselves, you and others around them by being headstrong.

I remember working with one young prophetic girl who was flirting dangerously with the world. One night, I got so exasperated I flung at her, "That does it, I'm not praying for you anymore!" It was probably the best thing I could have said because I had been remarkably patient (oh, the grace of God)—maybe too much so. She later told me I had scared her so badly that she immediately repented and got right with God.

Mentoring in the realm of the prophetic can be accomplished in a variety of ways. One important way to mentor is to judge the words the disciple uses to communicate what he or she is receiving from the Lord. I cover this in more detail in the next chapter, "Spiritual Protocol." Sometimes I sit down with the person I am mentoring and we discuss the style of prophesying the person uses and its effectiveness. Some people use so much typology that their effectiveness is greatly diminished, as was Chuck Pierce's when I met him.

Is it important for you to tell the person the Lord gives you to mentor that you are being a mentor? Not necessarily. On occasion, I share that information with someone. When people tell me they want to be an Elisha (or a protégée), I will usually pray with them and agree that if this is what the Lord wants, He will bring it to pass in His time and in His way. On the other hand, if you are to have a serious, ongoing mentoring situation, it's a good idea to talk about it together. I have found that commitment comes out of relationship and making a covenantal agreement together is powerful. Ruth made this kind of an agreement with Naomi. Ruth 1:16,17 provides a strong and moving pledge of allegiance:

> But Ruth said: "Entreat me not to leave you, or to turn back from following after you; for wherever you go, I will go; and wherever you lodge, I will lodge; your people shall be my people, and your God, my God. Where you die, I will die, and there will I be buried. The Lord do so to me, and more also, if anything but death parts you and me."

TESTING

I watch those with whom I am working to see how they are coming along in their servant-leader growth. Occasionally, I will give them a verbal test to see if they will rise to the bait in pride. This may be in the form of asking them to do something that might seem menial, and then listening to their responses. One thing that impressed me about Chuck Pierce was that when he came to work with us, one of his first comments was, "What do you want me to do? I'll sweep the floor, type a letter or anything." This was from a man who was getting his master's degree in cognitive systems! Needless to say, I was impressed. No wonder God has raised him up so quickly in the past couple of years.

This area of testing is one where many young leaders flake out on the call. They don't want to pay the price to be tempered. I know of one pastor who for six months watches those in his church who are prophetically anointed before he approaches them in any way. Many of them become angry and just move on. They fail the test. Just because you're anointed doesn't mean you deserve a position in the church. God can anoint anyone He wants to. He's more interested in your character than your anointing.

Waiting is a hard part of the testing process. I remember thinking that "wait" must be God's favorite word, because each time I asked Him when He was going to use me, all He said was, "*Wait!*" How I hated that word. Great prophecies would come for everyone else and all I got was "wait." One day, God quietly spoke to me in my heart, "Cindy, I don't waste the anointing. Be patient."

"But," I wailed, "I think that Jesus is going to come before I get to preach one time!" Of course, I've since preached thousands of sermons throughout the world. No telling what I would have done to the Christian community if I had been loosed on it too soon. Perish the thought!

The Lord uses this waiting time to season us. One of His favorite ways to season us is through the fiery furnace. Remember the story of the three Hebrew princes in the book of Daniel? The only thing God burned from them in the fire was their bindings (see Dan. 3:25). In the same manner, waiting, suffering persecution for His name's sake, and living through other "fun" adventures only burn off our bondages. I always tell those I mentor, "The first one into the furnace, the first one out!" Just say to the Lord, "Whatever it is I need to change, show me, Lord. Whatever You need to do, do it." One of my favorite Scriptures in regard to this testing is Jeremiah 12:5:

> "If you have run with the footmen, and they have wearied you, then how can you contend with horses? And if in the land of peace, in which you trusted, they wearied you, then how will you do in the floodplain of the Jordan?"

An interesting point about mentoring and servanthood in Scripture is brought out by Frank Damazio in *The Making of a Leader*:

> Joshua was known in Israel as "the servant of Moses," his official title. He was not called "the servant of Jehovah" until the book of Joshua, after Israel had entered Canaan. The word "to minister," used throughout the Old Testament concerning Joshua, meant to attend as a menial worshiper, to contribute, to serve another, to wait upon others. The word for servant in Exodus 24:13, "Moses and his servant Joshua," would be equivalent to the New Testament Greek word "diakonea," or deacon. Joshua was willing to serve Moses and be known as Moses' deacon. The leadership principle found here in the life of Joshua is for a leader to be faithful to others as servant. Afterward, this ministry will realize its full potential in direct service to God.[6]

I believe it is important to interject something for balance at this point. Several books have been written on the subject of leaders who spiritually abuse their followers and this, of course, includes those they have mentored. The Lord does not want us to suffer abuse when He asks us to be servants. Horror stories abound of those whose leaders took advantage of them to the point that they had no family time but were required to be at the church day and night. Others had physical breakdowns from the long hours they worked for little pay. What I have been talking about is the necessity of having the attitude of a servant and the willingness to do any job, no matter how small.

PRESUMPTION

One of the greatest problems a young prophet or prophetess can have is an attitude of presumption. The person hears something from God and immediately moves on it. I spoke of this in the opening paragraph of this chapter when I told the young girl she had a demon of drugs. An aspect of prophesying I still work on is the timing of when to give a prophetic word. This will be amplified in the chapter on prophetic styles and gifts (chap. 9).

The area of presumption is one stronghold in which many watchmen leaders who hear God in advance of others become blinded. It comes from presuming we know what to do without checking it with other leaders. This is where a good relationship with your pastor, your mentor or peers is critical. I always meet with my pastor, who is also on our ministry's (Generals of Intercession) board of directors, during the year to look over my schedule. Last year, he strongly believed that my schedule was overbooked. (Actually, an understatement!) We prayed separately and together about which meetings should be canceled and which should be kept. I canceled trips to six nations and shortened others. One area of presumption I deal with is saying yes when I am already overextended. Because of this, I become exhausted, which not only hurts my body but also robs my family of time together.

A good mentor will work with an emerging prophetic voice in the area of personal pacing. Prophets who are not properly tempered have one speed: fast-forward. They are usually typical Type A personalities (i.e., hard-driving, task-oriented). They want everything to happen yesterday and they don't like to wait on anything or anyone. God in His mercy has placed some wonderful gifts in the Church, such as the gift of pastor, to temper the prophets. Otherwise, most prophets would burn themselves out, as well as everyone around them. I love the illustration Dutch Sheets uses to explain the difference between a prophet and a pastor:

If you tell a prophet that a mountain needs to be taken for the kingdom of God, he will get the church to the top, pushing and pulling the Body up the slopes. Everyone but two people will be dead, but he will have taken the mountain.

If you tell a pastor to have the church take the mountain, the prophet will become terribly impatient. The pastor will be taking his time, helping each little lamb over the big rocks—taking time to tend their hurts and bruises. The prophet usually gets frustrated and says something like, "Pastor, if you take this long with every little sheep we'll never take the mountain."

I believe God needs both gifts to function to bring balance to the church. Pastors at times can be so slow in their wanting everyone to enter the new things of God, or "the mountain," that they might miss the season of visitation. Yet, it is the Lord's will for as many of His children as possible to make it up the mountain.

The young prophets are so busy accomplishing the goal, they oftentimes don't see what their pushing and pulling are doing to relationships in the church. They are only concerned with their own agendas and put agendas before relationships. Yet, they can be a real blessing at reminding the church to keep moving up the mountain if they avoid being obnoxious in their exhortations.

I believe a divine tension exists between the prophet and the pastor, but by working together, they get the mind of the Lord on His timing. It's a sad elders' meeting when the two gifts are butting heads and not working together, each wanting his or her own way. The prophetic voice must be willing to submit to the pastor as the authority. However, if the two take the time to sort out things without insisting on being personally right concerning the procedure and timing, they (and the church) can be blessed.

INSECURITY

A person's insecurities provide another area of work for the mentor. Many insecurities originate out of a fear of man (or woman). The Bible says that the "fear of man brings a snare" (Prov. 29:25). The word for snare in the Hebrew means "bait or a lure in a fowler's net."[7]

Fearing humans goes along with pleasing humans. We have to walk a tightrope to maintain that fine line between giving the word with God's character or with the strongholds of fearing humans and of pleasing humans. Not all prophetic words are pleasant, but when we are in the right timing and have the right heart, attitude and wording, grace is the spoonful of sugar that helps the medicine go down.

I remember years ago I was so afraid of people that I trembled just asking my pastor a question in our large church. The thought of giving a prophetic word publicly would have positively undone me. Even after I had experience in talking with our pastor, I would still shake inside and rehearse what I was going to say again and again. It seemed that the things I said came out backward. Basically, I had experienced some hurts from other pastors and was afraid of being hurt again, which caused me to have a tremendous fear of people. I finally was confronted with the truth during a prayer time. I cared more about what that pastor thought than what God thought! That's pretty strong. If God hadn't shown this fault to me, I would have hotly denied it. I also put the leaders on such pedestals that they weren't merely people anymore.

Caring too much about every little thing someone says to you is crippling. You are never free to just be yourself. The other end of the pendulum is not caring at all what others think, and consequently you hurt people. Some young prophetic people are too harsh and others are too timid. Sadly, the balance between these two extremes is hard to find. Once I discovered I was out of balance in my fear of man (or woman), I had a "no holds barred" approach for a while until I learned the things I'm writing about in this book, and was able to move toward a proper balance.

INFERIORITY

Inferiority is closely akin to insecurity. Check those you mentor for signs of inferiority. People who are inferior will often mask it with "hostile humor." They will cut others down to build themselves up. This is also a sign of a critical spirit. If the person you are working with tends to make unkind comments and then laughs as though it were a joke, he or she has a personality problem. Humble learners will not be offended when this is brought to their attention. Hostile humor or remarks often point to feelings of inferiority, in which case the mentor needs to pray with the learner to help discover the root causes so he or she can be healed.

Another indicator of inferiority is excessive boasting. I do not think it is boasting to share testimonies from the places where we have ministered. All of us need to be able to share and hear from one another what God has done in and through us. It's a testimony to the goodness of God. I love to hear stories of my friends' ministry trips. The Bible says to "rejoice with those who rejoice" (Rom. 12:15). Some people, however, always have to top everyone else's story. Frankly, I find this rather obnoxious.

Leaders have to be careful not to engage in excessive boasting when those who are just starting out tell about the exploits God is doing through them. Most people who have been in the ministry for a long time could top almost any story a younger Christian would tell. The danger of the more experienced leaders being blasé about what God does through the younger Christians is also possible. One of the attributes of good mentors is that they keep silent about the things God did with them in the past, when the learners are telling how God is using them today. Mentors also need to rejoice with the learner as though it's the best thing that ever happened, because for the learner, it is.

Again, this kind of humility is often hard to maintain and I've made the mistake of overshadowing others without being aware of what I was doing. A good example would be when the younger leader shares, "Today I prayed for my neighbor who has a bad back and the Lord healed her." The older leader could pop the youngster's bubble and steal his or her joy by saying, "Oh, that's nice. Last week I prayed for twenty thousand and there were an incredible number of physical healings!"

A WORD OF CAUTION

As I've looked back on my years of mentoring, most of my experiences have been positive. However, God shows each generation certain practices of the past that were once viewed as sound, but should now be seen as negative. For instance, my dad became burned out in the ministry. He worked day and night and maybe in his sleep as well! I wasn't aware of it, but I modeled my own style of ministry after him. His lifestyle had many positives, but the negative part was that he missed out on some of our growing-up days because he was busy starting churches. Was he an abusive parent? Far from it—quite the opposite. In reflecting upon his death, I feel privileged to have had such a dad. His pattern of giving all for the ministry, however, was rooted in me to the extreme.

How did this affect me? When I first started traveling in 1982, I asked other leaders in my position, "What do you do to keep in balance on the home front?" I took this very seriously.

The leaders said, "Well, just give the kids quality time when you get home."

I heeded their advice. I would take Mary (or Madison, as she likes to be called) out by herself and then Daniel out by himself. Now, in later years, I can see this wasn't enough. I have found out they need you *and* your time—period.

In retrospect, my children tried to tell me, "Mommy, do you have to go so much?" Sadly, the old tapes from my childhood were playing and I thought I did have to travel a lot. I can't blame my dad or the people from whom I got advice for my mistakes. I should have listened to my family more. Sometimes I just thought it was spiritual warfare, and sometimes it was. Do I have great teenagers? Yes, I do. However, there has been some cleaning up to do from old hurts.

Looking back, should I not have done any traveling? No, that isn't the answer. Would I have traveled less? Yes. Although in the early days I would not be gone more than two or three days at a time, I believe I was away too many weekends a month.

Many leaders who don't travel are still away from their families many nights during the week as well as on weekends. Physically, they may be nearby, but the children still feel cheated. Pastor Ted Haggard of New Life Church in Colorado Springs is committed to keeping a proper balance in this area. He clearly states, "My family is my top priority, and then the church." I'm sure this will be reflected in his five children as they grow up.

Another area of which to be aware is the telephone. You can be home, but if you're spending your time on the phone, the children suffer just as much from emotional abandonment as though you were gone. I'm very jealous of my time at home with my family. I try to clearly separate the ministry from my home life. At times, the phone encroaches and my family lets me know. A useful tool for a ministry person during "off hours" is an answering machine. Some ministry families have two phone lines at home, one is a special unlisted number and the other is more readily available to their congregations.

REJECTION

A couple of the people I have mentored had deep wounds of rejection and were hurt by the least little correction I gave them. One woman went home from church being very upset because I didn't smile at her when I walked past her. To tell the truth, I didn't even see her that day. On occasion, I do get caught up in what I'm thinking and am totally oblivious to those around me. The thing that puzzled me was, "Why such a big reaction from such a small oversight?"

As I prayed, I felt the Lord telling me that as a little girl this woman had been terribly wounded by her mother. I called her and probed a little. "Yes," she said, "my childhood was awful." She went on with a catch in her voice, "Cindy, I was so neglected as a child that I would go to school smelling like urine from when I wet my pants. My hair was filthy from a lack of care."

I gently queried, "Do you think maybe you are mixing the two of us up inside?" She had taken to calling me "Ma" or "Mom" because I was mentoring her and I was reaping from those things what her mom did or didn't do. The light came on for both of us that day and we switched our relationship to one that brought rich fruit.

It isn't always healthy for deeply wounded people to call you a spiritual parent. Playing the role of mentor to them would be best in my opinion. I am happy to say that the lady in this story is now a mature, wise leader in the Body of Christ and I am proud of her accomplishments in the Kingdom.

Rejection is a real crippler when it comes to being accurate in the prophetic realm. Old wounds leak out and color what we say. Many leaders carry battle scars from past times when they gave prophetic words and they weren't received or they were misunderstood. As mentors, we must be careful that our own bitter roots do not spring up and defile the student (see Heb. 12:15). This is extremely important because young leaders will often hang onto your words as if they were gospel. Whether you like it or not, if you have any biases, those you are teaching will pick up on them.

One day, the Lord dealt with me regarding a bias I had against a certain leader. I had never met this person, nor heard him teach; and on a personal level I knew very little about him. But when I thought about why I had such a bias, I remembered that a person I looked up to in the Spirit had made several negative comments about the ministry of this leader. Much to my chagrin, I had totally misjudged the person. I had an opportunity to minister with and get to know the man against whom I had a bias and was ashamed at things I had repeated against him. What a lesson! I repented to the Lord in earnest and have caught myself several other times being opinionated about a person when I really didn't know what I was talking about. At times, I have been convicted of participating in nothing more than "glorified gossip."

Interestingly enough, it has happened to me in the reverse. After I've known other ministers for a while, they'll confide in me that they had totally misjudged me as a person as well as my teachings. Most of them had never bothered to find out about me, but had just listened to someone else misquote me. Hmmm, I wonder if this could be a case of, *What you sow, you reap, Cindy!* Ouch, what a thought!

PRIDE

Although I've said a lot about pride and humility, both in this book and in *Possessing the Gates of the Enemy* (see the chapter, "The Clean Heart Principle"), one area I haven't touched on is the area of pride in revelation.

There is actually no copyright on God's revelation. I do believe in credit where credit is due, and I attempt to share where I learn certain truths or pick up certain teachings. Some people, however, become angry if you teach a lesson you have learned from them. It may be just a personal thing, but I think this is pride. For me, it is a great compliment when someone takes notes and teaches what I taught them. I tell young leaders to teach what they learn from me as though they had discovered it on their own, as if they had received it straight from God. If it is a *rhema* (alive word) in their hearts, then I pray they did receive it as being from the Lord Himself.

Often, I'll offer my notes to young beginners to help jump-start them in the ministry because they don't know how to prepare messages on their own. This doesn't mean I don't insist that they study on their own and receive messages straight from their own times of study. As part of a mentor relationship, however, I have seen the lessons they've received from me become a starting place to help them launch their own ministries.

We've received reports of leaders from around the world who take the messages written in *GI News* (the Generals of Intercession newsletter) and teach them in their Sunday services. They tease and say, "I'm so glad to receive the newsletter; it gives me fresh food to feed my congregation!"

RECEIVING MENTORING

If the Lord brings you a mentor, you can take certain steps to make the most of the relationship. Here are some guidelines for receiving mentoring.

A Teachable Spirit

No one wants to work with a know-it-all who has an argumentative spirit. Some people always have their defensive shields up and have chips on their shoulders. This is a shame because it makes them difficult to instruct. Recently, I was talking to my teenage daughter about this subject. I asked her, "Am I more defensive than usual?" The reason I asked this was that 1994 was probably the best year of my life as well as the worst year. Situations occurred that caused me to walk in a great deal of forgiveness and I was concerned that it was taking its toll on me. She was quiet for a minute, thinking, and then answered, "You know, Mom, I think you are getting pretty defensive these days."

The Word of God says that the truth sets us free (see John 8:32). Upon hearing my daughter's reply, however, I'm sad to say, my first feelings were *defensive!* I checked my emotions and went to my prayer closet (I have a special place where I pray in our basement).

"Lord," I asked, "why am I so defensive?" He began to show me situations where people had been critical and had taken potshots at me.

"These things," the Lord went on to say, "have caused you more pain inside than you have been aware of and you're not acting like yourself anymore." When He said this to me, a well of pain started rising up within me. I had not been in touch with how much I was actually hurting inside. That day, the Lord showed me one instance after another and I not only forgave, but I also asked Him to give me His special grace for the wounds to be healed. Where would I be without grace? I'd be one very defensive mom.

When a mentor is giving us advice, a good rule of thumb to follow if it is corrective is not to close up immediately and try to justify ourselves. Instead, take it to the Lord. Even if you don't agree with everything the mentor says, some of it may be true. Usually more of the advice is true than we want to admit. Whenever I'm criticized or corrected, I always try to spend time seeking the Lord and talking to others to find out if what has been said has any truth to it. I try to consider if perhaps I need to make some adjustments in myself, in the way I minister or in what I'm teaching.

Proverbs 27:6 says, "Faithful are the wounds of a friend." I've found that those who won't listen to a friend who is correcting them will have extremely painful experiences with enemies who are trying to correct them. I've seen people receive repeated criticisms about certain areas, but because of the person who criticized, or the style of the criticism, they refused to listen and instead rebuked the devil. When critical issues or concerns are brought to our attention, we need to deal with them immediately.

Again, this is a balancing statement. Every new move of God is usually severely criticized. This doesn't mean it is not truth. You may take a critical word shared by someone back to the Lord and He will simply say, "That person has a religious spirit" or "This stems from that person's own personal problems." At times, you simply have to put it before the Lord, forgive and go on.

One day, I was complaining to the Lord that I was tired of being controversial. It kind of went like this, "Lord, it's hard enough being a woman minister without also teaching on the subject of spiritual warfare! How about if I teach on color typing or how to bake a cake or something like that?"

Rather than answering my question directly, the Holy Spirit quietly spoke to my heart, "Cindy, controversial people do great things for God and the controversial things of yesterday are the commonplace of today. Teach My Word." End of discussion. What do you say to such a statement?

"Yes, Sir, You are right. You are always right. *Selah* (pause and think on it, amen)."

Undemanding

Through the years, it has been my delight to work with many young people who are growing in prophetic ministry. One of the character qualities I have enjoyed the most is when these young people are not demanding of my time, but are looking for ways to give to me as a person. Often, people only want to take from leaders without thinking of them as individuals. My heart is warmed by those who want to give without demanding anything in return. These are the people who are pleasant to be around, and you don't mind investing quite a bit of time to see that they receive all they need in the way of mentoring.

Conversely, some people are petulant and follow leaders around, demanding to have lunch and then becoming angry when they can't comply. Pushy people are a thorn in the side of busy leaders. They always go to the bottom of my list and I rarely will have anything to do with them unless the Lord really speaks to me to help them.

Self-Initiating

Those who grow fastest are those who do not sit around and wait to be spoon-fed from their teachers, but study and glean from every godly source they can. Some of my students have positively delighted me by bringing a nugget of gold they have dug out of the Word that I, myself, have not seen. This is important to me because I want them to grow beyond where I have been. It is my opinion that each succeeding generation should surpass the one that came before it.

Submissive to a Local Church

Being submitted to a local church can be challenging for some young prophetic people. It used to be difficult for young, fiery, prophet-types to find a church that understood them and encouraged them as their gifts emerged, yet reigned them in when needed. It is a blessing to be in the church I now attend because the people understand and embrace the prophetic gift. My pastor, too, is a prophetic teacher.

I have seen some young leaders refuse to submit to a pastor because they claim that the pastor "just doesn't understand my gift." This is haughtiness in the highest form. If you pray, God will send you to the right church and to the right pastor. However, it may not be the church you would like in the form you would personally enjoy. In certain stages of development, the Lord might have you submit to a pastor who doesn't have a handle on everything you do prophetically, but he has deep wells of wisdom and the common sense you need to absorb.

If a pastor senses resentment from a young prophet or prophetess, this will make him pull back. One of the biggest problems for those who prophesy is a critical, judgmental spirit against their pastors. The tendency of a young leader is to run off, start his or her own home Bible study and be a "lone ranger."

My advice to those who are dissatisfied is to get the counsel of some nonbiased leaders concerning their situations. Don't make hasty decisions. You may be wanting to run because of hurt and misunderstanding. If you feel you must leave a church, running isn't the way to handle it. You need to ask the Lord, "Is this the church you have for me or do I have a release to seek another church?" He may be giving you a release, or Satan may be trying to bring estrangement to your relationship with the church or the pastor.

MENTORING PROPHETIC CHILDREN

I want you to know that I approach this section with fear and trembling because my children are now teenagers and the process is yet to be completed. I learned some things when my children were young that might be helpful.

Prophetic children sometimes seem to be out of step with the rest of the world. They are often very headstrong. Although my children have distinct separate personalities, they are both prophetic. When Mary was little, she did not like the word "no." I used to believe that James Dobson wrote his book *The Strong-Willed Child* (Tyndale House Publishers) just for me. Parents who have prophetic children wear out several copies of Dobson's book, if they've discovered it, before their children are three years old.

Specific prophetic acts or words are the most obvious clues that a child might have a prophetic gifting. Personality style, however, can also provide insight in this area.

For instance, one of the first indicators that Mary (or Madison, as she calls herself) was prophetic was our altercations concerning the electrical outlets. Upon learning to crawl, she decided she would stick her fingers into every outlet in the house. We bought little plug guards but she found a way to work them out of the wall. No matter how many times we would spank her little hand, she would go back for those outlets.

Another significant sign came when she was almost four years old. I said to her, "Mary, go upstairs and pick up your toys."

She mounted the steps, whirled around and pointed her little finger at me (pointing her finger was a strong clue) and announced, "I'm going to go tell God on you!"

This evolved into a finger-pointing match in which I said back to her, "You do, and He'll tell you I'm right!"

And since her early childhood, Mary's prophetic giftings have continued to blossom in more overt ways.

Daniel's prophetic gift is much different. He is more of an intuitive seer (i.e., one who literally or figuratively sees things in the Spirit), being aware of others' feelings and needs. His rebellion is more inward than outward. Each prophetic person is unique and different. The chapter on prophetic style and gifts will go into this in detail.

Prophetic children are born with a built-in spiritual radar. Although most children have a certain sensitivity to the spirit realm, it will be greatly amplified in those who are prophetic. For example, let's assume that a certain household is under spiritual attack. Two children are asleep in the same room. The prophetic child wakes up screaming that monsters are present in the room, while the other child, gifted in other areas, sleeps blissfully on.

What is happening? The prophetic child is keenly attuned to the spirit realm and will be in touch with the fact that he, or his family, is probably under some kind of spiritual attack. Please do not rebuke the child and tell him the monsters are only imaginary. This shuts down his spiritual acuteness or simply leaves him unprotected in his vulnerability. He doesn't have the skills to counter what he is sensing in the Spirit. At times, of course, children do have dreams that are only imaginary. At other times, however, nightmares are the result of demonic attack.

I remember at times when we lived in Weatherford my children were more spiritually sensitive than I was. One night, both Mary and Daniel awakened me by saying, "Mother, there are spirits all over the house. Would you please get up and pray now!"

To which I groggily replied, "Where are they?"

They answered in an exasperated way, "In our bedrooms and the laundry room."

They were frustrated that I hadn't awakened before they did. I guess they were the watchmen that night, however, and the Lord was letting Mom have a rest! Needless to say, I rolled out of bed to pray.

We trained our children at an early age to know how to rebuke satanic attacks that were coming against them. I believe that one particular stronghold many prophetic children have is fear. Satan wants to intimidate them so they won't rise to their calling in full spiritual authority. Daniel was waking up night after night when he was around four years old. I began working with him, teaching him 2 Timothy 1:7, "For God has not given us a spirit of fear, but of power and of love and of a sound mind."

One night, there was tremendous spiritual oppression around us. It was so thick you could cut it with a knife. In the wee hours of the morning, we heard loud shouting coming from Daniel's bedroom. It was Daniel and he was yelling at the top of his lungs. "Devil," he proclaimed, "God hasn't given me a spirit of fear. I command you to leave my room right now. You have no authority or right in this room because I'm a child of the living God!"

Mike woke up, rolled over, only partially awake and murmured, "Cindy, can't you teach him to do that quietly?" I just laughed. Was I ever thrilled at what I had heard Daniel do!

Mary has also been fiercely attacked in the night during times when I have ministered in Argentina. She used to say, "Mother, I can tell the minute you get up to teach on spiritual warfare." One night when I was in a city in southern Argentina, Mary was back home in Texas. As I lay down to sleep, a dark presence filled the room. Both my roommate, Doris Cabrerra, and I felt it enter the room. At the same time, a dark presence appeared in Mary's room back home.

After I got home and Mary told me about what happened, I asked her, "Why didn't you wake your daddy to help you pray?"

She quickly said, "Oh, Mother, it was just a demon, and I knew what to do. Why bother Daddy and wake him up in the middle of the night?"

Here are some practical ways to deal with prophetic children:

Teach them about the spirit realm. I talked to my children about demonic powers and angels because they were seeing both.

Encourage them to intercede. Pray with the children and listen to their prayers. If they begin to pray prophetically, talk to them about it. For instance, they may pray for a sick grandma without knowing beforehand that Grandma was indeed ill. Find out if she indeed hasn't been feeling well and then give the report to the child. Build them up in their most holy faith in this manner.

Teach them the Word and their authority and security in Jesus Christ. Read Bible stories as well as stories of heroes and heroines of the Christian faith to them.

Pray with your prayer partners for them.

Watch and see if they have any major personality changes. Sometimes prophetic children will be attacked by demonic spirits or a denomic spirit guide. These can take the form of imaginary friends. Although it is possible the children are simply pretending, I would quiz them to see what the "friends" are telling them. They might be demons who want to try to control the children by telling them they are their friends. At times, the demons will manifest themselves as cartoon characters.

Daniel got up for breakfast one morning when he was three years old and announced to me, "Mommy, a spiderman was on my bed last night."

I immediately knew that a demon had taken the form of a spider-type man to try and trick him.

"Daniel," I asked, "is he here now?"

"Oh, yes, Mom, he's always here."

"Daniel," I countered, "he is not your friend, he is a demon. Rebuke him and tell him to go."

At this point, Daniel spouted out in a clear voice, "In Jesus' name, GO!"

I questioned, "Did he leave?"

"Yes, Mama," he said, "he left."

Many children have told me that cartoon characters appear to them and tell them things such as, "Don't obey your parents" or "Why don't you run away?"

Listen to your children. Prophetic children tend to be sensitive in nature, even the most strong-willed children. They may be suffering demonic attacks in the night and need your help. One of our prayer partners, Sandy Grady, told me that when she was a child, spirits would come around her bed at night to torment her, and because her family was not a Christian family they didn't know how to help her. Daniel would say that his stuffed animals would move around in the night. Mary said things with long claws would try to grab her in the night from under her bed.

Sometimes you may need to pray through their rooms to cleanse them. If they have used furniture, the previous children who slept in the beds may have been subject to terrible nightmares and thus "hitchhikers" of demonic powers. Their fear or terror may be tormenting your children.

Be careful and don't let them watch horror movies. These open the door to the spirit of fear.

Use wisdom in your disciplining. Children may be so stubborn and disrespectful with their mouths that you may tend to spank them too much and that can break their wills and wound them. We used to have a spoon in every room because Mary talked back so much. Other people in our church would tell me I needed to discipline her more. Of course, their children were passive, compliant children, and there was no comparison between Mary and them.

As children grow both spiritually and physically in the Lord, there is a time of letting go. When in the past they would want your opinion and advice, now they no longer welcome it. This can be painful at times if you don't realize what stage the child is experiencing. It is much easier, in a way, to realize that they may be going through these stages because of their physical ages. When you are mentoring someone in a spiritual sense, facing these stages is much more difficult.

One day I was talking to a young leader I had mentored. We had a difference of opinion concerning what she should do in a particular matter. In the past she would have greatly leaned on my advice, but now she was defensive. This hurt me. I couldn't understand what was happening. She told me, "Cindy, I prayed about it and I'm not going to go."

Puzzled, I hung up the phone and the Lord immediately spoke to me, "She's a 'spiritual teenager' making her way. Leave her alone in her decisions." Of course, she was becoming her own person! The way she reacted was just like a natural teenager. Because my kids were teenagers, this was a *rhema* word to me. I backed off and found she made very wise choices.

John and Paula Sandford offer some good pointers on letting go in their book *Restoring the Christian Family* (Victory House, Inc.), which is certainly helping Mike and me as we walk through the teenage years with our family.

Hand in hand with mentoring the prophetic gift is having an understanding of spiritual protocol. The next chapter will probably be one of the most practical chapters in this book as either you or others you know begin to move into prophesying.

PROPHECY IN PRACTICE

1. What kinds of mistakes do young prophetic people generally make?
2. Do you know anyone who is young in the prophetic ministry who has hurt people through premature prophecies?
3. Have you ever asked the Lord for a spiritual mentor?
4. Give examples of the ways good mentors helps those they mentor.
5. Are there those in your life who are younger in the spirit than you that you could help mentor and answer their spiritual questions?

Notes

1. J. Robert Clinton, *The Making of a Leader* (Colorado Springs: NavPress, 1988), p. 130.
2. Ibid., pp. 131-32.
3. Frank Damazio, *The Making of a Leader* (Portland, Oreg.: Trilogy Productions, 1988), pp. 74-75.

4. Earl O. Roe, ed., *Dream Big: The Henrietta Mears Story* (Ventura, Calif.: Regal Books, 1990), front cover.
5. Ibid., jacket cover.
6. Damazio, *The Making of a Leader*, p. 136.
7. F. Brown, S. R. Driver, and C. A. Briggs, *A Hebrew and English Lexicon of the Old Testament* (Oxford: The Clarendon Press, 1951), p. 430.

CHAPTER SEVEN

SPIRITUAL PROTOCOL

■

Several years ago, I attended a prayer meeting in the Los Angeles area called "Love L.A." The meeting was jointly led by Jack Hayford, pastor of The Church On The Way in Van Nuys, California, and Lloyd Ogilvie, chaplain of the United States Senate and former pastor of First Presbyterian Church of Hollywood. Excitement and joy filled the air as evangelical pastors and leaders came together along with charismatics and Pentecostals to intercede for Los Angeles. The unity was beautiful to behold and we could sense the blessing of God in the midst of His people.

As we sat in the beautiful jewellike First Presbyterian Church, there was freedom, yet an order to the time of prayer. Microphones had been set up at various stations along the aisles for those who sensed God was leading them to pray about certain issues. The sweetness of the power of the Holy Spirit was tangible as leaders from various parts of the Body of Christ stood and cried out to God together. It was as though a divine fusion of hearts and souls was taking place. We were becoming a body rather than disjointed parts. I marveled at the unity in diversity as the leaders told the names of the churches and organizations they represented.

All of a sudden, just as though a bomb had been thrown in our midst, a man who had wild-looking eyes starting yelling from the back of the church. His voice and body language expressed intense anger, and legalism oozed from his words as he proclaimed something to the effect, "Thus saith the Lord, Woe to the shepherds who build fancy homes for themselves and do not take care of My people. They do not feed the poor and the homeless nor see the hurting."

The congregation turned and stared at him, aghast at what was happening. I started to pray for Jack Hayford and Lloyd Ogilvie. One could almost imagine demonic forces whispering into the ears of those who had struggled to come to a meeting with "those weird Pentecostals." I personally felt a deep embarrassment. Questions ran through my brain: *Would people who had never heard a prophecy think this was condoned by the Pentecostals? Where did that man come from? How did he get into this closed meeting?*

Pastor Hayford spoke up with the graciousness for which he is noted and addressed the shouting man in a gentle voice, "Sir, would you please restrain yourself. According to the Word, the spirit of the prophet is subject to the prophet. You can control that. You are out of order." He then asked the ushers to escort the man out, who continued to yell as he was taken from our midst. Pastor Ogilvie concurred, and the two gifted men of God set about putting the shards of the gathering back together. Their teamwork was like that of David and Jonathan.

Looking quietly into the eyes of the leaders, Pastor Hayford softly apologized for what had occurred. Rather than skirting the issue, he stated, "I frankly feel embarrassed by what just took place. Please forgive this brother. He was out of order."

The authority in which the two men walked was evident and we were able to smoothly make a transition back into our prayer time. Later in the meeting, an evangelical leader stood and began to pray. His voice broke as he uttered his petition to the Lord. "Lord God," he said, "we have not always noticed the needs of others in our busyness of service. Father, help us to be sensitive to others' needs."

A sound of soft weeping filled the room. "Ahhh," I sighed, "this was the correct word God wanted to speak to His people." He had not wanted to beat His leaders for their oversights, they were already pressed enough by the enormity of the pressures and needs around them. He simply wanted to remind them that they needed to get back on center and to refocus their priorities. These leaders already had softened hearts toward the things of God and didn't require a stern rebuke. They so loved the Savior, all it took was a gentle nudge of His presence to steer them into a clearer focus.

The presumptuous intruder had heard something from God but interpreted it through a religious filter of bitterness against leaders. Perhaps he worked with an organization that focused on feeding the poor and suffered from a lack of support from local churches. These kinds of so-called prophecies, however, can actually do a lot of damage to the cause of unity.

God is a God of order. First Corinthians 14:33 states, "For God is not the author of confusion but of peace, as in all the churches of the saints." The margin note in *The New King James Version* (Slimline Reference Edition, © 1988) defines the word "confusion" as meaning "disorder." The end of chapter 14, verse 40, strengthens this point, "Let all things be done decently and in order." In the Greek, "decently" has the connotations of "decorously, decently and honestly." Its root meaning connotes "being noble (in rank), and honourable."[1]

Why a chapter on spiritual protocol? Many churches lack an understanding of how prophecy should be handled both corporately and individually within their midst. Done properly, and having correct scriptural protocol, the prophetic word is a catalytic, powerful influence on a church. Ministered incorrectly, it can cause enormous confusion and church splits. Through the years, I've seen many mistakes made through giving and receiving prophetic words that could have been cleared up simply by understanding protocol.

One dictionary definition of the word "protocol" states that "in diplomacy, protocol is the ceremonial forms and courtesies that are established as proper and correct in official intercourse between heads of states and their ministers."[2] Every kingdom on the earth has a form of protocol. The same is true for God's kingdom. The king of an earthly kingdom has delegated authority to carry out his desires, and there is a parallel in the spiritual Kingdom that is not of this world. This spiritual Kingdom carries on its affairs through the local church and through delegated authority.

Protocol for Corporate Prophecy

As I have talked with beginning prophetic voices, many are confused and puzzled about why they were rebuked by their pastors after giving a particular prophecy in a corporate setting. They were reprimanded without receiving instruction on exactly what it was they did wrong. Not only are there clear biblical guidelines for corporate prophecy, but each church and group seems to have its own rules, culture and boundaries. It is entirely possible for you to bump against some unwritten code within a church and be clueless about why people become upset after you give a prophetic word.

In addition, leaders have certain rules of ethics among themselves that those who have been in the ministry a long time just assume everyone knows. Sadly, young leaders usually learn the hard way and suffer bruises and wounds to the heart. This is why the mentoring process is critical.

I remember a conference where I asked to give a corporate prophetic word during one of the meetings. As far as I knew, I had followed all of the protocol. I had asked permission, shared a little of what I was going to do, and was given a go-ahead to prophesy. I gave the word, and then the speaker gave her message.

Later, after the speaker had concluded, one of the other leaders rebuked me as she prayed, "Lord, teach Cindy not to preempt what You are doing." Needless to say, I was in a state of shock! How did I preempt? Quickly my mind raced through what I had done to clear the prophecy, and I could find no fault with the procedure.

One of the other leaders drew me aside, sensing how crushed I felt. "Cindy," she said, "the Lord's anointing in the word you gave was so strong that the other lady's message following your prophecy seemed flat in comparison."

Personally, I learned a number of lessons from that experience at the conference. First, I will never rebuke a young leader through a prayer. Second, I will take responsibility to know the flow of a meeting. I will protect those under me by not giving permission for a certain person to prophesy if it will change the flow of the meeting in a detrimental way. Next, if I am asked to introduce someone, I will not prophesy before I introduce him or her unless I am flowing with the speaker and his or her message.

AUTHORITY AND ORDER IN PROPHECY

To understand order, it is imperative to grasp the concept of spiritual authority. Without proper spiritual authority, anarchy will occur. Where a leadership vacuum occurs, someone will fill the void. It may be a person acting in the flesh or it could be a person sent by Satan to disrupt.

Churches that have a grasp on this subject rarely have problems in dealing with flaky people. Responsible leaders know who they are in Christ and are not intimidated by strong, sometimes controlling, people. They rely on the Holy Spirit's guidance and are secure in the place of leadership God has given them.

Part of my training as a leader was through the study of spiritual authority. On one of my many trips to the local Christian bookstore, the manager, Joyce Bogle, suggested I read a book entitled *Spiritual Authority* by Watchman Nee. The contents of the volume were delivered in Chinese by the author in 1948 during a training period for the workers, held in Kuling, Foochow, China. The speech was then translated from the edited notes taken by some people who attended the training.[3]

When I received my call to ministry from the Lord, the subject of authority was heavy on my heart. One day in prayer the Holy Spirit cautioned me, "Cindy, if you want to move in great authority, you must be subject to others in authority. Your anointing will grow in proportion to your understanding of spiritual submission. Remember the centurion who came to Jesus and asked Him to heal his servant boy. A great miracle occurred because he understood authority." I pondered on this and went to read the story in Matthew 8:7-10:

> And Jesus said to him, "I will come and heal him." The centurion answered and said, "Lord, I am not worthy that You should come under my roof. But only speak a word, and my servant will be healed. For I also am a man under authority, having soldiers under me. And I say to this one, 'Go,' and he goes; and to another, 'Come,' and he comes; and to my servant, 'Do this,' and he does it." When Jesus heard it, He marveled, and said to those who followed, "Assuredly, I say to you, I have not found such great faith, not even in Israel!"

THE AUTHORITY OF GOD AND HIS WILL

Submission to the authority of God and His will is modeled by Jesus Christ, Himself, in the Garden of Gethsemane. Nee expressed it this way:

> Some think our Lord's prayer in Gethsemane when His sweat fell like great drops of blood was due to the weakness of His flesh, to His fear of drinking the cup. Not at all, for the prayer in Gethsemane is on the same principle as 1 Samuel 15:22. It is the highest prayer in which our Lord expresses His obedience to God's authority. Our Lord obeys God's authority first, more than sacrificing Himself on the

cross. He prays earnestly that He may know what is the will of God. He does not say, "I want to be crucified, I must drink the cup." He merely insists on obeying. He says in effect, "If it be possible for me not to go to the cross," but even here He has not His own will. Immediately He continues with, "but Thy will be done."

The will of God is the absolute thing; the cup (that is, the crucifixion) is not absolute. Should God will it that the Lord not be crucified, then He would not need to go to the cross. Before He knew the will of God, the cup and God's will were two separate things; and after He knew it was of God, however, the cup and God's will merged into one. Will represents authority. Therefore, to know God's will and to obey it is to be subject to authority. But how can one be subject to authority if he does not pray or have the heart to know God's will?

As God's servants, the first thing we should meet is authority. Before we can work for God we must be overturned by His authority. Our entire relationship with God is regulated by whether or not we have met authority. If we have, then we shall encounter authority everywhere, and being thus restrained by God we can begin to be used by Him.[4]

SUBMISSION TO DELEGATED AUTHORITY

I like what the *Amplified* version has to say about submission to authority:

> Obey your spiritual leaders and submit to them [continually recognizing their authority over you], for they are constantly keeping watch over your souls and guarding your spiritual welfare, as men who will have to render an account [of their trust]. [Do your part to] let them do this with gladness and not with sighing and groaning, for that would not be profitable to you [either] (Heb. 13:17).

When you join a church, you make a covenant not only with the local Body of Christ, but also with God to obey the leadership. You may not understand this, but one follows the other. Conversely, the leadership over that church has a responsibility before God to keep watch over your soul. Any pastor who truly understands his role in the church will take his oversight of the sheep very seriously. Many members do not fathom the times when this heavily weighs on their pastor. It is painful for leaders of a church when young prophetic people—or other church people—reject the counsel and wisdom they could be given through local church leadership.

SUBMISSION TO THE LOCAL CHURCH

Through the years, I have learned to discern a prophetic person who is submitted to a local church. The person is at peace and feels protected. Not all churches understand how to protect the prophetic person, which is sad. Nevertheless, there is protection in being submitted to a local assembly, whether it is the kind of covering you desire or not.

Many leaders attend my home church, Springs Harvest Fellowship. One reason for this is that Colorado Springs has a large proportion of Christian leaders compared to many other cities. As of the writing of this book, approximately 80 Christian ministries are based in Colorado Springs. Our church has a vision for covering leaders. We have a cell group attended by about 30 people that is intended only for ministry leaders and their spouses.

Each of the ministry leaders' families has been adopted by another cell group for intercessory prayer as well as by the ministry of helps, which provides meals or whatever they may need. Those who are traveling are prayed for from the pulpit on Sunday mornings and have hands laid on them when they leave on major trips, as well as when they return. At present approximately 600 people attend our rapidly growing congregation. It is a wonderful feeling to be prayerfully covered by a local church.

I know I have talked about this earlier, but I believe it cannot be reiterated too much. Don't be a "lone ranger" prophetic minister. Pray and search until you find the church you need. You may have to move to another location and come into covenant relationship with a church in another city.

Discernment and Submission
Do I think you need to submit to everything your pastor says regardless of what it may be? Of course not. I am greatly concerned about some

churches that call themselves "prophetic churches" but are actually part of the old shepherding movement—under the guise of the prophetic. For those of you who aren't familiar with this movement, it was highly dysfunctional and told the members whom they were to date, marry, how to spend their money and so on.

Some churches do not let their members marry outside of their own congregations. Even within the church, couples are not allowed to marry unless the church prophets receive a "word from the Lord" that the couple is divinely called to be husband and wife. Such an operation borders on being a cult, or may already be one.

Prophetic churches that have valid ministries do exist and are a great blessing to the Body of Christ. My pastor, Dutch Sheets, is a prophetic teacher and our church has an abundance of prophetic people. The flow between the prophetic word that is given corporately from the congregation and the teaching gift is beautiful. One Wednesday night, the prophetic word came that we were to sing in our barrenness and the next week Pastor Dutch taught a powerful prophetic message on "Singing in Barrenness."

Submission to delegated authority is not always easy because the authority figure placed over you may not be a person you would have selected. This usually occurs when the senior pastor appoints another leader with whom you may not get along. Many times this is a test for you because you may think your leadership abilities surpass those of the person who was chosen.

Promotion and Submission

In his book *The Making of a Leader*, Frank Damazio has written an excellent section called "The Parable of Promotion." This material is drawn from a passage in Judges 9:6-24,50-57, where the word "promotion" is used three times. The parable is about four trees that went forth to anoint a king over them: the olive tree, the fig tree, the grapevine and the bramble bush. Each of the trees, except the bramble bush, knew its place of authority. Damazio says:

> The "parable of promotion" also demonstrates through nature the spiritual principle that every leader must know his own place of ministry, and stay in it! Jotham's parable describes how all but one tree knew the place that God had given to them in nature, and were content to stay there. The bramble bush, however, expressed its desire to go beyond the realm

that God had given to it in nature. It wanted to be promoted over all the other trees, and to upset the natural order of all things around it.

In applying this parable to leadership and promotion, we see that every leader must adopt the attitude of ministry acceptance expressed by the olive, fig and vine. So must every leader accept the place of ministry which God has given him in His vineyard. Much strife, jealousy, and hurt feelings could be avoided if God's leaders would just find their ministries and stay within their boundaries.

A tragic example from recent history illustrates this. William Branham, a prophetic minister in the 1950's, desired to function beyond the ministries of prophecy, word of knowledge, revelation, and healing which God had so obviously given to him. He wanted to be a Bible teacher also. It was at this point, according to international traveling Bible teacher Ern Baxter, that Branham's pride put his ministry off the track. Branham had a great prophetic ministry, yet the end of his life and ministry was tragic.[5]

One top evangelist was called to be an evangelist—a great one—but when he tried to be a prophet, he ripped up many ministries and made a mess. Another young psalmist-evangelist tried to be a prophet, critic and guide—and died for it.

In learning to submit to delegated authority, personal pride issues may need to be addressed. One of the hardest situations is when a leader who is younger than you or has been in the ministry a shorter time is brought into a position to which you must submit. This often exposes what I call an "elder brother" spirit. This is taken from the parable of the prodigal son in Luke 15 when the elder brother is furious that his younger brother is receiving blessings from their father's hand. Jealousy is an ugly thing. God promotes on a basis different from the world. He raises up people based on how advanced they are in the spirit and not necessarily according to their physical ages or years in the Kingdom.

Through the years, I've taken some hard knocks from those who thought I was too young to be in the positions I've been placed in by those in authority. One day my friend John Dawson said to me, "Cindy, I'm usually the youngest one in my peer group and it has been difficult at times. I can't even imagine what it's been like for you as the youngest and, often, as the only woman." Afterward, he went on to pray for me. That prayer deeply touched my heart because only the Lord knew how much I had struggled with the things he had mentioned. Being physically young in leadership can be a challenge and I, at least, have often marveled at where God has placed me. Believe me, I've read Jeremiah 1:7—"Say not, I am only a youth" (*AMP*)—many, many times late at night when I have felt inadequate.

The good part about being criticized (and some would ask, "Is there a good part?") is that it tends to keep you humble. It can also keep you tender toward those whom others might look down upon. When I was growing up, my daddy would point at drunks on the street corners and say, "Don't you ever judge those people. Except for the grace of God, that could be you!"

One of my prayers for myself is, "Lord, when I reach the place where I need to step down or make way for the new generation, let me do it with grace and be a blessing." I am grateful for those who have gone before me who have prayed similar prayers and paved the way for those of my generation. I know we are reaping from their hard labors and are blessed to follow in their big footsteps.

David's Model of Submission

One of the greatest examples in the Bible of understanding delegated authority is that of David to Saul (see 1 Sam. 18—19). Saul was extremely jealous of the attention David received after his victories in battle. He became obsessed with passion and suspicion against David to the point of repeatedly trying to kill him. David, in all these things, kept his heart right. David had the opportunity to kill Saul but refused to touch God's anointed. David had great authority because he understood authority. Saul, however, was abusive in his authority, which left David in a quandary. Although David protected himself, he did not overtly attack the king because Saul had been appointed by God.

Earlier in this book, I shared how I have been mentored by many people through their writings. An exceptional book, to be read both by those in authority and by those who have been abused by leaders, is written by Gene Edwards, and is entitled *A Tale of Three Kings*. It essentially tells the story of Saul, David and Absalom and is incredible for attitude adjustments. This is one of those books a person needs to reread every few years or so. The story is one of submission and brokenness—even in the midst of dealing with a mad king called Saul.

Rejection and Submission

Years ago, I was part of a church that didn't understand the prophetic gifts. The hard part was neither did I. Because of this I did things that were out of order. Looking back, I see that a number of things occurred because we were all so young in the gifts of the Spirit. Many things, however, could have helped the church if it had been in a position to hear. One of the problems was that I was a woman, and women didn't share from our pulpit. Thus, I was in an awkward situation.

One day I noticed that a chill in the air developed each time I entered a room. I still led worship and taught the children's church, but something was terribly wrong. Finally, I asked the Lord, "What is going on?" The answer I received shocked me!

Quietly an inner voice said, "They think you're practicing divination. Go talk to the associate pastor and his wife." As couples, we had been close friends for several years but things had seemed strained lately.

I shared this with Mike and he said he would be glad to go with me to talk to the associate pastor. He, too, had noticed a strange withdrawal among our friends and acquaintances. As we talked with the associate pastor and his wife, they became very still. After a few moments they admitted, "Yes, it's true. The senior pastor told us you were practicing divination and even laughed at the times you had prophesied. Not only that, but he also has told this to other leaders in the area." To say I was crushed would be the understatement of the century. It was like a bad dream; this couldn't be happening to me.

Later that day, I called another leader and asked if he had been contacted. The answer was affirmative.

"But Cindy," the person said, "I never believed it. He just doesn't understand about the prophetic word and feels threatened. In fact, he's rather jealous of you." I didn't know about the jealous part, but some rather painful things had occurred while I was in the church. On a few occasions, for instance, I had been rebuked in prayers from the pulpit.

I thought, *I'm going to talk to the heavenly Father about this!* I went before the Lord and poured out my heart. I announced, "Lord, you know what this man said about your daughter?" (Of course, He knew!) "I ask you to vindicate me."

While praying, I drifted off in my imagination about exactly how God was going to answer my prayer. In my mind, I saw Him calling fire down from heaven upon the pastor's head. The man was going to be crispy critters! (Good Texas terminology for "toasted with fire.") The picture expanded as I saw the pastor come crawling back on his hands and knees, begging for my forgiveness.

Right in the middle of my beautiful imaginings, the Lord interrupted me with His fatherly voice, "Cindy, I'd like to use you more but you're too sensitive." There was compassion in that Voice. I didn't doubt that He cared that I was hurt, but He was trying to teach me a lesson.

What did I learn from all of this? The voice inside my heart went on to explain, "Leaders deal with rejection many, many times. If you can't resist rejection and deal with it on this level, you'll never survive where I'm taking you." At that moment, the grace of God flooded my heart.

The upshot of the situation was that we didn't leave the church until we were released awhile later. Instead, we met with the senior pastor to talk. He still didn't apologize, but the Lord assured me that if I would keep my heart right, everything would be all right in the long run. Years later, the pastor did apologize and we ministered together in a conference, which brought great healing.

Obedience and Submission

In looking back on my life, I've learned more from the painful situations than from the good ones. Many of them have been tests for me as a person. What the devil meant for evil, however, God turned around for my good.

On another occasion, I had been invited to be one of the main speakers at an outdoor crusade. To say I was excited would be minimizing my feelings. I had prepared the message, sensed the anointing and couldn't wait for the night to come. In addition, it involved traveling a long, long way to speak.

The afternoon of the meeting arrived. The leader overseeing the outreach came to me and said, "Cindy, the pastors' committee feels I should preach tonight."

I gulped and murmured, "Okay, if that's what they feel." The blood rushed to my head and I headed to my room. Mike found me there, being very spiritual—I was crying my eyes out. He comforted me the best he could while I poured out my hurt feelings. At last I calmed down and got very still before the Lord. All of a sudden, I knew this was a test. *Do I think I have to be the instrument of God for His people?* I pondered. I then thought of the ways the other speaker could reach this particular audience better than I could. I decided to pray that God would bless his message much more than the one I had prepared, and that as a result many would come into the kingdom of God.

That night as I sat on the platform interceding, my heart was at peace. When the invitation was extended, people poured to the front with tears streaming down their faces. "Oh, thank You, God," I sighed. "You are so good. You knew just the right person to minister Your Word tonight for these people."

You might say, "But what if the leaders were wrong and you were supposed to preach? Could that happen?" Of course. It doesn't matter to me. What matters is that I was obedient. I so believe in submission to delegated authority that even if the pastors' committee was wrong, God made it right. Later on as I ministered, the anointing was stronger than I had ever felt up to that time. God blessed obedience. It is better than sacrifice.

Let me quote a small portion of the book I recommended to you earlier, *A Tale of Three Kings*:

> David had a question: "What do you do when someone throws a spear at you?"
>
> Does it not seem odd to you that David did not know the answer to this question? After all, everyone else in the world knows what to do when a spear is thrown at them. Why, you pick up the spear and throw it right back!
>
> When someone throws a spear at you, David, just wrench it right out of the wall and throw it back. Absolutely everyone else does, you can be sure.
>
> And in doing this small feat of returning thrown spears, you will prove many things: You are courageous. You stand for the right. You boldly stand against wrong. You are tough and can't be pushed around. You will not stand for injustice or unfair treatment. You are the defender of the faith, keeper of the flame, detector of all heresy. You will not be wronged. All of these attributes then combine to prove that you are also, obviously, a candidate for kingship. Yes, perhaps you are the Lord's anointed.
>
> After the order of King Saul.[6]

RESPECTING AND HONORING GOD'S ANOINTED

In some cases, respecting and honoring God's anointed can be a real challenge. A situation I have touched on is when you are under the leadership of a person who is either a Saul or is in the process of becoming one. Most leaders don't start out as Sauls. In fact, they were once great and mighty people of God. Something happened to them that spoiled the anointing; it might have been a deep personal tragedy, or perhaps pride has become a stronghold. My friend Ed Silvoso says that pride is like bad breath—you're the last one to know you have it!

The tendency of a young leader, especially a young prophetic-type leader, is to want to rebuke the one who has become a Saul. This is not the biblical pattern. First Timothy 5:1 spells this out, "Do not rebuke an older man, but exhort him as a father." The *King James Version* uses the word "elder" for "older man." The connotation of "Do not rebuke" is "to not upbraid or chastise."

Years ago, a leader my age was greatly upset by something an older leader had done. He wrote a letter of correction and called to ask my advice about sending it. I thought a moment and said, "You know, if you send that letter, the person won't receive it from you. Besides, the Word says we are not to rebuke an elder. The person will chalk it off as criticism."

"What should I do?" he asked.

"We can pray."

What did we pray? We agreed that someone who was a peer to that leader, and a person from whom he would receive correction, would speak to that person. Further, we asked God to soften the person's heart to listen to the correction when it came.

The person in question had hurt many people through the years by harsh words and insensitive remarks, but was a great Bible teacher. But this wasn't the first call I had taken from other young leaders who were fed up with the treatment they received from that particular older leader.

God remarkably answered our prayer that day. I later heard this person speak and share publicly how God had been dealing with his harshness and hardness of heart.

Great leaders are vessels of honor in the Body of Christ. These vessels are handled so much by so many people that they can become rough around the edges. Through life's circumstances, they become so chipped and cracked as vessels to drink from that they can cut the ones who try to drink from their wisdom. An admonishment to young leaders: Remember, dear friends, love covers a multitude of sins (see 1 Peter 4:8). Treat older leaders as you would want to be treated in similar seasons of your life.

The Saul Spirit

In the past 12 years, I've listened to heartrending stories of pastors who had one or more of their congregations come to them and accuse them of having a "Saul spirit" (i.e., jealous, controlling and manipulative). Some of these pastors have been my close friends, and I *know* they do not have a Saul spirit. This is a wounding experience for pastors because most of them take their jobs seriously. It hurts them to think that the very people for whom they stayed up all night and for whom they prayed at the hospital could possibly turn on them in this way.

What were some of the things Saul did? Saul was jealous and controlling as well as a potential murderer. He refused to listen to God's prophets and did what he wanted. When given an opportunity, Saul bent God's rules to fit his own desires and then tried to manipulate the prophet of God into saying it was for the sake of God he had done it. Remember how Saul disobeyed Samuel's instructions (see 1 Sam. 15)?

Although a few Sauls are running around, more pastors are are simply in process, as you and I are. Be like David and refuse to touch God's anointed. If you start speaking behind the pastor's back, you will be responsible to God for your actions. Remember, God hates those who sow discord among the brethren (see Prov. 6:16-19).

What if you are under the thumb of a Saul and he is hurling javelins? First of all, seek the Lord regarding whether you are to go or to stay. If you believe you are to leave that church or ministry, do it correctly. By this I mean, do everything you can to receive a blessing when you leave. Don't just run off into the wilderness without saying good-bye. This is painful and can give you a bad reputation.

Years ago, my husband and I left our denominational church incorrectly out of ignorance. The church had appointed us as youth leaders and we took our job seriously. Our youth group wanted to study the book of Acts and so we began going through the book chapter by chapter with them. After a while, we realized that if we continued through Acts, we would have to say that we believed in miracles and that God heals today. Our church took a strict stance against healing and so we resigned our position and then left quietly.

The mistake we made was that when we resigned, we didn't tell anyone we were leaving. We just left. Looking back with hindsight, we should have talked to the pastor, explaining why we thought it wise to leave. The issue was that our new church believed in healing and we thought the previous church wouldn't have understood. Basically, we took the easy way out, and thus left in a way that broke a covenant. If we've broken a covenant, we need to repent and make it right with the churches we've left or it can hinder the blessing of God upon our lives.

The Jezebel Spirit

In addition to accusing someone of being a Saul, I am concerned about another area. It concerns the glib way Christians call people "Jezebels." Certainly people can become Jezebels, but this is a serious accusation. Revelation 2:20 describes Jezebel as a prophetess who taught God's people by her modeling to worship false gods. In that false religion was cult prostitution, thus, immorality. By teaching God's people to worship idols, they were sucked into wrong behavior.

I do believe Jezebels get into the church. A leader told me about a group in which the female leader eventually became a Jezebel and took the men of the church to bed with her. This kind of deception does happen.

Other attributes of a "Jezebel spirit" can be taken from the instance described in 1 Kings 21. Here, Jezebel has Naboth, a righteous man, killed to give her husband, Ahab, his vineyard. She is a controller, deceiver and murderer. I believe a Jezebel spirit that manifests these attributes is present in the Church today. Men *and* women are affected by this spirit (a demonic power has no sex), which causes them to act in ways similar to the Jezebels I have mentioned.

On the other hand, presently, an "accuser of the brethren" spirit seems to be running rampant that brands any strong leader as a Jezebel. We need to have the fear of the Lord on our lives when we label someone with this horrible woman's name.

The Absalom Spirit

Another problem that arises in churches surrounds those who display a spirit similar to Absalom. Absalom tried to take over his father's kingdom. This is an area I cover in *Possessing the Gates of the Enemy* concerning intercessors. This attitude of rebellion or betrayal, however, not only affects intercessors, but also young prophetic people. They are highly susceptible to becoming like Absalom. Here are some reasons for this and problems it causes:

Prophetic people tend to discern the faults and vulnerabilities in other leaders. This is because the Lord wants them to grow in the area of intercessory prayer.

Prophetic people often try to give corrective words with incorrect protocol. When the correction isn't received or acted upon in the fashion or with the timetables they prefer, they become bitter. They don't understand that they may have discerned accurately but are wrong in their delivery. In other words, they are right, but they are also wrong.

Bitter young prophetic leaders tend to "spout off" or tell others what they see in the church or among the leadership. This can cause a critical spirit to rise up against the leaders. Critical people in the church can then gather together like birds of a feather flock together.

Deception can easily enter at this point. Such prophets can become seduced into believing they know better than others or they should be the pastor themselves. Others under deception may claim they know who should be the pastor instead of the current one.

Such deception and dissension can lead to full-blown mutiny. Though at first the prophetic person may have identified a real problem, he or she handles it in such a wrong way that he or she becomes like Absalom, full of rebellious leadership.

A word of caution to those who have young prophetic people under their leadership: Try to listen to the young leaders and see past their arrogance and their incorrect delivery of the word. Then, tenderly share with them the part of the prophecy you believe is accurate (if any). Find some way to affirm them and gently give them instruction about the correct protocol for the delivery of a prophecy to eldership.

Honor and Authority

One little-understood concept in the Church today is that of honoring those in authority over us. This is probably because a lack of respect for authority is becoming rampant in the youth of many cultures. Webster has this to say about honor:

1. The esteem due or paid to worth, high estimation; reverence; veneration.
2. A testimony or token of esteem; any mark of respect or of high estimation by words or actions; as, military honors, civil honors.
3. Dignity; exalted rank or place.[7]

These are good points to ponder. Of course, we are not to venerate leaders over us, but we do need to understand how to esteem and respect them. We honor them not just as people, but also for the positions in which the Lord has put them.

As I have traveled across the world, a number of churches have left a deep impression upon my life in the way they honor their leaders. Many African-American churches seem to have a grasp on honor. In Buenos Aires, Argentina, Vision de Futuro, pastored by the Reverend Omar Cabrera, and his wife, Marfa, honors those in authority over them, as well as those who travel to minister to its congregation. I always feel valued when I am with the congregation. Unfortunately, some churches don't know how to treat traveling ministries and this makes the guest ministers feel devalued.

Even under great duress, Paul modeled an attitude of honor when he was dragged before the Sanhedrin in Acts 23:1-5:

> Then Paul, looking earnestly at the council, said, "Men and brethren, I have lived in all good conscience before God until this day." And the high priest Ananias commanded those who stood by him to strike him on the mouth. Then Paul said to him, "God will strike you, you whitewashed wall! For you sit to judge me according to the law, and do you command me to be struck contrary to the law?" And those who stood by said, "Do you revile God's high priest?" Then Paul said, "I did not know, brethren, that he was the high priest; for it is written, *You shall not speak evil of a ruler of your people.*"

Think about it. Paul had just been hit in the mouth and reacted naturally, even quoting the law. However, he was immediately submissive in his spirit, *not to the abuse but to the position*. This is what David understood about Saul. He did not submit to abuse—nor should we—but he kept his attitude right.

Abuse and Submission

The balance between not submitting to abuse and keeping our attitude right can be delicate. When we have an adverse reaction to something a leader tells us, it is time to search our own hearts. We need to ask: Am I reacting out of past hurts and wounds or is this really abuse? Is this person really like Saul? The truth may not be evident at first but may require a prayerful time of seeking the Lord.

A passage of Scripture I touched on earlier that has been a great blessing to persecuted leaders, but has also been taken out of context to "beat the sheep" is 1 Chronicles 16:22: "Do not touch My anointed ones, and do My prophets no harm."

This has wrongly been taken to mean that the people in the congregation cannot think for themselves nor question anything a leader says. This is dysfunctional and not what the verse means. It *does* mean that even in the midst of our questionings, we need to keep our hearts right and not attack. If we unjustly come against a leader, God will protect and take care of the leader and we will answer to the Lord for what we've done.

RESOLVING CONFLICTS AND DISAGREEMENTS

Although this isn't meant to be a book on settling disagreements, in some instances you will be involved in leadership and will need to sit down with someone and mediate. Matthew 18:15-17 gives a clear biblical model on this subject:

> "Moreover if your brother sins against you, go and tell him his fault between you and him alone. If he hears you, you have gained your brother" (v. 15).

This first step is often skipped. It is more usual for us to tell 15 friends about the problem without approaching the one with whom we have the disagreement. Almost every relationship has occasions when offenses occur. Most people in a friendship need to "clear the air" once in a while. Christians are oftentimes so nice to each other that these things build up until they blow sky-high! An offense can act as a snare or trap. The "little foxes" of offense can mount up, one upon the other, until they ensnare us in bitterness and hostility (Song of Sol. 2:15).

Before you go to someone regarding an offense, pray and ask the Lord to soften both your hearts. Seek the Lord for the power of the Holy Spirit to be in the midst of the meeting. You might use the authority of binding to stop Satan from interfering with the meeting or causing rejection to enter into the process (see Matt. 12:29; 16:18,19; Luke 10:17-19).

> "But if he will not hear, take with you one or two more, that 'by the mouth of two or three witnesses every word may be established'"(Matt. 18:16).

This is the second step. If you have tried to talk it out and have not been successful, ask a mediator or two to join you. Sometimes each side brings a person they trust to the meeting or you can mutually agree on a neutral mediator. Ask the Lord for the correct timing when the person you are confronting can emotionally take the intensity of such a meeting.

> "And if he refuses to hear them, tell it to the church. But if he refuses even to hear the church, let him be to you like a heathen and a tax collector" (v. 17).

We hope most offenses will never get this far. You would have to be extremely hard-hearted to be declared a pagan and a tax collector. This has at times been a much-abused step. People have sometimes been excommunicated in front of their congregations without step two ever having taken place and were almost destroyed. Oftentimes, the accused people are never able to bring in neutral mediators, and the situation turns into a setup against them.

Churches need to be careful about what they say to large groups regarding people who have fallen into sin. After a person repents and changes, the comments can follow him or her and his or her family for the rest of the person's life. It is better to deal with these people in a private setting. Many who have truly repented have been treated as pagans and have been exposed in public settings. Obviously, this can send people over the edge for years.

PROTOCOL FOR DELIVERING
PROPHETIC WORDS TO LEADERS

"All right, Cindy," you may be saying, "you've put the fear of the Lord in me concerning prophesying. What do I do if I believe I have a legitimate word from God concerning my church or a leader in the church?"

Sharing a Personal Prophecy with Leaders

If you have established credibility as a prophetic voice with the church or person you feel the word is for, you need to share it with someone who can judge it for you—whose confidentiality can be trusted (see 1 Cor. 14:29; 1 Thess. 5:19-21). Ask the Lord who this person should be. Come with a humble spirit and submit it without claiming it as God's divine revelation. Be willing to receive correction if it isn't right. Don't go to someone who will be harsh with you, but gentle.

If you have not established credibility in your local church, the protocol is to ask one of the leaders in your church to judge the prophetic word. This may in fact be the very thing that establishes credibility for you if the word is accurate.

One mistake many people make is giving the word to be judged to someone who doesn't know how to judge a word, or isn't in a leadership position in the Body of Christ. If the word is for a church, it would be wise to find someone who is recognized in that church as being accurate in both giving and judging the prophetic word.

If you believe you have received a prophetic word for a specific person, again, if you are young in the ways of prophesying, find someone who knows that person well—and you trust will keep the matter confidential—and have that person look at the word. Ask if it seems accurate and/or if that person would go with you to give the word. At times, young prophetic voices will have prophecies for leaders who are fairly well-known and will want me to give the prophecies to the leaders on their behalf. I usually look at the words and pray about them. Sometimes I say, "I'll call them, give the gist of the word and see if they want to talk to you personally about it." On other occasions, I suggest they write down the word and then I will tell the leaders I think they might want to consider reading it.

It is important to note that busy, visible leaders often have people hounding them, thinking they have heard words from God for them. This can be trying. I never want to discourage people from prophesying to me, yet I often receive some flaky, unsound prophecies. At times, however, I have received something that was a rich blessing to me— sometimes through the mail from an unknown person.

In sharing the prophetic word, rather than using a "thus saith the Lord" kind of approach, you might say, "I received this while I was in prayer for you. Would you look it over?" Once you have delivered the word, leave it and trust the Lord to bring it to pass if indeed it is from Him. I'll cover this, especially the area of timing, more in the next chapter, "Releasing the Prophetic Gift."

Sharing Corporate Prophecy

If a prophecy is for the church congregation as a whole, and you receive it before the service, write it down and give it to an elder whom you trust. If what you have received is more than a simple prophecy, and it has a forthtelling element or direction for the church Body, you need to have it judged and approved before you give it to the congregation. Don't just blurt it out on Sunday morning. If the prophecy is accurate, the elders will be able to determine when it should be given, and they will ask you to hold it until the proper time in the church service. People who give corrective words but are not recognized prophetic voices within a church need to be very careful. If they have not had the word judged beforehand by the church leadership, they are out of line. They have broken proper spiritual protocol. This can lead to great confusion within the church Body. Some of the congregation may side with the out-of-line prophecy and become offended with the leaders, not knowing the various circumstances and inside knowledge the leaders are employing to weigh the timing and import of the word.

SPIRITUAL PROTOCOL FOR PROPHECY IN THE LOCAL CHURCH

This section will be full of gleanings from various successful churches on how they handle prophecy. As I travel to various nations and work with a spectrum of churches and organizations, I find that not only do they follow biblical guidelines for prophesying, but they also each have a culture of their own. You'll hear them make comments such as, "Here at First Church of the Desert, we have these guidelines for our services:..." Nothing is wrong with such distinctions. Each church needs to be true to the vision God has given it, and this means handling prophecy in individual ways.

Many churches are not aware of the do's and don'ts that have become built into its system of leadership until an outsider tries to become part of the inner circle. When this happens, you'll hear church members start to say, "That's not our way." Sadly, many churches become ingrown because they do not have fresh voices speaking to them.

Women's Aglow Fellowship International is a cutting-edge organization for women. The group has been progressive in wanting to have prophetic input from beyond those within its circle. The organization has created several positions on its board of directors for leaders who have not grown up in Aglow, which keeps an openness toward change in its leadership. This openness has proven extremely fruitful for the group. Other groups, such as *Charisma* magazine, invite known leaders and prophetic voices to come and share with their staffs from time to time. This stops a "not invented here" mentality.

Community of Joy, Glendale, Arizona

One of the most unique and exciting churches I interviewed was Community of Joy, an ELCA Lutheran church in Glendale, Arizona (near Phoenix), pastored by Walther Kallestad. (Earlier in this book, I quoted some information about the church's prayer ministry.) Kallestad describes his church as a third-wave evangelical congregation (i.e., one that is open to all the gifts of the Spirit) with a major emphasis on evangelism.

Community of Joy has a vision to build a church for the unchurched. During the week, around 10,000 people will be ministered to, of which 7,000 consider themselves members. Founded in 1978, the church consists of 65 percent unchurched people, 40 percent of whom have no church background whatsoever. At present, the church is getting ready to build a new campus having a strong focus on children. They are using Disney designers to build a kid-friendly environment. Even the shrubs will be in special animal topiary designs. What a delightful concept!

I share all of this to give you an understanding of Community of Joy's philosophy of prophecy. Pastor Kallestad says that prophecy is very much a part of the life of the church. The leaders, however, do not let people prophesy on Sunday morning because the church is reaching for the lost, and nonbelievers would not understand a prophetic word.

Although Sunday morning is not the appropriate place at Community of Joy for prophecies, they do receive a lot of prophetic words from their intercessors, which they take very seriously. According to Pastor Kallestad, his wife, Mary, is quite accurate in spiritual discernment. He relies upon her, among others, to judge the prophecies that come to the leaders. If the prophecy is one they believe is from God, the prayer ministry, headed by Bjorn Pedersen, gives it to the intercessors for prayer.

Pastor Kallestad shared about a time when he received a personal prophecy from an unlikely source at a low point in his life. The church was struggling financially and he was very discouraged. A woman who could barely write gave him a prophecy in writing. To begin with, it was miraculous that she was even able to write the note. When she gave him the note, she said with a shaking voice, "This has never happened to me before!" The message was on target. It said, "You are called of God and

do not be disheartened." Simple, but exactly what he needed to hear.
Prophecies don't have to be complicated to hit the mark.

First Assembly of God, Phoenix, Arizona

Leo Godzick, pastor of special projects for First Assembly of God in
Phoenix, Arizona (pastored by Tommy Barnett), was most gracious to
give me his time to talk about the way this booming, evangelistic church
handles prophecy. Pastor Godzick says, "We encourage anyone to
prophesy. Although we do not have a written policy on prophecy, we do
have order in our meetings. It is our desire for the Holy Spirit to have
free reign and so we do not have specific rules on who should speak. We
believe prophecy is a gift of God and we are open to His moving in a
variety of manifestations.

"Usually, if people have a prophetic word, they come to me during
the service to have it judged or to ask if they can give it. I consider the
word in light of what is happening in the Spirit in the service, and when
or if it is appropriate I let the pastor know. There have been times when
people have been out of order and we have had to ask them to be still.
Upon occasion, someone that we do not know will prophesy and we will
send a pastor to talk with them and get to know them."

Springs Harvest Fellowship, Colorado Springs, Colorado

My home church, Springs Harvest Fellowship, puts the following
announcement in the bulletin each week, stating the protocol for giving
a prophetic word to the congregation:

> A NOTE TO THE BODY:
> Regarding the operation of the gifts of the Holy Spirit:
> Anyone who has something to contribute to the service
> should check with one of the leadership team sitting in the
> front row of the sanctuary. We ask that this procedure be
> followed for the sake of order. Please do not approach the
> person with the microphone at the pulpit.
> Pastor Dutch and the Elders

So many people who have mature prophetic gifts attend our church
that Pastor Dutch teases they need to take a number when they wish to
prophesy. The prophecies given are taken very seriously. As I shared
earlier, Pastor Dutch will build teachings around the prophecies to bib-

lically amplify what has been prophesied. In addition, the prophecies are always taped and kept as part of the spiritual history of the church as confirmations, and as spiritual guidance. The intercessors take these prophecies and pray over them in their early morning prayer times as the Lord leads them.

The Church On The Way, Van Nuys, California

The Church On The Way in Van Nuys, California, has the reputation of being a model church in many ways. Pastor Jack Hayford is noted for his wisdom. His associate pastor, Scott Bauer, is also a profoundly wise man. Pastor Bauer and I talked for quite some time about the philosophy of the church concerning prophecy. The Church On The Way integrates the teaching gift in regard to mentoring those who prophesy.

One way the leaders establish protocol in The Church On The Way is by teaching about the philosophy and biblical foundation of the church. Pastor Bauer has shared a three-part message called "Demystifying the Will of God," which establishes the boundaries of what is acceptable in the way of the prophetic word. For instance, if a prophecy said, "It is not My will that all may be saved," the church would immediately know that the word was incorrect. For the Word of God says that it is not God's will "that any should perish" (2 Pet. 3:9).

As is the case in some of the other churches, The Church On The Way does not have a written policy regarding public prophecy. Bauer, however, says they encourage anyone who has a valid word to come to the front of the church and use the microphone. One of the reasons for this is that the church has two campuses and this enables the word to be recorded for everyone to hear. Some who prophesy in the church—actor Dean Jones for one—usually come to the front and wait until they are recognized, while others simply launch out wherever they are seated. If the pastor is in the middle of something else, he will simply ask them to hold on to the message until a later time.

Pastor Bauer is clear that the church does not allow inappropriate messages to go uncorrected. If the word is biblical but has a legalistic tone, the leaders will approach the person privately later and give instruction. They may ask the person to listen to some tapes or to take a class on the gifts of the Spirit.

The Church On The Way works diligently through pastoral counsel, as well as through the teaching ministry, to mentor and give people who desire to prophesy every opportunity to learn to flow with what God is doing in their church. Some people, however, do not listen and still give inappropriate prophecies, sometimes in one-on-one situations outside of the sanctuary. In such cases, when a person refuses to observe the guidelines, the leadership team approaches the person and asks him or her to find another place to worship.

The Sanctuary of the East Valley, Mesa, Arizona

The Sanctuary of the East Valley, in Mesa, Arizona, pastored by Daniel and LaNora Van Arsdall, takes the prophetic words given to the congregation very seriously. Each of the words is written down and put into a book of remembrance (or journal of prophecies) for the intercessors to pray over.

They experienced a major breakthrough as a church after having a 21-day, 24-hours-a-day prayer meeting in 1994. The book of remembrance was placed at the front of the room along with a separate journal for each prayer watch. The intercessors logged what the Lord had told them during each watch. At the end of the 21 days of prayer, they experienced a visitation (i.e., a time of revival, conversions, repentance and healings) of the Holy Spirit that hasn't left them yet.

Atlanta Metropolitan Church, Atlanta, Georgia

Elder Yul Crawford of Atlanta Metropolitan Church in Georgia discerns prophetic words as they are brought to him during the church service. Yul says that his pastor, Bishop Flynn Johnson, has highly encouraged and mentored his prophetic gifting by taking Yul along as he travels. For Yul and others in the church, mentoring occurs in the services as they realize they are hearing the same things that are given by the more mature prophetic voices of the church.

Is one method better than another? I believe the best method is the one that is biblical (according to 1 Cor. 12—14), works in the local congregation and brings maximum blessing through the release of the prophetic word. In my opinion, it is always wise to remain open to better ways of honing the use of the prophetic gift in the church. Also, as churches grow, they sometimes will change the way their services flow.

PROTOCOL REGARDING TONGUES AND INTERPRETATION

Tongues and interpretation can be sensitive areas and I've considered the best way to explain protocol regarding these two subjects. As I see it, there are three perspectives concerning tongues and interpretation:

1. *Cessationist: Tongues ceased with the last apostle.*

The spiritual protocol for those who attend a church that holds the cessationist view is that it is out of order to give a prophecy using tongues and interpretation. It would produce confusion. This perspective is also true for mixed gatherings that are promoting unity. Tongues is a hot issue that is much debated and so its use does not edify the Body of Christ at large in mixed meetings.

One of the greatest movements promoting unity for the sake of world evangelization is the A.D. 2000 and Beyond Movement, which has an emphasis on "a church for every people and the gospel for every person" by the year 2000. The prayer track, headed by Peter Wagner, brings together a diverse group of people to intercede for the lost. It is so cross-denominational that guidelines have been written for the meetings.

In 1989, Lausanne II in Manila, Philippines, was one of the largest gatherings of various cultures and denominations the Church has ever witnessed. Approximately 4,500 leaders came from throughout the world to this invitation-only meeting. One plenary session was disrupted by a man yelling in tongues during the service; he then continued to speak what he felt was an interpretation. This was totally out of order for a number of reasons. For one, it was divisive. For another, it brought confusion. Also, it polarized some camps while it simply puzzled others. One brother told me he heard an evangelical leader tell his friend in hushed tones, "There was someone in the meeting today who thought he was God!"

2. *Third wave: Tongues is a gift of the Spirit given to some of the Body of Christ.*

Peter Wagner is one of the major leaders of the third-wave movement. His definition of the gift of tongues and of interpretation is as follows:

> The gift of tongues is the special ability that God gives to certain members of the Body of Christ (A) to speak to God in a language they have never learned and/or (B) to receive and communicate an immediate message of God to His people through a divinely anointed utterance in a language they have never learned.
>
> The gift of interpretation of tongues is the special ability that God gives to certain members of the Body of Christ to

make known in the vernacular the message of one who speaks in tongues.[8]

Third-wave churches, such as Community of Joy, often embrace prophecy in meetings other than the regular congregational services of the church. Some people in the church would be opposed to tongues and interpretation while others would not. If you are new to a church, it is best to clearly understand its policy and beliefs before you launch out into tongues and interpretation.

3. Charismatic or Pentecostal: Tongues are available through the empowering of the Holy Spirit to every believer. A private devotional tongue is given to every Christian as found in Acts, and the ability to give public tongues and interpretation is found in 1 Corinthians 12:10 and 14:5. The private devotional tongue has been described as the man or woman speaking to God through the power of the Holy Spirit. The second type, which is given publicly, is God speaking through a man or a woman to His people.

I realize that by putting the charismatic movement together with the Pentecostal denominations I am making some broad generalizations. Most of these groups, however, would support public tongues and interpretations in their regular congregational services.

For those who are not familiar with the use of tongues and interpretation, it is sometimes confusing that the tongue may be short while the interpretation might seem lengthy. The reverse can happen, where the tongue is long and the interpretation is short. One possible explanation is that the tongue is being interpreted and not translated word for word. It is possible that an interpretation gives the gist of what is being said through a person who may be more verbose or, on the other hand, through someone who may be given to concise speaking. It is similar to one person interpreting by using *The New King James Version* and another person interpreting by using an extended paraphrase such as the *Amplified* version.

I have seen cases where a long tongue was given and the interpretation came through three, short interpretations, each with a piece of what was said through tongues. When I am personally responsible for meetings, an interpretation may be given and I might sense that it is not all the Holy Spirit wants to say to us through the tongue. I will ask, "Is there anyone who has the rest of the interpretation?"

At times, a person who has a prophecy for the service will tack it onto a tongue as an interpretation. However, it may not be the correct interpretation at all, but rather a separate prophecy. Sometimes, if it is appropriate and will not destroy the momentum of what God is doing in a service, I will mention that I feel the prophecy was from the Lord but not the interpretation of the tongue. I will then ask the person with the interpretation to please give it.

At times, the tongue is simply an adoration to God, but giving the adoration so lifts up the person or another hearer that it prompts a prophetic word to be given. This could also be a reason a person may give a long tongue and the interpretation is short, or vice versa. It could be that when the tongue is given from God to the congregation a translation will follow, but when it is simply an adoration, an interpretation will be given.

Leaders need to be aware of their responsibilities regarding interpretation or translation whenever a tongue is given in a corporate meeting. The protocol is that if a tongue is given and no one else can interpret, the leader or one of the other leaders of the meeting should be prepared to ask God to give him or her the interpretation. This has happened many times to me. On the other hand, the leaders should not assume they are the ones who always have to, or should, interpret. God might want to use others. I have found that when leaders always interpret the word it loses its freshness, because God wants to use the whole Body of Christ to speak and not just the church leadership (see 1 Cor. 14:26). If only the leaders interpret, it can create a "spiritual elitist" mentality both in the leaders and in the people.

If a tongue that is simply adoration to God is given, God at times has given me the exact translation of the adoration. For instance, the person may have said something like, "Oh Father, thank You for Your presence in our midst. You have so graced us with Your comfort and joy." I have often found that God through the Holy Spirit will touch a person to express the corporate feelings the church is experiencing at that moment, and it releases a greater level of adoration through the whole Body.

It is possible for a tongue not to be of the Lord at all and, instead of releasing peace in the meeting, it produces unrest and agitation in the hearts of the congregation. The tongue might be strident, angry or harsh, and be of another spirit other than the Holy Spirit. If this is the case, it is entirely appropriate for the leader to ask the person to be restrained, as Pastor Hayford did with the man at the Love L.A. meeting in the story at the beginning of the chapter. Pastor Hayford says if someone is publicly out of order in his church and refuses to be silent, he simply encourages the whole congregation to lift up their voices in worship to the Lord so the praises of God's people drown out the other voice!

Spiritual Protocol for Conferences

Properly given at conferences and large gatherings, the prophetic word can be a great blessing. Protocol will depend on the size of the conference, where it is held, if it is held in a church or conference center and the purpose of the meeting.

Prophetic words given at a church conference for the church's own people will usually follow the guidelines of the church itself. If the church, however, is opening the conference to people from other churches and still wants to release the prophetic gifts during the worship services, it is appropriate to give some kind of explanation to those visiting to avoid confusion. For instance, after a prophecy is given a leader might say, "What you have heard is a prophecy in which we feel the Holy Spirit was speaking a message to us through this brother/sister. You will find this described in the Bible in 1 Corinthians 12 and 14." Others might make a stronger statement indicating that what was given was a direct word from God.

Conferences designed to promote unity should probably require that prophecies given by attendees be written down and given to one of the conference leaders. In this way, the leaders can still harvest or glean from what God is saying to the whole group without exercising public prophecy. Some may not want to draw this much attention to prophecy in their meetings by giving such instructions. I've found, however, that if you have a mixed group and do not give any guidelines, someone may launch out in the middle of the meeting in an inappropriate way.

It also may be wise to state that the group is from diverse backgrounds, some where prophecy is not embraced, and that the reason for the meeting is to promote unity. The request can then be made from the lectern that people are to refrain from public prophesying. I have been in meetings where this kind of announcement wasn't necessary because it was commonly understood. I have, on the other hand, been in other meetings where something should have been said at the beginning of the meeting.

Conferences that range in attendance from 4,000 and greater might consider putting together a prophetic team. The reasons for doing this are practical. In large meetings, those who speak from the floor without a microphone simply cannot be heard. Also, large meetings attract flakes as bees are attracted to honey.

Prophetic teams can be chosen in various ways. I have been a part of the prophetic teams of both the North American Renewal Congress (NARC) and Women's Aglow Fellowship International. The NARC committee sends recommendations for possible prophetic team members and then issues invitations to those they want to include on the team. The teams have appointed leaders who judge the prophetic words and decide when they should be given during the meetings.

For large conferences, Aglow has regional chapters send in names of gifted prophetic women to the conference committee, which then chooses about 50 women to be on what they call their "Word Gift" team. The ladies come to a leader when they feel they have a word, and at certain times during the worship service a microphone is set out for them to prophesy. In addition, the board of directors, officers and platform people prophesy from time to time.

I'll never forget one night when one of the leaders, Dee Finck, gave a word that God was going to use Aglow to "unravel the garment of Islam." It struck a deep chord in our hearts as an organization, and since that time Muslim women have been a primary target of our prayers.

Two other topics could be included in this section on spiritual protocol—releasing the prophetic word and receiving the prophetic word. They are so intertwined with prophetic style, however, that I thought it was best to leave them for the next chapter, "Releasing the Prophetic Gift."

PROPHECY IN PRACTICE

1. Have you ever witnessed a service where proper spiritual protocol was not practiced?
2. What were the effects on the meeting as a result?
3. Have you ever had a time when you thought you might have a prophecy for a service but you didn't know how and when to give it?
4. Are you willing to prophesy during a corporate setting if the Lord wants you to do so?
5. What do you do if you have a corrective word for your local church congregation?

Notes

1. W. Bauer, W. F. Arndt, W. F. Gingrich, and F. W. Danker, *A Greek-English Lexicon of the New Testament and Other Early Christian Literature* (Chicago: University of Chicago Press, 1979), p. 327.
2. Noah Webster, *Webster's New Twentieth Century Dictionary* (New York: Simon and Schuster, 1979), p. 1448.
3. Watchman Nee, *Spiritual Authority* (Richmond, Va.: Christian Fellowship Publisher, 1972), preface page.
4. Ibid., pp. 14-15.
5. Frank Damazio, *The Making of a Leader* (Portland, Oreg.: Trilogy Productions, 1988), pp. 191-192.
6. Gene Edwards, *A Tale of Three Kings* (Wheaton, Ill.: Tyndale House Publishers, 1992), pp. 15-16.
7. Webster, *Webster's New Twentieth Century Dictionary*, p. 872.
8. C. Peter Wagner, *Your Spiritual Gifts Can Help Your Church Grow* (Ventura, Calif.: Regal Books, 1979; revised edition, 1994), pp. 204, 206-207.

CHAPTER EIGHT

RELEASING THE PROPHETIC GIFT

■

Through the years, many people have asked me, "Cindy, how do I get started prophesying? When do I share the prophetic word I'm receiving? How did you get started in all of this? Were you ever nervous?" This is one of those chapters where I've tried to think of the myriad questions with which I've often been barraged. Because of lack of time and personal contact, I will never get to meet or worship with many of you. For that reason, I offer the following ideas that have proven to be practical truths I wish I had known a long time ago.

I don't know if you have ever leaped out and prayed some extremely radical prayers in your life—prayers such as, "Lord, I'll do anything You want me to, anytime, anywhere!" This is really dangerous-type praying. Quite some time ago I started giving myself wholly to the Lord, every part of me—everything I owned, did and said, and everywhere I went. Do you know the Scripture, "He must increase, but I *must* decrease" (John 3:30)? I was doing my best to live it. The funny thing about praying those kinds of prayers is that the Lord takes them seriously! Very seriously.

During this Radical Praying and Commitment (R.P.C.) season, one particular prayer stands out to me today. It was the time I said, "Lord, I'll be a fool for You. Just ask me to do anything, no matter how foolish it looks." During the next Sunday evening service, I felt that heavy presence of the Lord I mentioned earlier in the book.

Oh no, I thought, *surely the Lord doesn't want me to prophesy out loud in the congregation*! Fear struck my body like an 18-wheel truck. As you know by now, I'm famous for negotiating at times like this. "Lord, I have a friend with me here from a church where they don't do stuff like this. I'll embarrass her, Lord. She may never come back to visit here again. She already thinks we're all a bit crazy." There was silence from heaven; just the same heavy presence of God. "Lord," I continued in desperation, "there are nine thousand members in this church. Can't you use one of them?"

The church Mike and I were attending at the time had no official protocol for prophesying and those who gave a word simply "launched out." I never got the courage to launch out that night. Later I talked to the pastor about it and he gently said, "Cindy, this is your family. If you miss the prophecy God is speaking to you, we'll help you."

As I walked away I murmured to myself, "If you miss it, we'll help you! Pastor, there are nine thousand—count them, *nine thousand*—people here." I didn't know if I could take being chastised in front of so many people and I was unsure if it had been God that touched me to prophesy or not.

About a year went by, and the experience with the Lord during that service never returned. Finally, I decided that maybe He was waiting for me. "Father," I prayed, "I confess to You that I really blew it. Please give me another chance. I'll be a fool for You like I promised." That was what He had been waiting for! By this time, we had moved to another city and attended a church that only had around 1,200 in attendance on Sunday morning. (*Only 1,200!* Lots of people were there!)

The next Sunday morning, I was minding my own business, worshiping the Lord, when His presence came upon me just as it had a year previously. *Oh no*, I mused, *He certainly didn't waste any time.* Again, the church had no established protocol, so during a lull in the service, I stood up. The part that was really alarming me was that I was receiving no English words. *That could only mean one thing*, I reasoned, *tongues.* I thought with alarm, *He wants me to give a word in tongues!* Panic hit my body. As I described in the previous chapter, if you give a prophecy, it doesn't have to be interpreted, but a message in tongues does. Unless it was "in adoration," I knew if I gave the word in tongues and no one interpreted it, I would be totally out of order (see 1 Cor. 14:5,6,13).

After I stood to my feet, no one recognized me or did anything and so, not knowing what to do, I sat down—greatly relieved, I might add. "Well, Lord, I was a fool. I did what You asked." The pastor got up for the message and I felt relief flood my whole being. I thought, *The spirit of the prophets is subject to the prophets. God isn't going to interrupt Himself.*

Just at that moment, the pastor looked at me and said with a smile, "We never want to miss something that the Lord has to say to us. So if anyone has a word, let them give it now." My heart banged in my chest and my mouth felt like it was full of cotton. I knew that this was the opportunity God had opened for me. He was calling me on my prayers. If I didn't give the word now, I'd be in direct rebellion to God.

I cautiously stood and opened my mouth to speak and out came a tongue. It flowed for a minute or so and then I sat down and looked expectantly at the pastor. He was looking around for the interpretation. *Oh no*, I thought with panic, *He doesn't have the interpretation!* After a long minute, no one else spoke up either. My husband, Mike, was earnestly praying, "Oh God, give it to me, I'll interpret it. What did she say?" Neither of us had done this before.

All of a sudden, I knew what I had said. The whole thing just flooded my mind. I quickly stood and began to speak. I remember to this day the essence of the interpretation:

> Some of you are saying to Me that your back is up against the wall. You are in a room with no windows or doors and everywhere you look there is no way out. I say to you, My children, you are looking in the wrong place. For I say, "Look up, and begin to praise Me." For as you praise Me, I will reach down with My strong right arm and lift you out of your circumstance from which there is no way out.

It blesses me today as much as it did then! The members of the congregation began to clap their hands. A few of them also had tears rolling down their faces. I sat down with great relief and a deep sense of satisfaction and sighed to myself, *It was worth the fear, cotton mouth and panic. What a blessing the word of the Lord can be to His people.*

The fear I had to deal with before giving the tongue and interpretation is not unusual, as I found out later after talking with others. Some big strongholds in my life had been the fear of humans and the fear of missing God. Both of these had been purged before I gave the tongue and the interpretation. It could also be that Satan was throwing a few fiery darts of fear my way because he certainly doesn't like God's people being blessed through prophecy.

RELEASING YOURSELF TO GOD

Suppose you have considered praying some radical prayers like I did or perhaps you already have prayed them. I encourage you to follow the guidelines I'm going to present if one of the things God asks you to do is to prophesy. If you haven't already prayed and given all of yourself to the Lord, maybe you'd like to do that now with me.

> Lord, I give all of myself to You. Take every aspect of my life and use me for Your kingdom to glorify Your name. I'll do anything You want me to do, go anywhere You want me to go, and say anything You want me to say. Father, there isn't any gift that You have for me that I don't want. If You want to use me in a way I'm not used to, I yield myself to that. I trust You, Lord, to teach and guide me as I dedicate my life to You. In Jesus' name, Amen.

Hearing from God

Some of you who are reading this book know the Lord wants you to prophesy. Perhaps you already have prophesied and want to learn more. You may just be getting started and a few friends have mentioned to you, "I think you have the gift of prophecy." It is my personal belief that everyone in the Body of Christ does occasionally exhibit—in some way—supernatural knowledge of things to come without the person being aware of it. Usually, people will mention after an event, "I kind of had a feeling this was going to happen."

God gives parents who are praying for their children many of these impressions so they will know how to intercede for them when they are in a mess, in danger or upset. They may not know what to do with what they are hearing from God, or recognize that it is the Lord wanting them to pray prophetically to avert the danger, or so forth, but this kind of knowledge does happen.

Shirley Dobson once told a story at a conference in Washington, D.C., that touched my heart. She is a great woman of God who knows the Voice of the Lord and is sensitive in her spirit. Here is the story in her own words about the prophetic prayer she prayed for her daughter, Danae, and the resulting supernatural protection she received:

> I was at home one rainy weekend and looking forward to working on several projects I had set aside for just such a time. Both Jim and Ryan [their son] were in Northern California on a hunting trip, and Danae had plans for the

evening with one of her friends. She had previously asked for permission to use the family car for her outing.

Secretly happy to have some time to myself, I turned on some music and was busy at work when suddenly a heaviness descended upon me. Feelings of unexplainable anxiety and fear for Danae washed over me. I thought, *This is silly. She's out with her friend, having a good time. I'm sure she is all right.* Instead of lessening, the apprehension I felt grew more intense. Finally, I slipped into the bedroom, closed the door and got down on my knees.

"Lord," I prayed, "I don't know why I am experiencing such fear about Danae, but if she is in any danger, I ask You to send guardian angels to watch over, protect and bring her home safely." I continued praying for a time and then got up and went back to work. The burden lifted to some degree, but I still sensed an uneasiness.

Forty-five minutes later I heard a knock on the door. Opening it, I found a policeman standing on my porch. He asked me if I owned a red car and I replied in the affirmative. "I found it upside down on a mountain road, Mrs. Dobson. Who was driving? Was it your husband?" he questioned. Danae had been driving the red car. I now realized why the Lord had impressed me to pray. Later I was to realize just how powerful that time of intercession had been on her behalf.

While he [the policeman] was there, the hospital emergency room called. They wouldn't tell me details. I found Danae very shaken with her left hand badly injured, swollen and bleeding. She had used her left arm and hand to brace herself as the car rolled over, and the car had actually rolled on her hand. We were told she could have lost her hand had her palm been facing down. Fortunately, a noted hand surgeon was in the hospital that night and was able to operate immediately. Another answer to prayer.

Later, we were to learn the whole story. Even though she had been driving very slowly, the rain had washed gravel over the oil-slick road, causing her to skid as she rounded the curve. She became very scared and lost control as most young drivers would. The car landed upside down in the middle of the road. If she had gone another 30 feet, the car would have plunged off the road and down a 500 foot embankment. There was no guardrail. With much gratitude in my heart, I thought about my prayer in light of the accident and saw legions of angels lined up against the road, keeping her car from sliding over the edge. Another answer to prayer!

Danae quickly recovered, regaining full use of her left hand and we give much praise to the Lord.

Pastors may come from a tradition where they aren't familiar with prophesying. Many may feel that prophesying is simply preaching the Word of God. Pastors may preach under a prophetic anointing at times, but there is more to the gift of prophecy, and anointed preaching is not its only use. Sometimes I'll ask pastors who aren't familiar with prophecy, "Have you ever had a time when the Lord awakened you and suddenly you had every point for your sermon? The Holy Spirit just gave it to you point after point. You may have joked and said, 'I wish they all came that easy!'" This is the Lord giving the message prophetically and it is one way a prophetic word comes to a person. It isn't the only way, but it is one way.

THE OFFICE OF PROPHET AND THE SIMPLE GIFT OF PROPHECY

The gift of prophecy is demonstrated in the book of Acts. Peter Wagner talks about the gift of prophecy in *Lighting the World*, the second book in his three-book commentary on Acts. Note his comments on Acts 11:27,28 and the differentiation he makes between the simple gift of prophecy and the office of the prophet:

> 11:27 And in these days prophets came from Jerusalem to Antioch. 28. Then one of them, named Agabus, stood up and showed by the Spirit that there was going to be a great famine throughout all the world, which also happened in the day of Claudius Caesar. 29. Then the disciples, each according to his ability, determined to send relief to other brethren dwelling in Judea. 30. This they also did, and sent it to the elders by the hands of Barnabas and Saul.

This is the first time prophets and the gift of prophecy is mentioned in Acts. Many other aspects of power ministry have been introduced, but now we see the Holy Spirit speaking specific words to the church by recognized prophets. Not that prophecy was unexpected. On the Day of Pentecost, Peter had announced that Joel's prophecy was now being fulfilled, part of which was, **"I will pour out My Spirit in those days; and they shall prophesy"** (2:18). I would imagine prophecy was actually an ongoing part of the normal life of this early church, although Luke postpones spotlighting it until now.

The spiritual gift of prophecy is mentioned in Romans 12:6 and 1 Corinthians 12:10, and the *office* of prophet, which is second only to apostle, is mentioned in Ephesians 4:11. An office means that a person's particular spiritual gift has been recognized by the church and that the person is authorized to engage in open ministry centered around that gift. Agabus and the others had both the gift and the office because they were recognized prophets.

The office of prophet is gaining more stature in Christian churches around the world these days than it has in the recent past. The postdenominational churches particularly—representing the fastest-growing segment of global Christianity—are giving new prominence to prophets, but they are not doing so exclusively.[1]

This prophecy in Acts 11:27,28 is important to us as a precedent setter. Evidently, the word was given corporately and it warned of something that was going to happen in the future, giving specific instructions on how to prepare and provide for relief. The elders received the word and the disciples each gave what they could to send to the brethren in Judea.

Agabus stood in the *office of the prophet* as he gave this word to the church. It is different from that which would be given with the simple gift of prophecy. Prophecies given through the simple gift of prophecy will not be as detailed and rarely include any *foretelling:* Simple prophecies will be edifying, exhortative or comforting, but will not tell of things to come. Notice that the prophecy through Agabus not only told of a coming drought, but also gave instructions to the disciples to send relief to Judea.

Although budding prophetic people may occasionally flow with detailed words that include foretelling, that does not make them prophets. God's training for His prophets takes years. One leader said he believes it takes about 20 years of intensive instruction in God's boot camp before He sets a person into the office of the prophet.

Years before I was actually set into the office of the prophet, people would often ask me, "Are you a prophetess?" Each time they would ask, I would reply in return, "No, I'm not a prophetess. I'll know when He sets me into the office."

One evening in the midst of a powerful time of corporate intercession, the Lord began to speak to me in my heart. By this time, I knew His Voice better than I did as a nine-year-old child. "Cindy, this night I set you in as a prophetess to the nations." A few moments later, the leader of the prayer time prayed for me and I was overcome with God's power. The next thing I remember hearing was, "And the Lord says, 'This night I stand you up as a prophetess to the nations.'"

In ways that are hard to describe, I was different from that night forward. The closest thing I can liken it to was when I was ordained as a minister through the laying on of hands. I had a new anointing and more authority in the Spirit. The prophecies I gave were more detailed and precise.

Today as I prophesy there are times when I operate with the simple gift of prophecy. These prophecies usually include exhortation and are uplifting in content, similar to the first prophecy I wrote about earlier in the chapter. At times, however, I sense the anointing of the office of the prophet and the power of God will come with great intensity. Many times, these prophecies will be intended for nations. It is amazing to see God use such prophecies as catalysts for change and intercessory prayer in a particular country.

Remember the prophecy I gave about the power of the Marches for Jesus stopping the carnivals in Brazil? In addition to what I shared earlier, I discovered that in 1994, São Paulo had the largest March for Jesus in the world, having eight-hundred-and-fifty-thousand people marching in the rain. Five thousand Christians entered the carnival in Rio, marching and worshiping the Lord in the midst of the devil's festival.

Prophecy and Natural Disasters
Does God warn His children today to protect them before natural disasters take place? Absolutely! Chuck Pierce, the prayer leader for

Generals of Intercession and a pastor in Denton, Texas, gave this unusual prophecy in Houston, Texas, on September 21, 1994:

> *I would say, the next 24 days are critical.* Though the enemy has stood against you as a city, I have brought you to a crossroads and you are about to make a transition and crossover. My eyes are upon this city and the remnant of this city, and I will overcome the structures that are set against My Spirit in this city. Revelation that has been withheld is going to begin to come down to people like rain. *Look to the river of the east.* As that river rises so will My people.
>
> [At this time he saw a vision and described it.]
>
> Watchman, what do you see? He replied, *"I see a fire. It is a literal fire. Fire is on the river."* Then the Lord said, "My fire will begin to come to the city."
>
> [The next part of the prophecy gave detailed instructions on what to do with what had been shown to Chuck as a watchman.]
>
> I would call you to the night watch. Gather together in the night watch. Sing in the night in the hard areas of the city and evil will be uncovered and deliverance will come. If you will enter into the night watch you will overthrow the impending destruction and doom that is set for the area.

One of the prayer leaders, Deborah DeGar, took the prophetic word from church to church, leading a prayer watch from 3:00-6:00 A.M. *At the end of 24 days, it began to rain in Houston.* There had never been a flood exactly like it in the history of the city. Houston was brought before the eyes of the nation. The San Jacinto River *(the river to the east)* began to rise and flood the entire territory. Gas lines erupted underneath the river and the flooded river *literally had a fire that burned in its midst.* In the middle of all this chaos, the Church came together in great unity.

In the case of this prophetic warning, the flooding was not averted but it did not do the damage it could have done. My in-laws live in the area that was flooded and their house was totally spared. I know others whose homes were not spared, but God's promise to work good out of evil will come true. Sometimes crises will force the Church to come into unity when nothing else will. Regardless of what Satan might have wanted to do in the midst of it all, the Church rose triumphantly in spite of the flooding.

KNOWING WHEN TO RELEASE PROPHECY

How do you know when to release the prophetic word? (If you haven't yet read the chapter on spiritual protocol [chap. 7], go back and do so, because what I'm going to write now builds upon it.) Here are some simple guidelines:

Are you released to prophesy according to the local church protocol?
As a general rule, I do not prophesy in a church I am just visiting. At times, however, I have felt the Lord give me a word for a church where I am simply attending the service. If the word is a true one, the Lord always opens a door for me to give it. If you are visiting a church and feel you have a prophecy, this is what you might do:

- Ask an usher if you can speak to the elder or leader who judges the prophetic words given to the church. It is often good to write it down so he or she can read it rather than trying to talk to the person in the middle of the service.
- Pray for favor and then release the giving of the word back to the Lord. He might use someone who is already recognized in that local Body to speak the word.
- Wait and trust the Lord and the leadership in the church to discern if and when the prophecy should be given.

What is the timing to give the prophecy?
I used to think that a strong anointing meant I had to give the word immediately. I have found, however, this is not the case. At times, I have felt the anointing so strongly it was like fire burning in my bones, but I didn't give the particular prophecy for another year. Also, at times a prophecy should not be given out loud at all, but should simply be used for intercessory prayer.

Here are a few confirming signs to help you know whether a prophecy is for a given church service:

- It will be in the same flow as what God is doing with the whole service. In other words, it will be similar in nature (i.e., gentle and comforting or strong and bold) to how the Lord seems to be moving with the worship, with other Scriptures and with the general direction of the service. I don't think God would give a blasting, loud word in the midst of a quiet move of the Spirit. Rather, He probably would give it in a still, small Voice.

- The leaders will confirm that the timing is right and find a place for it to flow into the service. There have been times when I have had a prophecy for one part of the service, but I didn't get it judged by a leader or elder in time. The Spirit flowed another way and it would then have been out of place for me to give the prophecy. I usually write down this kind of prophecy and give it to the pastor, or share it when I get up to speak (if I am the speaker).
- If the word is correctional, unless I am a recognized prophet in that local church, I do not give it publicly. Correctional words need to be submitted to the leadership for them to pray over and judge.

In terms of a corporate setting, it is possible that the word you receive will be for a person, rather than for the congregation. If this is the case and you are new at prophesying, have the word judged by someone you respect rather than just blurting it out. This is very important. Otherwise, if you have given an incorrect word to a member of a congregation, you may be called and corrected by the leaders of that church.

I will always talk to the pastor about a word I have for someone in his congregation to see if he feels it should be given at that time. Remember to always preface such prophetic words by saying something like, "I am sensing this" or "Could it be that God wants to do this in your life?" Also, if you are a recognized and established prophet or prophetess with that certain congregation, you have a lot more freedom to give prophetic words.

The danger in these guidelines is that a fledgling prophetic person might be so afraid of missing God that he or she won't step out at all. This is not what I am trying to accomplish. In fact, I hope just the opposite happens—that these guidelines give you the proper boundaries needed to leap out in faith to prophesy.

How do I know if I am on target with the word I think I have for this person?

One question I'm asked is, "How do I know if what I am discerning is from God?" Of course, there are times when you must move out in faith, just as I did when I prayed for the Jewish man in chapter 2. One way of finding out if I should give what I think is a prophecy from God is through the interview method. This is simply probing the person through questions to get some kind of feedback.

For instance, if you think you have a prophetic word about a person's daughter you might ask, "Do you have a daughter?" If the answer is yes, and what you think you've heard from the Lord is that the daughter is sick, you could proceed with, "Does she have any physical problems?" If the answer is no, don't give up yet. The sickness might be emotional or relational. The word may need to be fine-tuned; you may have heard a partial word.

Ask a few more questions, along the lines of what I suggested regarding other kinds of possible problems or sicknesses. Something usually surfaces about which you can pray and the impression you received from the Lord will be clearer to you. Ask the person if it is all right to pray with him or her for the daughter. I always like to get people's permission to pray for them; it opens their hearts to the Lord and His power. If they are uncomfortable about praying at that time, tell them you will pray for the daughter later by yourself. Leave them with the knowledge that God cares for them and their daughter.

Is what you're receiving a prophetic word or an impression?

An impression is vague, usually just a sensing of something from the Lord. I believe an impression is a feeling that God is communicating to you but it isn't as crystal clear as when the Lord is speaking a direct word to be given as a prophecy. In these situations, I will couch my words with something like, "This isn't strong and clear enough for me to call it a prophetic word but I do have the impression that your current situation will clear up in two years' time." However, if I am certain what I am receiving is directly from the Lord, I will say so.

When you are given a prophetic word about a person or a group of people while you are alone or not in the presence of that person or group (i.e., ahead of time), it will probably come as words that form inside your spirit. The Lord will speak the same things again and again. At times, you may feel as though a balloon has been blown up within your inner person. If it is not the right moment for you to give the word out loud, it may be difficult to contain yourself. Still, you need to submit the word to the Lord's direction and timing, and wait for the appropriate time to share it.

Unless you are a recognized prophet or prophetess in the Body of

Christ, I would be cautious about giving a prophecy in the first person (i.e., "I, your God say..."). Even those who are set into the office of prophet should be careful about using the first person and should do so with the fear of the Lord upon their lives.

Much of what is given in the way of prophetic words is the gift of exhortation operating through a prophetic vehicle. The Lord sometimes gives exhortative words through those who have the simple gift of prophecy in order to give hope to His people and encourage them not to give up or despair. On the other hand, if the word of exhortation is given through a prophet, it will be much more detailed and directional. This kind of prophetic word usually results in a strong, positive response from the person or congregation receiving the prophecy. At such times, the people may break out in spontaneous clapping or shouting. Other times people weep at the personal way God has spoken to them.

GETTING STARTED

As 1 mentioned in chapter 2, one of the primary ways people start to prophesy is during prayer times. A person may ask for prayer and your prayer may become a prophecy. This is actually a good and safe way to begin. Ask the Lord to anoint your mind with His thoughts. Then believe God to do so and as you pray, launch out and pray the details you are hearing in your thoughts. If you need to, stop and use the interview method I described earlier.

At times, you will miss what the Lord might be saying to you. (This is why I suggest you should not speak in the first person.) If you do miss His word, apologize and admit that you must not have been hearing correctly. This will keep you clean with the Lord and in your relationships; don't let pride get in the way. A person recently gave a prophecy regarding a specific event and specific date, and missed what God was saying. His prophecy had been heard by many in the Body of Christ. As a man of God, however, he had the integrity to print an apology in a major Christian magazine. I really respect him for that and believe God will bless him.

We are responsible for what we give to others as prophecies. You might ask, "Cindy, have you ever missed a prophetic word?" Yes, I have. A prophecy may not come to pass for several reasons. Here are two reasons a prophecy may not be fulfilled:

1. The person being prophesied to does not meet the conditions the Lord gives in the prophecy or falls into sin (see 1 Sam. 10:1; 13:13,14).
2. The person prophesying did so out of the flesh or only has a partial understanding of what God was saying—this affects what he or she gives as being from the Lord.

Human love can taint a word. I am careful about prophesying to people who are close to me because my own personal love for them or my emotions may get in the way of what God is really saying. Usually I will simply say, "I feel I am possibly hearing this prophetic word from the Lord but I would like to have it confirmed by someone who doesn't know you as well (or doesn't have a vested interest in what happens)." Sometimes love blinds the prophet, causing him or her to give a good prophetic word when the Lord wanted to give a word of correction.

David and Nathan
A passage that could shed light on this is 1 Chronicles 17:1-4:

> Now it came to pass, when David was dwelling in his house, that David said to Nathan the prophet, "See now, I dwell in a house of cedar, but the ark of the covenant of the Lord is under tent curtains." Then Nathan said to David, "Do all that is in your heart, for God is with you." But it happened that night that the word of God came to Nathan, saying, "Go and tell My servant David, 'Thus says the Lord: "You shall not build Me a house to dwell in."'"

It is possible that God was impressing upon David what would later become his job—to prepare the materials to build the Temple. David was musing about this and Nathan made some assumptions. Perhaps Nathan had been thinking the same thing and thus leapt to the conclusion that David was ordained of God to build a house for the Lord. Whatever the case, Nathan spoke out of turn, out of an impression that was not properly interpreted, and he missed God's message. He then received a true prophetic word from the Lord and had to go and correct the impression he had earlier left with King David. The Lord wanted David's son to build the house rather than having David build it (see vv. 11,12).

Paul and Agabus

Agabus is another case from the New Testament in which a prophet may not have been 100 percent accurate, but the basic gist of the prophetic word was correct. Agabus was evidently a proven prophet from the way the Church responded to the prophecy he gave about the famine, which also happened in the days of Claudius. Acts 21:10,11 records the prophecy he gave:

> A certain prophet named Agabus came down from Judea. When he had come to us, he took Paul's belt, bound his own hands and feet, and said, "Thus says the Holy Spirit, 'So shall the Jews at Jerusalem bind the man who owns this belt, and deliver him into the hands of the Gentiles.'"

It appears from later accounts that Agabus missed the part of the prophecy where he said that the Jews *would bind* Paul and deliver him into the hands of the Gentiles. Paul was delivered to the Gentiles, but was not bound until Acts 21:33 when the Romans themselves put him in chains. I have some thoughts about this account:

Agabus was possibly given a vision of Paul being bound and of the Jews being the instrument through which this would happen. From this, Agabus assumed that it was the Jews themselves who would do the physical binding. The place where most people get offtrack as they prophesy is in the area of interpreting what they have heard and/or seen. (Compare Dan. 7:15,16; 8:15; Acts 20:22,23; 21:4,12,13.)

A possible interpretation of what happened is that Agabus's vision of Paul being bound may have been a symbol of the Jews declaring that Paul was bound (or prohibited to speak or preach) according to their law. The Greek word for bind is *deo* and is used both for being physically bound and for being bound or forbidden under the law.[2] As no record was made of the Jews actually declaring the preaching Paul was doing as being bound in their courts (using the same word *deo* for bound), this cannot be proven. However, it is evident from what the Jewish leaders said that they considered his preaching bound or forbidden (see Acts 21:27,28; 23:12-15; 24:1-8). In this case, Agabus would not at all have missed what he said under the inspiration of the Holy Spirit regarding the Jews binding Paul.

We could "spiritualize" the point that the actions the Jews took caused Paul to be delivered to the Gentiles, although the text indicates that they would physically deliver him. In actuality, they did not want to deliver him to the Gentiles. They simply wanted to kill him themselves.

Jonah and Nineveh

Another Old Testament prophecy that did not come true was the one given by Jonah for the city of Nineveh. Jonah walked through the city proclaiming, "Yet forty days, and Nineveh shall be overthrown!" (Jon. 3:4). Not only did the people believe Jonah gave a prophetic word from God, but it also caused an incredible proclamation to come from the king himself as given in Jonah 3:7-9:

> Let neither man nor beast, herd nor flock, taste anything; do not let them eat, or drink water. But let man and beast be covered with sackcloth, and cry mightily to God; yes, let every one turn from his evil way and from the violence that is in his hands. Who can tell if God will turn and relent, and turn away from His fierce anger, so that we may not perish?

This so pleased God that the Bible says He relented from the disaster He was going to bring upon them.

God changing His mind? Absolutely! What a great precedent in understanding that God never desires to bring judgment. He wouldn't have warned the people if He had actually wanted the judgment to occur. He would have just done it. God gives prophetic warnings to His people to cause them to repent and turn from their wicked ways so He can heal their land (see 2 Chron. 7:14).

Again, we see that Jonah was not stoned although he was carnal in his response to the mercy of God on Nineveh. He had not given a false prophecy even though it was a word that did not come to pass.

Examples Today

This happens today also. A couple of years ago, a prophecy was circulating that said a major earthquake would hit the Pacific Northwest of the United States on a certain date. Many churches took this seriously and repented for the New Age involvement and witchcraft of many in the region as well as the complacency of the Church. The day came and went and there was no earthquake. Was it a false prophecy? We'll probably never know. It very well could be that the prayers averted a disaster. The sad part is that if the pastors don't explain this kind of prophetic process to their people it can result in confusion, giving prophecies a bad name in the region and causing skepticism.

What should you do if you are in a region that is given a prophecy such as this? First, the prophecy needs to be judged to determine whether or not it is accurate (see 1 Cor. 14:29). This is what the churches did in the Northwest. They prayed, repented and sought God for mercy. Some people took it a step further and left town on that day.

The hard part is that we can become so caught up in such prophecy that the door to deception may open; or we do not hear when the Lord says to His people, "I have received your prayers and the disaster will not come." I am not saying the ones who left were in deception. I don't know what I would have done in that case myself. I'd have to pray and discern.

Where there has been a foretelling prophecy of impending disaster, the leaders of the community or area need to come together in prayer. They need to carefully listen to the Lord, and listen regarding whether or not He has changed His mind. Tremendous peace will accompany this assurance. This, of course, is a great responsibility because if they are wrong in their discernment regarding a possible disaster, the effect can be dire.

California often receives such prophecies and that state certainly has more than its share of earthquakes. I believe if the Lord was going to really shake California with what some have called "the big one," He would give a clear prophetic word to very respected leaders that His people should clear out and be protected. I know that godly people have died in natural disasters, but I believe in the case of such a widespread earthquake the Lord would warn His people, just as He warned Lot that He would destroy Sodom and Gomorrah (see Gen. 19:12-17).

Heeding God's Warnings

Sometimes stories of dire upcoming events are true and should be heeded, as in the fascinating story of a prophecy of persecution that comes from the life of Demos Shakarian. It affected his entire family and resulted in their coming to America.

The Shakarian family lived in Armenia in the village of Kara Kala, located in the rocky foothills of Mount Ararat—believed by many to be the mountain where Noah's ark came to rest. The whole family was strong in the Lord, having received a special visitation from God as a result of the testimony of the power of the Holy Spirit from Russian Orthodox Christians at the end of the nineteenth century.

In the village of Kara Kala, there lived a "boy prophet" who had had a remarkable visitation from God when he was 11 years old. His name was Efim Gerasemovitch Klubniken. One day he heard the Lord calling him to a time of prayer and fasting, which he was often given to do. As he persisted for seven days and nights, the Lord gave him a vision. This is how the story is recounted in the book *The Happiest People on Earth*:

> Efim could neither read nor write. Yet, as he sat in the little stone cottage in Kara Kala, he saw before him a vision of charts and a message in a beautiful handwriting. Efim asked for pen and paper. And for seven days, sitting at the rough plank table where the family ate, he laboriously copied down the form and shape of letters and diagrams that passed before his eyes.
>
> When he had finished, the manuscript was taken to people in the village who could read. It turned out that this illiterate child had written out in Russian characters a series of instructions and warnings. At some unspecified time in the future, the boy wrote, every Christian in Kara Kala would be in terrible danger. He foretold a time of unspeakable tragedy for the entire area, when hundreds of thousands of men, women, and children would be brutally murdered. The time would come, he warned, when everyone in the region must flee. They must go to a land across the sea. Although he had never seen a geography book, the boy prophet drew a map showing exactly where the fleeing Christians were to go. To the amazement of the adults, the body of water depicted so accurately in the drawing was not the nearby Black Sea, or the Caspian Sea, or even the farther off Mediterranean Sea, but the distant and unimaginable Atlantic Ocean! There was no doubt about it nor about the identity of the land on the other side; the map plainly indicated the east coast of the United States of America.
>
> But the refugees were not to settle down there, the prophecy continued. They were to continue traveling until they reached the west coast of the new land. There, the boy wrote, God would bless them and prosper them, and cause their seed to be a blessing to the nations.[3]

More than 50 years later, Efim again brought out the prophecy and announced it was time to make the move to America or all would perish. Several families throughout the area, including the Shakarian family, sold their goods and moved. Many—including Christians—were skeptical, not believing that God would speak so specifically and accurately.

In 1914, the Turks began a blood bath and more than two-thirds of the population of Armenia was driven into the Mesopotamian desert. A holocaust ensued, leaving more than one million Armenians dead, including every inhabitant of Kara Kala. Another half a million were massacred in their villages in a pogrom that later was to provide Hitler his blueprint for the extermination of the Jews. "The world did not intervene when Turkey wiped out the Armenians," he reminded his followers. "It will not intervene now."[4]

WHEN IS IT FROM THE LORD?

But how does a person receive prophetic words from the Lord? Actually, it varies quite a bit. For me, one of the most frequent ways I receive a prophetic word is by simply opening my mouth, starting to speak and trusting the Lord to give me His words. I realize that for beginners this is really scary. Other times I receive just a few words or a complete sentence. If I am faithful to share the little portion I have, more of the prophecy comes to me through the inspiration of the Holy Spirit as I go along. On some occasions, I receive the theme of the word and begin with that.

Many times when I have given a word I have experienced a lot of trepidation afterward. The devil has done a few tap dances on my head by making comments such as, "That wasn't God at all!" When I first began to prophesy to well-known leaders, I would struggle to give the word, and then if they didn't give me feedback about its accuracy, I would struggle after I gave it. This is partially because of the stronghold I have had to deal with concerning fear of humans.

Several times, I didn't know for years how much words had meant to particular leaders, and I chastised myself for even giving them, only to find out later that they had been life-changing for the people. I would think such thoughts as, *Cindy Jacobs, who do you think you are, giving a prophecy to so and so? They certainly don't need you sharing anything with them in their lives. Look how important they are, and besides, they hear God so well for themselves.*

Although it is true that leaders do tend to get overwhelmed with people who think they've heard something from God for them, you may be the one voice they need to hear. As long as you follow biblical protocol, I would encourage you to go ahead and share what you are hearing. It may be just what that leader is waiting to hear to confirm something God is saying to him or her.

Is It for the Church Service?

As I've mentioned, if the word is for a corporate church service, it should fit with the flow of that service. Pray and ask the Lord how to link what He is giving you with the worship that has preceded it. For instance, if you are receiving a word of encouragement about breakthrough for the people, ask the Lord to speak to you prophetically within the theme and context of the worship service. For example, if the worship includes the song "Great Is Thy Faithfulness," you might be led to begin with an exhortation of the Lord, reminding His people that He is a faithful God and will be true to meet their needs in difficult times.

The prophecies given should usually amplify—and flow with— what God has already been saying in the service. The exception to this would be when the service is going in a totally different direction from what the Holy Spirit wishes it to take and the prophecy moves the meeting in the way the Lord intended it to go. This is not the norm, as I've indicated, and should only be done by mature prophets who are under the leadership of that meeting. Prophecy should take God's people to a greater place in Him than where they were before the word was given. The prophetic word can also be used by the Lord to break spiritual bondages and oppression (see Ps. 107:20). Heaviness of spirit is often lifted and a time of rejoicing in God takes the place of sadness.

HOW DO YOU KNOW IF AND WHEN TO PROPHESY?

I've already talked about tongues and interpretation. One teacher I heard compared them to being two nickels that make a dime and prophecy being the dime. They both amounted to the same thing. Prophecy can be more powerful as it stands alone, but the tongue needs to be interpreted.

A question I'm often asked is, "How do I know that I am the one God has anointed to give the word?" Many times when the Holy Spirit is moving in a meeting, almost anyone who is prophetic can prophesy. This doesn't mean they are to do so, but they need to be willing and available to the Lord if He should desire them to prophesy. There are moments when I could give a word but I wait for those younger than myself who do not prophesy as much to move forward. Then, if there is more to be given, I will share the rest of what I believe the Lord wanted to say.

I always encourage people to ask the Lord to allow them to prophesy. Even if they don't have the gift, the Lord may use them occasionally. The Bible exhorts us to earnestly desire to prophesy (see 1 Cor. 14:39). There have been times when a person has given a word for the first time and we as a group or congregation experienced a powerful blessing from the Lord. It was a stronger anointing than if someone more experienced had given it.

So how do you know if and when to prophesy? You can trust the Holy Spirit to give you a deep sense of His presence and peace. One question to ask yourself is, "Is this a prophetic word God is speaking to me personally or is it to be shared with everyone?" Sometimes it can be for both. I have heard people get up and give a word that didn't edify the general Body of Christ and I thought, *Those words were for them alone and they projected them to the Body*. Another way to know whether or not to prophesy is to ask an elder what he or she thinks. Mature leaders are usually able to tell whom the presence of the Lord is upon and know that a certain person is the one to give a prophetic word. This is a gift God gives to many in leadership.

As I mentioned earlier, I found when I first started prophesying that the anointing would come on me so strongly at times that it was hard to contain it. This sometimes happens to me now, but not as often. Through long experience, I have come to know His Voice and He usually doesn't need to knock me over to get me to move; a simple nudge from His presence usually suffices.

When the prophetic word is shared correctly in God's timing and way, it will often confirm the message about to be given through the speaker. I've had times when the speaker joked that I just preached his sermon! Of course, what I prophesied was just a portion of the message, but the word hit the highlights of what God wanted to say. There are times when I have been the speaker and have asked God to confirm through music or a prophetic word the message I was about to give. It's amazing how many times this has happened just as I've asked.

YOUR PERSONAL PRAYER LIFE

One critical factor for anyone who is going to be used by the Lord to prophesy is to make sure his or her prayer life and time in the Scripture stays in balance. You can always tell a prophetic person who spends time steeped in God's Word. There is a richness to a person's prophetic gift when it is liberally enhanced with Scripture. This is also a great safeguard against deception.

At times, the Holy Spirit will manifest through prophecy in a meeting. When this occurs, many prophecies will be spoken and many who do not usually prophesy will be able to do so. It sometimes seems like a river of prophecy is flowing through the gathering as one person picks up where the last person left off. The song of the Lord (a spontaneous prophetic song) may take place during this time. One of the most moving services I've been in was when one person started with the song of the Lord and then one person after another picked up additional verses and sang. This kind of service leaves a person with a sense of awe.

Some churches are not currently incorporating the gift of prophecy in the lives of their churches but would like to begin. For those who believe they would like to release this gift in their local churches, check the excellent section in chapter 13 of Wayne Grudem's book *The Gift of Prophecy in the New Testament and Today*, called "Encouraging and Regulating Prophecy in the Local Church."

Here are a few suggestions along this line:

1. Teach on the gift of prophecy. If you are clear about how you want the gift of prophecy to function in your church, include it in your teaching.
2. Identify ways the gift has already been functioning in the church.
3. Encourage the people that a good place to begin to prophesy is in less formal gatherings.

THE PROPHETIC IN WORSHIP

The worship service itself can amount to a prophetic message that God is expressing to the church. When this happens, a powerful anointing will come upon the music. The worship will quicken within the hearts of the people. For instance, if the Lord is saying to His people "Fear not," and a song is sung that proclaims those words, life will spring up in those who are singing. It will give them special faith. They are not to fear, for God is with them through their trials.

For specific periods of time, a particular song will be prophetic for the local church. The congregation may sing it many times and never tire of it. For that season, it is what God wants to say to His people.

There may be times when God's power will so pour out during the worship service that the pastor recognizes God is speaking to His people through prophetic worship. The pastor may then choose not to preach, but to worship God for the entire service. My pastor is especially sensitive to these *kairos* times. I have been in meetings when the Holy Spirit was grieved because He wanted to receive the worship of the people that day rather than have them sit under the teaching gift. The leader, however, was insensitive and inflexible to changing the order of service. More traditional services where hymns are sung also experience these kinds of visitations, and the pastor may want to say, "Today, we are just going to sing to the Lord and glorify His name through our music."

A beautiful expression of the prophetic is when the Lord gives the song of the Lord or prophetic songs to the singers or instrumentalists. This is not a rehearsed song, in the same manner that a prophecy is not rehearsed. Rather, it is spontaneous. Those on the instruments, led by one of the musicians, may play a set pattern of three chords or so while the prophetic song is released. I have been in churches where the whole congregation started singing the words as they were repeated again and again. It is as if the Lord wants to give the message many times until it is indelibly printed on the pages of our hearts.

If an instrumentalist, such as a drummer, plays prophetically, the Lord usually wants to give an interpretation. It may be that the drummer was "warring" on the drums to break spiritual strongholds—such a prophetic act would then need to be explained to the people by the pastor. Various instruments were used to express warfare in the Old Testament: Isaiah talks about the tambourines and harps being used in battle (see Isa. 30:32). At the end of the prophetic songs, the people often experience a tremendous release of joy. The Lord may give the interpretation that He used the instruments to break the spirit of poverty that had been sent by the enemy against the congregation.

Prophetic Words with Songs

It is possible for those who give verbal prophetic words to interact with the singers and musicians. The prophetic word may be given verbally, followed by one of the instruments picking up the word in a musical theme and then singers joining in to amplify what God has said through the prophecy.

I have been in services where a person starts to sing and is off-key and flat. Instead of being a blessing, the singing is jarring and quenches the Spirit. For this reason, I believe it is best for those who are gifted in singing or who are part of the worship team to be used of the Lord as psalmists. I suggest if you are affected in your vocal technique through nervousness that pulls you off pitch, that you do not try to sing a prophecy. Instead, wait for the appropriate time and give the prophecy verbally rather than sing it. It will have a much greater effect if you do.

The worship service is meant to give glory to God, so it is critical that the Holy Spirit not be interrupted by a verbal prophecy given at the wrong time. This must be handled with great sensitivity. Although it is entirely possible to weave a verbal prophecy into the time of worship, it should not stop what God is doing through the worship team. Some churches prefer to hold all verbal prophecies until after the worship time to avoid quenching the Spirit.

COMMUNICATING THE PROPHETIC WORD

In understanding how to release the prophetic word, it is important to think through how you communicate the word. Some people who prophesy use so much symbolism and typology that at the end of the message the listeners are scratching their heads and saying, "I think that prophecy was from God but what does it mean?" If a person is going to use typology, it needs to be interpreted in the same prophetic word, especially if the meaning is not obvious to most Christians.

The use of typology in prophesying can be a tremendous blessing. Prophecies may also include allegories. Allegory depends on a correspondence between ideas, and typology depends on a correspondence between events.[5] *Wilson's Dictionary of Bible Type,* by Walter L. Wilson (Wm. B. Eerdmans Publishing Co.), and *Number in Scripture,* by E. W. Bullinger (Kregel Publications), are tools I would recommend for interpreting typology in words.

Some common uses of typology in prophecy include:

Type	Interpretation of Type
Crossing over Jordan	You're about to enter your promised land of great blessing. It might also

	mean you're about to enter into your destiny. Yet another interpretation migh be you are about to fight some giants!
Restoration of the years	The Lord is beginning the process of undoing what the cankerworm has eaten (i.e., what circumstances have destroyed in your life). Restoration can be painful at times because you may feel as though you are being taken apart—as an old car is during restoration—before God puts you back together.
God will make the crooked places straight	Situations in your life are troubling you and God is going to help straighten them out.
You will be given hinds' feet to climb to high places*	The Lord is going to give you the purity of heart and mind to do what He is requiring you to do. The call of God upon your life is a high one so the Lord isgoing to purge and sanctify you to accomplish it.
You are standing at the bank of the Red Sea	You are in a difficult place, but just as God delivered Moses, He wants to deliver you if you don't waver but trust Him. Many difficult circumstances surround you right now, but God will make a way where seemingly there is no way.

*Another possible meaning is given by John Sandford. A hind (the ibex in Palestine is what David referred to) can go up a steep cliff or down it safely because its rear feet track exactly where the front feet lead. A few centimeters off, and the deer would plummet to death. Our front feet are our minds and wills. Our hind feet are our hearts and spirits— our motives. To be given hinds' feet means that you will be so purged and sanctified, your motives will follow truly in whatever you set out to do.

God's Vocabulary

These are just a few examples. In addition to the use of allegories and typology, there are times when the Lord uses certain words that mean one thing to us, but quite another to Him. Dr. Bill Hamon gives some examples of prophetic terminology in his book *Prophets and Personal Prophecy*:

> "Suddenly or Immediately." On the surface, it may seem that a sudden event has happened spontaneously. But if we look below the surface we find that a long time of preparation has led up to the sudden manifestation. "Suddenly" on the day of Pentecost they all began to speak with other tongues...But this came about according to God's timetable, and man's preparation and placement.
>
> The word "Immediately" was used by Jesus in a similar way. When the grain is fully ripe, then "immediately" the farmer comes and harvests it. What is called "sudden" and "immediate," then is actually based on progressive growth and preparation.
>
> "Now." When we hear the word "Now" we usually think immediately, or within twenty-four hours...In the first two years of King Saul's reign, he received a personal prophecy from the prophet Samuel. Saul had prophesied judgment upon him by telling him that "now" his kingdom would not continue. The "now" was thirty-eight years later.[6]

In light of these things, Hamon interprets the following words in this way:

> "Immediately" means from one day to three years.
> "Very soon" means one to ten years.
> "Now" or "This day" means one to forty years.
> "I will" without a time designation means God will act sometime in the person's life if he is obedient.
> "Soon" was the term Jesus used to describe the time of His soon return almost two thousand years ago. "Behold, I come quickly."[7]

The fact that people perceive the meaning of a word in a different way from what the Lord is actually saying may confuse them. For instance, you may have received a prophecy that says God is going to give you a house. To some, the word "give" means you will receive a free house, as a gift. However, there are many kinds of gifts from the Lord and numerous ways He can give you things. I consider our house as a gift from the Lord even though we make payments on it. We got it for a very good price and it is a great blessing to us.

Waiting on God's Promises

Another area where people get confused is in receiving a promise from the Lord and thinking God is going to do it immediately. He may fulfill it next year or 10 years from now. You may receive a prophetic word in which the Lord says, "I will do this immediately" but the actual result might not occur for 3 years or more. However, God will begin to work behind the scenes now to set into motion the things that will bring about the fulfillment of the word. I once heard a profound prophecy that said: "For I the Lord am a behind-the-scenes God. I am constantly working in ways you cannot see because if you knew what I was doing you would get your hands into it and mess it up."

Lest you become totally discouraged and overcome by the definitions I have given, let me interject that it doesn't necessarily have to take 40 years for the Lord to fulfill His prophecy. Sometimes it does happen in a few days. The point is that we need to cling to the prophetic word and believe God has spoken whether it takes one day or 40 years to see fruit. If it is truly a word from the Lord, it will come to pass. This reminds me of the Scripture in Habakkuk 2:3, "For the vision is yet for an appointed time; but at the end it will speak, and it will not lie. Though it tarries, wait for it; because it will surely come, it will not tarry."

PROPHESYING TO YOUNG PEOPLE

When you are prophesying, it is important to communicate in a way that will be understood by the person receiving the word. In other words, how would God talk to that person? Some people are rigid in their prophetic styles, and never change their approaches. I believe God desires to make His will known to humankind so we can be encouraged to utilize what has been said to us. For instance, when prophesying to a teenager, the use of archaic *King James* language would probably hinder receptivity. Most teenagers think it's funny when people use "thee" and "thou." Most young people read from modern translations of the Bible in easily understood language.

One day I was with a minister friend who said to me, "Cindy, what kind of Bible translation do you use?" Wondering why he asked I replied, "Why, the *King James Version*." "Oh," he quipped, "that explains why you prophesy the way you do." Although I was somewhat taken aback, I gave some serious thought to what he said. Jesus didn't live in the seventeenth century so He wouldn't have spoken seventeenth-century English. In fact, He didn't speak English at all. Our traditions infiltrate our prayers and our prophecies.

Before I deliver a prophecy to someone, I stop and think about the person to whom I am going to give the word. I believe the Lord would speak differently to a child than He would to an adult. He would use words the child would understand and a tone of voice that would not intimidate the child.

I also factor in any knowledge I may have about the person. For instance, if I know the person is from an unchurched background, I use vernacular language that is as free of "Christianese" as possible. The way I minister to someone from an evangelical background is very different from the way I minister to a charismatic.

Ministering to Children

As we look at Scripture, it is easy to see that the Lord loves children. Oftentimes adults are rough as they minister to little ones and this can hurt them for a long time. My own daughter was pushed over by a minister who was praying for her when she was little. She has had a difficult time allowing herself to be prayed for by anyone she doesn't know very well because of this experience. Children consider the size of adults intimidating and do not like to be treated in a harsh or rough way by them. Here are a few keys for ministering to children:

1. Ask them if they want you to pray for them. Many times an adult has dragged children to the front of a church to be prayed for and they're either afraid or resentful. No adult would like to be forced against his or her will to receive prayer and neither do children. (Teenagers especially resent this.)

2. Talk to them for a moment on a personal level. Ask them their names. If you perceive that they might be afraid or nervous,

ask if they feel comfortable having you pray for them. I sometimes say that I understand their being nervous and that I
once felt that way too, but the Lord wants to bless them.

3. Watch your tone of voice. You might want to stoop down to
their level if they are very small. Don't use a religious tone
of voice. Keep it gentle. Some Christians have an affected
form of speech and deliver their words in a way that seems
to be an attempt to make the message clear, but their delivery actually takes away from their effectiveness. For
instance, they may end their words with something like
"word-duh" and "God-duh." Although this may be a habit
that is hard to break, I would suggest you consider dropping
any affectations and speak normally.

The Goal of Prophecy

Your aim as you prophesy or minister (in any manner to anyone) should
be to help that person receive a prophetic word from the Lord. You need
to be careful that your style of ministry does not turn the person off and
thus keep him or her from receiving a prophetic word. Your job is both
to receive the word from the Lord and to communicate it in such a way
that is most edifying to the person to whom you are ministering.

I remember one young man who came to me and said, "The Lord
doesn't want you to wear mixed garments of linen and wool."

Grinning at him, I said to him, "That's nice but what does that
mean?" Some people will give a veiled word such as this because they
are so unsure of what to say that they can't "shoot straight" or tell you
in clear words. If you are going to give a prophetic word, you need to be
able to stand behind it and ask the Lord what it means. Understand
though, sometimes God speaks in "dark speech" (see Num. 12:8;
Ps. 78:2). In such instances, the Lord may be planting something He
wants the person to ponder, the true meaning of which He will reveal
later. He may not give you or the recipient the meaning at the time.
Normally, however, it is good to ask and to know.

As I mentioned earlier, there may be times when what you are receiving from God doesn't seem very clear to you. This doesn't necessarily
mean you are not to give the prophecy, but you might preface it with,
"I'm not sure if this will mean anything to you or not" or "This might be

for sometime in the future and not be especially meaningful to you now."

Another option is to use the interview method. At times, God will intentionally veil from the prophet what He is saying to the one receiving the prophecy. The word may be between God and the person receiving it. On other occasions, God will give the word in a riddle that will require prayer and seeking Him for the answer. (For example, see Amos 7:8; 8:2; Acts 10:11,12.)

Years ago, I sat on the board of directors for a ministry dedicated to women in leadership. We felt God was leading us to do a conference in a city in Canada. Our leaders flew to the city and searched and searched but could not find a facility that would work for the meetings. At last, the intercessory network earnestly began to pray for a prophetic word from the Lord. Two prophetic words came out of the prayer times: "There was room in the inn" and "Jesus is the Lion of Judah over the city." These two clues helped us. The ladies found a bridge called the "Lion's Gate Bridge," which they had crossed to come to the International Hotel. There they found room at the inn for the conference.

God's Way of Working

One day when I was flying home from a ministry trip, I found myself sitting next to a lovely young lady. After speaking to her for a few moments, I realized she didn't know the Lord. As we talked, I silently prayed and sought the Lord for a key and an opening to witness about Christ. While we talked, I kept hearing these words inside me, "Cindy, ask her about Jeremy." This made no sense to me. I was concerned I would scare her if I wasn't careful and then the opposite of what I wanted to do would happen.

Finally, the conversation turned to her love life. She explained that she had a boyfriend but they weren't very serious. I felt this was my opening. "Do you know anyone named Jeremy?" I queried.

Paling, she confirmed, "Why, yes, he's helped me out of some rough places and is a good friend."

"Have you ever dated him?" I questioned.

"Yes," she said, "but when I liked him, he didn't like me and when he liked me I didn't like him. However, I've been thinking a lot about him lately."

"Perhaps you might make contact with him again," I suggested. This turn of events gave me a perfect opening to share about God's intimate knowledge of her and His abiding concern for her welfare. Before the end of the flight, I was able to present the plan of salvation to an open and interested young lady.

Giving Our Words the Right Voice

One area I have to personally be aware of in my style of ministry is not to get too loud. This is offensive and hurts people's ears. Loud doesn't necessarily equate to being anointed. This is not to say that prophecy will not be given in a loud voice at times, but we need to be careful.

A tip to women who prophesy—which I learned from a speech teacher—is that we can modulate our voices. People are turned off by high squeaky voices and the tonality of the voice may be unpleasant.

When I speak, I intentionally lower the tone of my voice so it will be more pleasant. My Texas accent was very strong and, although it is not entirely necessary, I have tried to moderate it to a degree (difficult for a Texan). You may love your accent and choose not to change it, and that is quite all right. But because I minister extensively with translators in foreign countries, it has been helpful for me to modify my accent. Translators have difficulty understanding thick American accents.

PROPHETIC PRESBYTERY

God's people have seasons in their lives when they earnestly set themselves aside to hear prophetic words from the Lord. Of course, He may or may not choose to respond through a direct prophetic word because He has many ways to speak to His children.

A prophetic presbytery is a group that is organized on a one-time or seasonal basis to offer counsel or insight to those needing it. Such a group is one place where those who fast and pray can receive ministry by the prophets or prophetesses of the local church or community. This kind of ministry by a group of prophets, prophetesses or prophetic people is particularly powerful. Oftentimes, the person being ministered to receives a fuller expression of what God is trying to say to him or her. Whereas, one person prophesying may receive a message about one aspect of the person's life or situation, another person providing ministry might amplify, clarify or interpret what was said earlier. Because prophetic people receive insight in ways different from each other, the presbytery is able to function in an edifying manner. One prophetic person may have a vision while another may receive a directional word.

Prophetic presbyteries employ a variety of protocols. Some presbyteries are more formal than others. The strongest kind of presbytery is when the local church announces it for a specific amount of time and asks those who are seeking ministry from the prophets or prophetesses to sign up. It is usual to ask the people who will be receiving the ministry to fast and pray for three days or so (by the direction of the Lord) to prepare their hearts for what God would say to them.

Processing What We Receive

A natural tendency when seeking direction from the Lord is to experience frustration when we don't get the kind of prophetic word we want or when God doesn't address what we think is our point of greatest need. Here are some thoughts on this:

What we think is the most critical issue at the time may not be what God thinks is most important. For reasons unknown to us, there are times when God simply won't reveal things to those prophesying to a person. Remember the time when the Shunamite woman's child died and Elisha said, "The Lord has hidden it from me, and has not told me" (2 Kings 4:27)? God sometimes hides things because it might not be the proper time for revelation, the hearer may not be prepared for the knowledge or perhaps it might stop an aspect of character development God is doing in the person's life.

The Lord may choose to reveal something to us in ways other than through the prophetic vehicle. There have been times when I have begged God to speak to me on certain subjects, set myself aside for prayer and fasting, but heard nothing at those times. Later on, while doing the dishes or driving the car, seemingly out of the blue, the answers finally came. The fasting was the preparation of the heart; the timing and circumstance in which God would answer was up to Him.

Does this mean God will never answer a question we have during a prophetic presbytery? Of course not. He often does provide an answer, but we must be willing to leave the how and when up to Him.

Other times, pastors of prophetic churches may call together an informal presbytery of known, proven ministers to pray over a visiting leader or speaker. In this case, it is important to tape the messages so the leader or person being prophesied over can listen to what was said at a later time.

Evidently, a group of prophets and teachers was at the church in Antioch and functioned as a kind of presbytery, as shown in Acts 13:1-3.

Now in the church that was at Antioch there were certain prophets and teachers: Barnabas, Simeon who was called Niger, Lucius of Cyrene, Manaen who had been brought up with Herod the tetrarch, and Saul. As they ministered to the Lord and fasted, the Holy Spirit said, "Now separate to Me Barnabas and Saul for the work to which I have called them." Then, having fasted and prayed, and laid hands on them, they sent them away.

David Blomgren presents a thorough list of the ways God uses this kind of ministry in his excellent book *Prophetic Gatherings in the Church*.

THE DIFFERENCE BETWEEN TRUE AND FALSE PROPHETS

Earlier, I discussed some characteristics of Old Testament prophets. Here is some further amplification. It seems that most people I know who are prophets or prophetesses have been called false prophets at some point in time. But there are more true prophets than false ones. I'll give some descriptions of false prophets just so you'll know what they are like.

Many cults and religions claim to have prophets or seers who speak for their god. This is the most obvious false prophet—one who says he or she prophesies in the name of another god (see Deut. 13:1-3; 18:20). The information they give is false or demonically inspired.

A second kind of false prophet or prophetess is one who claims to speak in the name of God but can be recognized as false by the fruit of his or her life.

Beware of false prophets, who come to you in sheep's clothing, but inwardly they are ravenous wolves. You will know them by their fruits. Do men gather grapes from thornbushes or figs from thistles? Even so, every good tree bears good fruit, but a bad tree bears bad fruit. A good tree cannot bear bad fruit, nor can a bad tree bear good fruit....Therefore by their fruits you will know them (Matt. 7:15-18,20).

In *Prophetic Gatherings in the Church*, Blomgren gives this definition of false prophets:

False prophets may be detected by their character and conduct. A false prophet will live a sinful and wicked life, while a true prophet will exemplify conduct and character which are consistent with God's character. A false prophet will bring forth evil fruit, and a true prophet will display good fruit.[8]

Here are some characteristics Blomgren gives of such false prophets:

Ungodliness in attitudes (i.e. violent, rebellious, despising authority)
Ungodliness in appetites (i.e. profane, greedy, immoral, lustful)
Ungodliness in actions (i.e. defrauded others, conspired to deceive, liars)[9]

False prophets will often take Scripture out of context for their own uses. Many will do this particularly to manipulate for better offerings or to "sell their gifts" by praying for those who give the most. The prophet of God needs to be above being bought or sold for money or influence and needs to be no respecter of persons.

Just as I mentioned about being careful in labeling someone a Jezebel or a Saul, you also need to be cautious in denouncing a person as a false prophet. Nathan wasn't labeled a false prophet even though he missed the prophecy at first in telling David he could build the Temple (see 2 Sam. 7:3). Jonah wasn't stoned because his prophecy didn't come to pass about Nineveh (see Jon. 3:4,10).

I have talked to young prophetic people who missed prophecies when they were getting started and were branded as false prophets or prophetesses. It so devastated them that some of them couldn't stand to go to church anymore. Others changed churches and vowed never to prophesy again and it took them years to live down the charges brought against them. Please, please, be extremely cautious in proclaiming someone a false prophet. If you are wrong, the stigma is horrible and not easily undone.

Seeking God's Direction at All Times

One time I was ministering in Canada and was stopped on the way out of a meeting by a lady who had given an accurate prophecy in the meeting. I was extremely tired from long hours of ministry and hesitated when she asked me to prophesy to her. In retrospect, I should have listened to the hesitation as a caution from the Lord.

The next day, I received calls from some very distressed people who were asking me what I had told the lady. I was shocked to hear that she had twisted what I had prayed for her into a direct confirmation that God was sanctioning her to leave her husband and children for a man 15 years her junior! Thank God a friend of mine had been with me when I prayed for her and could vouch for what I had said. Sad to say, it did hurt my credibility for a time in that city and I was simply crushed over the whole situation.

While I was working through this difficult time, my greatest distress was that somehow I had grieved the Lord and hindered His work. One day while praying, He gently said to me, "Cindy, you can't hurt My reputation. Just keep being faithful and everything will be okay." That was good news because I was sorely tempted to give up. I am grateful to report that the Lord has restored my reputation in that city (as far as I can tell) and I have experienced the favor of the Lord as I've ministered there.

When Prophets Get Offtrack

It is possible for weaknesses or character defects to grow, which, if not corrected, will set you up to eventually become a false prophet or prophetess (see for example 1 Kings 13:18). I've heard that people who initially followed false prophets such as Jim Jones have said that these prophets were true ministers of the Lord in the beginning. Eventually, Jim Jones went from being true to being completely deceitful. Just because people seem to display gifts doesn't mean they are true prophets of God. Character needs to match up with gifts.

A pastor I know went to hear Jim Jones when he was preaching in Los Angeles, and he shared how a person in the front jumped up and began to praise God. Jones commanded him to sit down, saying, "You're here to hear from me today. I taught you that, not God." At this point, the pastor I know said he quietly exited out the back door.

The thought that it is possible to deteriorate from a true minister or prophet to a false one is very sobering. Consider Balaam, who was so loved by God that He went to great lengths—even by sending an angel and speaking through a donkey—to keep Balaam from going astray (see Num. 22–24). The love of money, however, was so great that eventually Balaam became a false prophet and was killed. His name is now equated with false prophets as shown in 2 Peter 2:15, "They have forsaken the right way and gone astray, following the way of Balaam the son of Beor, who loved the wages of unrighteousness."

We need to keep the fear of the Lord upon our lives to keep us straight with God. Few people start out false; but time, circumstance and temptation can start a slide toward total corruption.

In summary, this chapter has given you some simple guidelines to help you avoid getting into error. As we move into the next portion of the book, you'll learn in an in-depth manner about several kinds of prophets and the ways they function.

PROPHECY IN PRACTICE

1. Have you ever experienced any intimidation when you considered prophesying?
2. List several ways in which you might know when it is appropriate to release a prophetic word corporately.
3. Are New Testament prophets or prophetesses ever inaccurate? Does this make them false prophets or prophetesses?
4. Name two examples in the Old Testament where prophets were not stoned when their prophecies were not fulfilled.
5. What are some characteristics of a false prophet/prophetess?

Notes

1. C. Peter Wagner, *Lighting the World* (Ventura, Calif.: Regal Books, 1995), pp. 108-109.
2. W. Bauer, W. F. Arndt, W. F. Gingrich, and F. W. Danker, *A Greek-English Lexicon of the New Testament and Other Early Christian Literature* (Chicago: University of Chicago Press, 1979), pp. 177-178.
3. John Sherrill and Elizabeth Sherrill, *The Happiest People on Earth* (Grand Rapids: Chosen Books, 1975), pp. 19-20.
4. Ibid., pp. 21-22.
5. J. I. Packer, Sinclair B. Ferguson, and David F. Wright, eds., *New Dictionary of Theology* (Downers Grove, Ill.: InterVarsity Press,   1988), p. 294.
6. Bill Hamon, *Prophets and Personal Prophecy* (Shippensburg, Pa. Destiny Image Publishers, 1987), pp. 120-123.
7. Ibid.
8. David Blomgren, *Prophetic Gatherings in the Church* (Portland, Oreg.: Bible Temple Publishing, 1979), pp. 59-60.
9. Ibid.

CHAPTER NINE

DREAMS, VISIONS, PROPHETIC STYLES AND GIFTS

■

This chapter includes information on discerning and interpreting dreams and visions, as well as how to know the difference between an open vision (i.e., strong and visual) and an inner vision (i.e., more subtle). Another section talks about the various kinds of prophetic gifts and people. Who knows, maybe you'll find out about yourself in these pages. Let's begin!

To really get a grasp on how important this first section on dreams and visions is, we must go back to the Scriptures in Joel 2:28, which describes what will occur when the power of the Holy Spirit is poured out in the end times:

> And it shall come to pass afterward that I will pour out My Spirit on all flesh; your sons and your daughters shall prophesy, *your old men shall dream dreams, your young men shall see visions* [italics added].

As I was growing up in the church, the area of prophetic dreams and visions was not understood. However, linking these areas with the moving of the Holy Spirit is undeniable. I am convinced that God tries to speak to many of His children through dreams or visions. Many people, however, don't understand what God is trying to say or what they should do with the experiences they have had.

DREAMS IN SCRIPTURE

The Bible is full of stories about dreams. Although it may seem strange to those reading this book who are of a Western worldview, God often spoke to His people through night visions or dreams. Here's an interesting passage from Job 33:14-17:

> For God may speak in one way, or in another, yet man does not perceive it. *In a dream, in a vision of the night, when deep sleep falls upon men,* while slumbering on their beds, *then He opens the ears of men, and seals their instruction.* In order to turn man from his deed [italics added].

The Bible shows that the Holy Spirit often spoke through dreams that caused critical changes in people's lives and the history of nations, as well as predicting the birth of the Messiah. Without the dream where God sent an angel to speak to Joseph, Mary might have been stoned or at least put away (see Matt. 1:20-23). Joseph was also warned in a dream to flee to Egypt to protect Jesus from Herod's wrath (see 2:13,14). In the first two chapters of Matthew, we find no less than five dreams.

According to John and Paula Sandford, the virtue of a dream is that in one fast-moving reel God may speak with minimum conscious interference. He can often teach us more profoundly by dreams because they stimulate us to think about subjects and help us make discoveries. The Eastern courtesy of speaking indirectly is founded upon this same principle—people retain best what they discover for themselves.[1]

DREAMS AND THE PROPHETIC

Scripture indicates a clear linking of dreams, visions and the prophetic. Numbers 12:6 says, "Hear now My words: If there is a prophet among you, I, the Lord, make Myself known to him in a vision; I speak to him in a dream."

It is not uncommon for God to speak to His people in dreams. Unfortunately, many people ignore most of their dreams or they wait so long to write them down that they forget them. Those who have a prophetic gifting will remember their dreams more often; God says in His Word that this is one way He speaks to His prophets. For some prophets, dreams are one of the main ways God speaks to them (see Joel 2:28; see other examples in Gen. 28:12; 31:10,11; 37:5-9; Matt. 1:20; 2:13,19).

My entire family has prophetic dreams from time to time. In *Possessing the Gates of the Enemy*, I wrote about the warning dreams my husband, Mike, has had for our family. One of his most frequent warning dreams is of tornadoes coming at our house or at other people. We know these are not fate, but rather the Lord wanting us to pray and avert what is coming.

DREAMS AS WARNINGS

I am convinced God often tries to warn of disasters through dreams, but His people do not always understand what to do with the information in such dreams (see Matt. 2:12,22). As well, certain prophetic people are stronger than others in their abilities to interpret dreams (see Gen. 40:8; 41:16; Dan. 2:19,27,28; 4:18). Through the years, I have often interpreted dreams, but I am not as strong in this ability as are people such as John and Paula Sandford.

When I was a senior in high school I had a terrible dream. I woke up from the dream crying with big wrenching sobs. I dreamed that my dad had died. It was so vivid, it was kind of like I was half asleep and half awake. In the dream, we were together and I said to him, "Daddy, what's wrong?" He looked gray and sick.

Daddy answered me in his affectionate Georgian drawl, "Darlin', I'm just so very tired."

Four years later, the last time I was home and saw my daddy alive, he was sleeping on the couch. He was so still, I went over and touched him. I felt uneasy and wanted to see if he was all right. Dad stirred as I gently put my hand on his arm, "Daddy, are you feeling okay?"

My sweet dad looked up at me and said these words, "Darlin', I'm just so very tired." Three months later, he died of a massive heart attack at age 49.

If I had had the knowledge I now have when I dreamed that dream as a senior in high school, I would have prayed and asked that his early death be averted. On the other hand, I would also have relinquished him to the Lord. That way, even if he died, I would have stood against any attacks of Satan.

You might say, "Well, Cindy, maybe God was just warning you that your dad was going to die early." That is possible; however, it is my personal opinion he had many more years of life left—49 is a very early age to die. I do know, however, that our times and seasons are in the Lord's hands. More than anything else, I am at peace knowing that Dad is waiting in heaven for the rest of our family.

A Vision of Comfort

The Lord did something very special for my family that brought us great peace concerning my dad. Dad died before he could see either of my two children. One day at church camp, my son, Daniel, was walking and praying. Daniel was 11 years old at the time. As he prayed, he was thinking about my father, Grandpa Johnson, whom he had never met. What happened next was related to me on the phone while I was teaching in Charlotte, North Carolina.

Daniel was praying, "Lord, I'd like to see my grandpa." At that moment, he looked up to see two people leaning against a fence. "Mom," he excitedly told me, "one of the men was Jesus and the other man was your dad."

I quickly asked, "How do you know that, Daniel?" It was kind of hard to understand him because his sister was also telling the story on the line and they obviously had been crying.

"Mom, I know because he told me. Jesus brought him, Mom."

By this time, I was crying too. "Daniel, what did he tell you?"

Softly, he said, "Mama, he said, 'Hello, Daniel, I'm your grandad. I know the Daniel from the Bible. One day I'll introduce you to him.'"

Although Daniel had never seen my dad as a young man, he went on to describe him exactly to me. "Mom, he said to say 'Hi' to Mary, and, oh yes, one more thing. He knows what you're doing for the Lord and he's really proud of you."

At this point, giant tears were rolling down my cheeks, just as they are as I write this. How comforted I felt! What a wonderful feeling it is to know that Dad is looking over the grandstand of heaven as part of that cloud of witnesses and cheering on his little girl.

Later on, I thought about the passage where the Lord brought Elijah and Moses to the Mount of Transfiguration to talk with Jesus (see Luke 9:30,31). I don't know why God chose to answer my son that day. I'm sure other people have wanted to have just such experiences, but God didn't answer them in this way. I also know that we have to beware of counterfeit spirits who want to deceive us—but I truly believe Daniel had a visitation that day and that it changed all of us.

DREAMS AS GOD'S INSTRUMENT

The Church in general has been leery of dreams. This may be because of the controversial work of Sigmund Freud and Carl Jung. To discount dreams, however, totally cuts off one possible biblical way the Voice of God is trying to speak to His people today.

How do you tell the difference between an everyday dream and a spiritual dream? For one thing, spiritual dreams are usually very vivid and real. They are the kind that cause you to think about them for a while. Sometimes you wonder if you are awake or asleep when they occur because they seem so real. These dreams are often etched in your memory, although it is good to write down the details immediately. Notice from the biblical accounts that people remembered the details of their dreams and could recount them. When we have a spiritual dream, the meaning may be clear or it may need to be interpreted.[2]

Dr. Glenn Clark told of how Stella Holbrook, a Minneapolis woman, dreamed that she saw her best friend, Mrs. Simpson, walking back and forth in a room holding her head between her hands. She had gone insane. Horrified by the dream, Stella was unable to sleep for the remainder of the night. Early the next morning, she telephoned the friend saying that she had to see her. When they met Stella told her, "You are in a deadly peril. You must see a doctor immediately."

"But I've never felt better in my life," Mrs. Simpson remonstrated.

"No matter. I plead with you to see a doctor. I've never had a dream so real."

As much for her distraught friend's peace of mind as anything, Mrs. Simpson made an appointment with her doctor. He found a brain tumor located where it would probably cause insanity without prompt surgery. Her friend had dreamed the truth after all.[3]

The story goes on to tell how Mrs. Simpson went to the Mayo Clinic where Dr. Will Mayo found out the strength of her faith. "Let's wait," he suggested, "for three months, live healthily and apply all the faith you have."

Mrs. Simpson went away and prayed for three months in a cabin, closing any possible breech between herself and the Lord. At the end of the three months, she went back to see Dr. Will and Dr. Judd (a colleague), who, after many tests, could find no trace of the brain tumor! It was proclaimed a great miracle of God by these notable medical physicians.

Thank God for the courage of Stella Holbrook to share the dream with her friend, even at the risk of appearing foolish. It probably saved her friend's life.

DREAMS AS PROCLAMATION

Prophetic dreams proclaim events, give warnings, direction, comfort and open the door to deep emotional healings, among other things. I know for certain the Lord sometimes announces the birth of a child as much as two years before it is conceived. This is what happened in the case of our son, Daniel.

One night when we lived in California, Mike had a dream. He was a financial analyst at the time and prophetic dreams were unusual for him during that period of his life. He dreamed that we were going to have a son, and in the dream the Lord spoke to Mike and said, "I want you to call your son Daniel. He will be constantly before the Lord, just as Daniel was in the Bible, and he will be a mighty man of God."

Mike woke up, sat up in bed, and shook me awake. "Cindy, Cindy, we're going to have a son!" Well, in my groggy state, this was quite a shock as I was certain I wasn't pregnant. Seeing my astonishment, he went on quickly to explain, "Not now. In the future."

This dream came two years before Daniel was conceived. In the meantime, we moved to El Paso, Texas, where Mike worked for American Airlines, and we decided it was time to have another baby. One night, we read all the portions of the Bible where the Lord remembered His promises to give a child to people such as Abraham and Sarah, and Hannah. We then knelt down and Mike prayed and asked God to give us the child of promise—our son, Daniel. The very next month I found out I was pregnant.

When I was in the delivery room, bets were flying back and forth at the American Airlines offices about the sex of the baby. But Mike never wavered in his conviction that God had spoken to him in a dream and that we would have a son named Daniel. We didn't know the sex of the child in the natural realm, only through Mike's spiritual dream. Later, when the baby was born, the question wasn't, "Is the mother okay?" Rather, everyone wanted to know, "Is it a girl or a boy?"

We've always been glad God spoke to Mike. One reason He told us beforehand may have been so we would be able to pray prayers of warfare for Daniel's life. You see, he was born with a condition that inhibited his body from reproducing red blood cells. All the hospital staff would tell us that first night was, "He's holding his own, but we can't make any promises." First Timothy 1:18 tells us we can wage a good warfare over the prophecies given to us. We took the dream and prophetic promises given to Mike almost three years previously and went to prayerful war for our son's life. The Lord healed him completely that night. Daniel is 13 years old at the time of this writing and is a great blessing.

Dreams as Intercessory Tools

Because I am a prophetic intercessor, many of my dreams are given for intercessory reasons. I have often ministered to a person and suddenly realized I received the key I needed to help that person in my dream the previous night. Just last Sunday, I had a dream where I was being chased all night by people who wanted to kill me, and I woke up with a prophecy to pray for the persecuted Church in Iran. My dream and the emotions that still lingered from my fear for my life as I slept intensified my praying. I had been touched with the feeling of the Iranian believers' infirmities and persecution.

At times, I have found that a dream may have more than one interpretation; it may have both a physical and spiritual meaning. God in His economy is able to accomplish multiple things with one situation. For instance, a person might dream of people who look old and sick even though they are young. They may have physical infirmities that are making them feel old before their time and they may also have deep inner needs that have aged them prematurely.

One night, I dreamed I was looking at my left hand and noticed two stems of leaves coming out of it. I pulled on one leaf and it had a long tendril and eventually a big bulb with roots on it plopped out. Then I yanked on the other one and it was even longer, bigger and had an even larger bulb with roots attached. The understanding of the dream came a few days later when I ministered to a friend's husband who was in depression. As we prayed and talked, it became evident that his depression had two major roots: his relationship with his mother, and even greater dysfunctional problems with his dad. When we started praying, he also asked me to pray for the healing of his left hand, which he had hurt in construction work.

Later, when I meditated on my dream, the Lord showed me two major roots in my life also. One interesting element is that I am left-handed, and the Lord showed me that this should be my stronger hand. I should have been strong in certain areas in my life, but because of these painful roots that needed healing I was weakened in these areas.

UNDERSTANDING YOUR DREAMS

To pull together some loose threads, here are some specific things to do if you have a vivid prophetic dream:

Ask if it is from the Lord or not. Satan can send tormenting dreams or deceptive dreams (see Eccles. 5:3,7). For instance, if a married woman dreams she is married to another man, this wouldn't be a prophetic word from God that she was to divorce her husband and marry the other man, but could be a lying dream.

Write it down so you will remember the details.

Pray for the interpretation. If you are not able to interpret it yourself, ask the Lord to send someone to you who can. I have found that the Lord will often let me know when a circumstance fits a dream I've had. The dream will come to my remembrance and it will be like the pieces of a puzzle fitting together.

If the dream remains a mystery to you and no one else is able to interpret it at that time, don't throw it away. If you sense it is from the Lord, keep it somewhere for a later time. Dreams can be like time-release capsules; they can take years to come to pass. Consider Joseph's dreams, which he related to his father and brothers (see Gen. 37:1-11). It was years before they came to pass.

Be careful with whom you share the dream. Like Joseph, you may tell your dream too soon and it may seem outlandish or prideful—especially if it seems rather grandiose (see v. 5). Years ago I had dreams of speaking to packed stadiums, praying for the sick and seeing many dramatic healings. It was a long time before I shared these dreams with anyone, and then only just a few people. Today, the night visions I saw long ago are coming to pass.

If the dream seems to indicate a change in life's direction, seek guidance from those in spiritual authority to confirm what you believe God is saying to you.

The dream may be for someone else. Ask the Lord if and/or when you should share it with the person. It may be something you need to pray about yourself, thus allowing the Lord to avert the situation without worrying the other person.

One of my prayer partners was greatly disturbed when she had a dream that I had died in a shipwreck. She woke up and prayed for me and also shared it with my sister, who also prayed about it. Later on, my sister, Lucy, told me about the dream. I understood immediately what it was about. In the past, I have preached a sermon on being shipwrecked in faith. At the time, I was totally overwhelmed with many responsibilities and the pressure was so heavy that I felt as though I were drowning. Perhaps these two intercessors averted some physical disaster that might have been brought on by such stress. Thank God for their prayers and great wisdom.

If the Lord is giving a warning, pray about it. Seek wisdom from someone you trust. It may be that you need to share it with your prayer group. At times, God gives a warning dream so you can "sound the alarm" for disaster or judgment to be averted.

Frank Hammond, who is a pioneer in the area of personal deliverance, had a dream or night vision on February 5, 1985. At first, he didn't understand the dream, but then he received the interpretation in another dream seven nights after the first dream. He was praying for the interpretation of the dream when he fell into a supernatural sleep. Frank wrote the vision down, writing almost nonstop until it was finished. It has since been published in a little book entitled *God Warns America. Arise, O Church!* (Impact Books, Inc.).

In his night vision, Frank dreamed of three eagles: one green, one red and one blue. They represent judgments coming against America and the Church in the United States in the areas of the economy, judgment for the sin of murder and abortion, and third, a direct judgment against the Church in the form of persecution from state and federal governments. The Lord was clear in the vision that the intercessors would be able to stay these judgments at least partially if enough prayer were made on behalf of America. We are already seeing the judgment in the form of persecution of Christians by the government, but many are praying and I am believing that full-blown judgment will be turned away through intercession.

VISIONS

There are many similarities between dreams and visions. John and Paula Sandford call visions "the picture language of God." They go on to state that the important difference between dreams and visions is that when we receive a vision we are awake, so visions are much more subject to our control. Visions come in many degrees. Sometimes the Holy Spirit flashes pictures across the inner screens of our minds with or without interruption of conscious thoughts. Some think such visions are less "in the Spirit" because they happen less dramatically than do trances. Not so. God simply chooses how He will communicate to us according to His wisdom. Such visions are not less valuable, forceful, imperative or truthful.[4]

Many people have minivisions but often don't recognize them for what they are. The Lord might flash a picture of your child being hurt, which will prompt you to go and find out what the child is doing. Right when you enter the room, see your five-year-old child standing on the ledge of the window of your two-story house and there is no screen to protect him from falling. You go over and pluck him from danger—just in the nick of time. Some remember the flash picture of the child just before they went to look for him, and others don't realize it was God who gave them the picture of warning.

My first full-blown vision happened when Mike and I were flying to Africa in 1979. He had been laid off from his job with Trans-World Airlines and we had one trip pass left. We were discussing his future and I was saying, "Mike, what would you like to do for a job anyway?" About that time the movie came on. When I looked at the screen, it looked like another screen had been rolled over the movie screen and I began to have a vision. This vision was of an airplane. It was sitting in a hangar and seemed to belong to Mike. I also saw him kneeling down, praying with two other men in a lovely office. One of the men had beautiful silver hair.

I sat transfixed by what I saw. In fact, I shook my head, closed my eyes and rubbed them a little to see if I was making this all up. When I opened my eyes again, the vision was still there. It lasted five minutes or so, although it seemed longer.

When the vision ended, I described the airplane to Mike. He said, "Honey, as far as I know, no plane like that exists." Years later, he came to me with a magazine about flying and showed me a picture of an airplane. "Is this the plane you saw in your vision?" he asked. Astounded, I looked at the picture of the plane I had seen in the vision years before. It was one and the same—a private business jet that had transatlantic capabilities.

As of yet, we do not own that airplane and we don't have the full realization of what it all means. Revelation is often progressive. God told Abram to leave and go to the land of promise (see Gen. 12:1,2). Later, God told Abram He would make his descendants like the dust of the earth (see 13:16). God often gives us just what we need for the present season of our lives and adds to it when there is a change, shift or addition to what He has said previously.

It is possible to receive a vision and to stop it in the middle portion. I believe I could have resisted what I was seeing, shaken it off, scoffed at it and likely aborted what God was trying to show me.

Visions and Prophetic Words

At times, what is called a word of knowledge couples with a vision. Many people have commented to me how they were searching for objects they had lost and had pictures in their minds of unusual places to look for them. Once when I could not find my passport, and after searching fruitlessly for days, I decided to ask the Lord where it was. (My children often admonish me, "Mom, why don't you think of that first?" You would think I would, but I get caught up in my anxiety at times and forget!)

Mike said, "Cindy, calm down and just get quiet before the Lord so you can hear Him." When I did this, I immediately had a flash of insight; I knew to look in our tall dresser behind the top left drawer. In a matter of seconds, I had walked to the drawer, pulled it out, reached behind it and had the passport in my hand. God is infinitely caring and was more than likely just waiting for me to ask Him where it was.

Open and Inner Visions

Two basic categories of visions are open visions and inner visions. An open vision is one where the vision seems as real as anything else going on around you. Angelic visitations would fall into this category. You are able to "see" into the dimension in which the angels exist. Gideon's visitation with the angel of the Lord would be an example of this (see Judg. 6:11). In Acts 10:3, Cornelius "saw clearly in a vision an angel of God coming in" and calling his name. I have found that certain angels seem to be messenger angels, and when they come they deliver messages from God.

It is interesting to note that although Cornelius was a God-fearing man, he wasn't a Christian. The use of visions and dreams given to unbelievers has been a powerful factor in many of them coming to Christ.

Intercessors throughout the world are praying and asking God to reveal His Son to the unreached people groups of the world. Because many of these groups have little or no Christian witness, it takes supernatural intervention for many of them to become open to the gospel message. The following story is taken from the September/October 1994 edition of the Anglican Frontier Missions newsletter, *Out of Sight.* The title of the article is "The Quashqu'i No Longer the Most Unevangelized!" and it tells a fascinating story that occurred in the nation of Iran:

> At a weekly Koran study—just like our Bible studies—a group of people were reading a passage which had frequent mention of Isa (Jesus). Actually Jesus appears more often in the Koran than does Mohammed. In this particular passage the frequency caught the attention of these people.
>
> They said to themselves something like, "You know, for as often as Jesus occurs in these passages we read, we ought to know something about him. Does anyone here know who he is?" No one could shed any light on who he was.
>
> That night one of the men had a dream in which somebody said to him something like, "I want you to know more about Jesus. If you go to the bridge on the road just over the mountain, I'll have some literature there for you. This will explain who Jesus is."
>
> Meanwhile, in Shiraz, a city near the mountains where the Quashqu'i live, two missionaries had arrived to pass out Christian literature. In a way that was uncharacteristic of that city, hardly anyone was interested in taking their literature. They decided to leave and drive to another city.
>
> On the way, as they were passing over a bridge over a mountain stream, their jeep stopped. Try as they could, they could not get it started again. At one point they looked up from under the hood and saw a man scampering down the mountain. So agile was he that they knew he must be one of the local Quashqu'i. When the man arrived at the jeep, he said something like, "I've come to take the literature about Jesus to my village."
>
> After loading him up and watching him easily ascend the mountain, they got back in the jeep and tried the key. It started right up and they drove off praising God and saying

something like, "Somewhere some people have been praying for the Quashqu'i to receive the Gospel of Jesus Christ."

An inner vision is what I described having when I was praying about the location of my passport. It wasn't as strong, and was something I pictured in my mind as opposed to the open vision where I felt I actually saw what seemed as real as anything else around me.

Acts 10 shows examples of a person having a vision and another falling into a trance. A trance is a much deeper experience than a vision. It seems that when God causes someone to fall into a trance it supersedes all else. In fact, the Greek word for trance used in verse 10 means a displacement of the mind, or "ecstasy."[5]

I have a theory on why God gave an open vision to Cornelius and a trance to Peter. Cornelius was open to receiving from God what was shown him. Peter was entrenched in the legalism of the Jewish religion and it took a deeper experience to create an openness to be used of God with the Gentiles. From what we know up till this time, it wasn't a matter of consideration for Gentiles to be converted to Christianity. Something big had to happen to cause Peter to have a paradigm shift (i.e., a shift in his worldview and thinking). Acts 10 tells us that the Lord showed Peter three times that what God had cleansed, he was not to consider unclean.

Saul's meeting with God on the road to Damascus could be considered a deeper trancelike experience (see 9:3-6), although Paul himself calls it a "vision" in 26:19. A bright light shone from heaven and Saul fell to the ground. He didn't actually see the Lord but was spoken to by God.

Modern-day accounts of God dealing with those who are resistant to the gospel are not uncommon. My sister, Lucy, married a fine young man named Mark. The only problem was that he wasn't a Christian, and Lucy, although she was raised in a Christian home, had wandered far away from Christ. I prayed for almost six years and finally she gave her heart back to the Lord. She then joined me in praying for her husband's salvation.

History reveals accounts of people falling into trances. One of these stories comes from the account of a revival led by Maria Woodworth-Etter. She was conducting meetings in Hartford City, Indiana, the first week of January, 1885, in the Methodist church. Because the church was cold and skeptical, she banded with five of the leading members to pray for an outpouring of power from on high that would shake the city and countryside for miles around. They cried out to God that Christians and sinners would be overcome by the power of God as had Saul, Daniel and the priests who could not stand in the Temple because of the glory of the Lord being poured out (see 2 Chron. 5:13,14). In Maria Woodworth-Etter's own account, this is how God answered their prayers:

> The Lord answered our prayers in a remarkable manner. The class leader's little boy fell under the power of God first. He rose up, stepped on the pulpit, and began to talk with the wisdom and power of God. His father began to shout and praise the Lord. As the little fellow exhorted and asked the people to come to Christ they began to weep all over the house. Some shouted; others fell prostrated. The power of the Lord, like the wind, swept all over the city, up one street and down another, sweeping through the places of business, the workshops, saloons and dives, arresting sinners of all classes. Men, women and children were struck down in their homes, in their places of business, on the highways, and lay as dead. They had wonderful visions, and rose converted, giving glory to God. When they told what they had seen their faces shone like angels'. The fear of God fell upon the city. The police said they never saw such a change; that they had nothing to do. They said they made no arrest; and that the power of God seemed to preserve the city. A spirit of love rested all over the city. There was no fighting, no swearing on the streets; that the people moved softly, and that there seemed to be a spirit of love and kindness among all classes, as if they felt they were in the presence of God.[6]

Again, let me give the caution I've been giving all along about deception. In some counterfeit religions, people meditate to go into a trance state. This is not the same as God visiting you with a trance. God gives a trance as a result of an outpouring of His Spirit or it may come upon you sovereignly as it did when Peter fell into a trance.

Types and Styles of Prophets and Prophetesses

Prophets and prophetesses are diverse, each one having a unique style, flavor and calling. This section will give you some general groupings modeled from biblical examples of the prophets, or prophetesses, as may be the case. The people talked about in this section may be prophetic people who, although not standing in the office of the prophet, move in the gift of prophecy and/or are prophetic intercessors.

How a prophetic word is received from the Lord, as well as the method used to deliver the message, are clues used to identify the type of prophetic gift in which you or someone else operates.

The Seer

Prophets in the Old Testament at one time were called "seers" (see 1 Sam. 9:9). This means that they literally or figuratively saw things in the Spirit. Some of the prophets were more pictorial in their gifts than others, such as Ezekiel who saw visions of heavenly creatures.

Certain prophetic people today receive their prophetic words mainly through pictures. Their prophecies will often be interpretations of pictures or inner visions they see.

Satan will try to give counterfeit visions to those who are seers. Also, I believe it is good to ask the Lord to close your vision to those things He does not want you to see. People who have been involved in the New Age movement or occult often are accustomed to seeing things that are inspired through spirit guides. This occultic influence needs to be renounced and cut off so the prophetic vision will not be affected by demonic influence.

Seers are usually emotionally empathetic people, as are some of the other prophetic types I will talk about in this chapter. Those who tend to take on others' burdens indiscriminately—regardless of whether the Lord wants them to or not—would benefit from reading the chapter on burden bearing in John and Paula Sandford's book *Healing the Wounded Spirit.*

Prophets and Prophetesses of Government

Daniel would be an example of a prophet of government. His prophecies spoke of monumental changes in world order. There are just such prophets today. Some of these prophets are actually in governmental positions. I have found that God places His gifts in people from all walks of life. Prophets seem to be sent to various institutions of society, such as legal, educational and governmental offices.

Governmental prophets may not give as many personal prophecies. They also understand trends and are watchmen on the wall for their nations. Although I do not know if Pat Robertson considers himself a prophet, in my opinion he certainly would fall into this category.

Counseling Prophets and Prophetesses

Some prophetic people may never give many public prophecies, but they possess a prophetic gift of counsel. They have a rare ability to point out pitfalls, serious problems and consequences of people's actions in a manner that releases an enormous measure of grace to the hearer.

One day I was listening to one of Jack Hayford's assistants relate how she handles the wide variety of calls that come to Pastor Hayford's office. Because of his visibility in the Body of Christ, people flock to him and want to relate some revelations they feel God has given them. Pastor Hayford's staff member shared how one man called, thinking he was Jesus Christ. Usually these people are almost impossible to reach because their deception is so deep. By the end of their conversation, however, he had been backed into a corner in a grace-filled manner and even showed signs of realizing his deep error. This staff member may not stand in the office of the prophet, but she does have a marked God-given ability at times in the area of prophetic counsel.

John and Paula Sandford's "Elija House" is a great example of a marriage of the prophetic and counseling.

Counseling is one area in which prophets are usually gifted because they are able to give a word of knowledge or wisdom supernaturally about a given situation. Nathan gave counsel to King David (see 2 Sam. 7:3; 1 Kings 1:24). Huldah would be an example of a prophetess who gave prophetic counsel (see 2 Kings 22:14-20).

Weeping Prophets and Prophetesses

Some prophets are used of God in the area of weeping in intercession for nations. This kind of weeping is different from that caused by personal emotions. You may not feel the least bit sad but find tears coursing down your face and a godly sorrow pouring out as you prophesy or pray for a person. Jeremiah was used by God to weep for his nation (see Jer. 9:10; 13:17; 14:17; Lam. 1:16; 2:18; 3:48).

Prophetic Dreamers

I discussed dreams at length earlier in the chapter and mentioned how some people receive clear, frequent direction from the Lord. A friend of mine in California has been repeatedly shown by the Lord through dreams regarding when physical attacks were going to come against her.

Prophetic dreamers will often be awakened by the Lord to intercede when warning dreams are given. They are called by God to take the night watch and are given keys to pray about in their dreams.

Singing Prophets and Prophetesses—Psalmists

David was certainly a good example of a singing prophet or psalmist. The psalms are a songbook that include many prophecies. Deborah sang a song with Barak after the victory over Sisera (see Judg. 5). Prophetic people such as Charles Slagel sing their prophecies. I will sit at the piano at times and play and sing as I prophesy. Prophetic song is a beautiful expression of the prophetic gift and, coupled with the anointing on the music, is an extremely powerful prophetic way.

Prophets and Prophetesses of Prophetic Administration and/or Finance

This is what I call the Joseph anointing. The Josephs who have prophetic anointing are raised up and put into positions of authority to bring order and release of finances in economic systems. God gives them supernatural strategies such as He gave Joseph for Egypt.

Some people are gifted in the area of administration and are able to bring order to organizations within a short time period. Our prayer leader, Chuck Pierce, is one of these, and my husband, Mike, also flows in this way.

Prophets and Prophetesses to the Nations

This would include those who have a call to minister in the nations of the world. Their theme Scripture is Psalm 2:8, "Ask of Me, and I will give You the nations for Your inheritance, and the ends of the earth for Your possession," or Isaiah 49:6, a prophecy of our Lord, but often a *rhema* for His servants.

Some will travel and prophesy in many nations. Others will be called to their own nations as prophets or prophetesses and the prophecies they receive will center around their nations.

My call is to the nations of the world. One of the major ways the Lord uses me is to prophesy historical changes that God wants to make through prophetic intercession being made on behalf of a nation. More about this kind of prophecy in the next chapter, "Warring in the Heavenlies."

Prophetic Orators and Teachers

These people are gifted to communicate God's prophetic messages. They are like the silver-tongued Isaiah and will be moved to give lengthy prophetic messages. Not all of the messages will be spontaneous—some may come in the form of prophetic teaching. As a result of studying God's Word, the Lord will give revelatory messages that will be a trumpeting of what the Holy Spirit is saying to the Church. My pastor, Dutch Sheets, is this kind of prophetic teacher. He sometimes will give a personal prophetic word but consistently flows in the very strong teaching gift God has given him.

Prophets and Prophetesses to the Local Church

I personally believe that God calls one or more prophets to each local church. They may not be recognized as such and their prophesying may take the form of prophetic intercession, but they will hear accurately from the Lord. Such people come to the pastor and say such things as, "Pastor, I was praying for the church this week and I believe we're going to experience a breakthrough in finance in the next few months." (I know some of you are thinking, *I'd like to hear that from my intercessors!*)

As Peter Wagner points out in his book *Prayer Shield*, some intercessors are assigned by God to pray and accurately share with the pastor the information they hear from the Lord. Although these people may not be prophets or prophetesses, they certainly are prophetic in their gifting.

The Deborah Anointing

God has called some prophetesses to be Deborahs—they have spirits of wisdom and counsel and are often spiritual warriors. They have strong gifts of leadership and many times the Lord will couple them with Baraks, as found in Judges 4.

How Prophetic Gifts Function

Steve Penny of Australia has some interesting insights on the various ways the prophetic gifts will function within the Body of Christ:

1. To awaken and activate the saints to the purpose of God for their time.

2. To be a governmental ministry with the apostolic ministries. (Prophets often bring directional and structural adjustments to churches, movements and even governments, which is usually administered through local apostolic leaders.)
3. To sound the alarm in times of transition, judgement, expansion and warfare.
4. To prepare the way for a visitation of God by addressing oppositions and difficult issues not able to be dislodged by other ministries.
5. To hear from God in unique ways and bring clarity and perspective to the church in difficult days.[7]

Steve also points out that strategic prophetic churches will be linked—and in some cases led—by strategic prophetic men and women.[8]

God still speaks to us in supernatural ways just as He did in the book of Acts. He wants to be involved intimately in our lives and wants to answer our questions, protect us and give us the guidance we desire. I pray that this chapter has helped you to understand the ways He is speaking through dreams, visions and special visitations of the Holy Spirit.

The final chapter is a window on the world concerning the prophetic realm and spiritual warfare. You'll learn how God is using prophetic people and principles, such as identificational repentance, to change nations for the kingdom of God.

PROPHECY IN PRACTICE

1. Can you remember a time when you had a prophetic dream?
2. How do you determine the difference between a weird or "pizza" dream and one sent from the Lord? Do you know anyone who is able to interpret spiritual dreams?
3. What is the difference between an open and an inner vision?
4. Have you ever known anyone who experienced a spiritual trance? Why do you think God might have caused this person to experience this?
5. Name at least three types of prophetic people.

Notes

1. John Sandford and Paula Sandford, *The Elijah Task* (Tulsa, Okla.: Victory House, Inc., 1977), p. 170.
2. Cindy Jacobs, *Possessing the Gates of the Enemy* (Grand Rapids: Chosen Books, 1991), p. 76.
3. Catherine Marshall, *Something More* (New York: Avon Books, 1976), pp. 90-91.
4. Sandford, The Elijah Task, p. 187.
5. W. Bauer, W. F. Arndt, W. F. Gingrich, and F. W. Danker, *A Greek-English Lexicon of the New Testament and Other Early Christian Literature* (Chicago: University of Chicago Press, 1979), p. 245.
6. Maria Woodworth-Etter, *A Diary of Signs and Wonders* (Tulsa, Okla.: Harrison House, 1916), pp. 63-64.
7. Steve Penny, *Look Out, the Prophets Are Coming!* (Sutherland, NSW, Australia: Prophetic People International, 1993), pp. 162-163.
8. Ibid., p. 165.

CHAPTER TEN

WARRING IN THE HEAVENLIES

∎

In July 1994, Brazil and Italy played the final World Cup soccer title match at the Rose Bowl in Pasadena, California. The eyes of the world were fastened intently upon the game. Television stations from across the globe had their cameras rolling to catch the final moments of this clash of giants to declare the victor. While reporters were announcing the natural news, a behind-the-scenes battle was taking place between two heavenly armies—the army of the King of kings and the army of the dark prince, Satan.

Little known to most people outside of Brazil was the exaltation of spiritism in that country's news and the reliance they have had as a nation on occultic power to help win their games. One of Brazil's top players is a young man named Romario. He is the most famous soccer player since Pele, who is noted as being the greatest player who ever lived. During the 1994 World Cup, a television camera was placed in the home of Romario's mother, a known spiritist. Every time her son scored a goal, she would throw a bottle of beer against the wall as an offering to the spirits.

This upset many Brazilian Christians who decided to take the battle to the heavenlies. They were determined to hinder Satan from being exalted in Brazil on public television. How did they fight the battle? On their knees—in corporate church meetings, praying to the King of kings, strategically wrestling to break the spiritist's power.

Amazingly, Romario played arguably the worst game he had ever played. He played so badly that Italy should have won. The Christians held the line in prayer, asking God to receive the glory. Six of the players on the Brazilian team are Christians. One of these is a famous player named Jorginho. Jorginho was offered $500,000 if he would give the sign for a Brazilian beer company—the number one sign held chest high—when he made a goal. He turned down that offer for a better one—that of giving glory to God and receiving a heavenly reward. Each time he scored, he held the "one way Jesus" sign high above his head at arm's length.

The game finally came down to a tie. In the rules of the World Cup, in case of a tie, each team kicks five goals with five different kickers to break the tie. The moment was tense. Christians were fervently praying. Italy's top player, Baggio, a professed Buddhist, attempted his free kick against the Brazilian goalie, Tafarel, a born-again Christian.

What was happening in the unseen realm between the two opposing armies we can only imagine. However, at times clues are leaked into the natural realm that give us a glimpse. Pele, who was the color man (the one who analyzes the game) and who is not a Christian, commented on how good it was to have Christians on the team at this time. The biggest show of hands from the heavenlies came through the other national sports announcer who declared over the airwaves, "This is spiritual warfare, Buddha against Jesus!"

In the end, Brazil won 3-2 after nine shots of overtime. This was an incredible power encounter! Baggio, the Buddhist, made such a bad kick that Tafarel didn't even have to block it! The next day, the biggest national newspaper in Brazil announced the heavenly victory, "Buddha loses to Jesus." Satan's army got thrashed that day through the power of spiritual warfare on a soccer field in California.

In analyzing this whole scenario, I can't help but feel the Lord set this up to show the world a prophetic picture of what is happening today around the globe through intercessory prayer. This is an example of God's power over Satan's power in the nations. The Church's eyes are becoming wide open to the fact that they do not wrestle against flesh and blood but against principalities and powers (see Eph. 6:12). Baggio is not the enemy. The Lord wants him to be saved. The unseen battle is against strongholds, such as Buddhism, that blind millions of eyes to the light of the gospel.

Two armies are fighting in a dimension not visible to the natural eye. Many places in Scripture provide insight into this dimension where angels do God's bidding and demons oppose God's children. Jacob made reference to this in Genesis 32:1,2. After being met by God's angels, Jacob named the place "Mahanaim," which literally means "double camp"—the place where he camped and the camp of heavenly beings.

In recent years, a new emphasis has been placed on the spiritual realm. People are hungry to study such subjects as angels and demonology, and books on the occult are filling bookstores. For many years, the Church in general has paid little attention to what is happening in the heavenlies. God has used many methods to open the eyes of the Body of Christ. One method has been through the books of Frank Peretti, *This Present Darkness*, *Piercing the Darkness* and *The Prophet* (Crossway Books).

I believe God has used the vehicle of fiction to get people to think about spiritual subjects in a nonthreatening way. In a way, these are prophetic parables. *The Prophet* is about the use of a prophetic word that begins a course of events that exposes the problems of abortion.

GOD'S PLAN FOR PROPHETIC PEOPLE

What role do prophetic people play in exposing Satan's schemes and warring in the heavenlies? A major one. Historically, the prophets understood and prophesied against the worship of the demonic gods of the Gentile nations. For instance, they didn't have to do any deep studying to find out what god the Philistines worshiped. It was common knowledge they worshiped Dagon.

The prophetic movement in the United States has for a while largely been involved in giving personal prophecies. I believe God allowed this focus for a season to cause people to become open to the prophetic word and to personally experience the truth God still speaks today. Just as the prophets of old prophesied against the false gods of nations, however, God is raising up a company of prophets to speak His word against the strongholds of cities and nations. This is not to say that God is not speaking and will not continue to speak individually in personal prophecy. He does and will continue to. The point I am making is that God wants us to be watchmen as prophetic people to see and hear beyond a personal level. Prophetic watchmen are reaching a level of maturity in which the prophetic word is catalytic in bringing changes to societies, cultures and, of course, the Church and nations.

Clifford Hill points out that the prophets in the Old Testament were keen students of contemporary affairs in social life, in economy, in political affairs and in the religious life of the nations. The prophets often referred to international events and, in particular, to the threat of foreign invasion. They saw a major part of their task as warning their nations of danger or

of the threat of impending disaster. Hence, they keenly followed the movement of foreign armies and the political intrigues of neighboring states.[1]

We've talked about watchmen earlier in the book. Not only do
watchmen sound the alarm through prophetic intercession, but the warrior watchmen are also proactive or militant in their war against Satan.
It can be summed up in Scripture through Jeremiah 1:10, "See, I have
this day set you over the nations and over the kingdoms, to root out and
to pull down, to destroy and to throw down, to build and to plant."

GOD'S PLAN FOR REGIONS

As an emphasis and understanding of prophetic people comes to the
forefront, we can see that God is establishing these servants in specific
geographic regions to prophesy and pray prophetically for their
assigned areas against the powers of darkness. This is beginning to happen and is having phenomenal results. Where prophetic intercession is
being utilized, captives of Satan's spiritual prisons are coming to Christ
in great numbers.

Through my travels, I talk with many people who are used in spiritual warfare and prophecy. As we compare notes, it is evident that there
are fertile seasons and years when God speaks similarly about coming
events and plans He has for the nations.

Rolland Smith tells of an extraordinary visitation of God in 1984.
This was one of those prophetic years when God spoke strongly to many
leaders and revealed major keys for the healing of nations through
prophetic intercession. While in Sweden teaching a prophetic conference, Smith was in the home of Kjell Sjöberg, a man of God who has a
worldwide prophetic intercessory ministry. The visitation was much like
what happened to Daniel.

> As we interceded for Kjell's ministry and his home and office
> where he would spend so much time communicating with
> the Lord and with watchmen from around the world, a
> frightening thing happened to me. The presence of the Lord
> came so strongly upon me that it pressed me down on my
> face to the floor. I was so overwhelmed by His glory that I
> could not look up or open my eyes. I became acutely aware
> that three angelic beings were standing in the room.

These angels told of the battles they had fought side by side with Joshua and David. I noticed a weariness on their faces similar to that of a battle-scarred veteran. I finally managed to whisper the nagging question, "Why haven't we won the war against the forces of Satan in the earth?" The answer they gave was embedded in my mind forever, "We have helped God's children to win the same territories many times, only to have them lost again to the Devil and his forces."

After this time of visitation, I traveled to Zagreb, Yugoslavia where I met some friends and we traveled together by car to our next destination. On the way we got completely lost on back farm roads. We started praising the Lord when, all of a sudden, there before me was an enormous host of angels. The Lord Jesus was the center of the host. So striking was His appearance that He dominated it all.

Jesus sat behind a huge desk with volumes of very old, leather bound books. He began to take the pages from the books one at a time. As He took a page, a trumpet blast was sounded and a band of mighty angels came forward and stood before the Lord in rapt attention. With great solemnity, the Lord Jesus Christ presented each band with a page from the book.

As He opened the last book, the pages became visible to me. About half of the page was covered with handwritten notes, and the other part was filled with geographical maps of a fairly large region, with rivers, mountains, roads and other landmarks drawn on them. Also, there were symbols and arrows identifying various locations and directions. These drawings were like those in a war room of a military headquarters where the commanding officers direct war operations.

I did not understand the interpretation of the vision until later during a communion session when the Lord Jesus spoke it softly into my heart. "What you saw," He said, "was not the angels going into battle alone. I was sending them to My servants all over the world. Today I have found faithful and trustworthy men and women all over the world."

Just as the military must subject soldiers to very severe tests to verify their trustworthiness with the secrets of war, defenses, weaponry, and battle plans; so I have also subjected my servants to the most severe tests of faithfulness. Now I have, for the first time in the history of the world, found such people positioned in every part of the entire globe.

Jesus continued in my heart, "The maps you saw were the assignments to My servants. The angels were sent to deliver them. Every geographical area in the world is included. These are My officers ready to assume the command of My army throughout the earth."

The final piece came later on New Year's Eve. Jesus spoke again. "Those who were given these assignments will begin to develop strategies of prayer and evangelism for whole nations, multi-national regions, and whole continents. Networks will be formed among vast numbers of God's servants and will stretch out over the whole earth in mighty outreaches. Even global strategies will be given."[2]

This vision has proven to be incredibly accurate. Today, global strategies are sponsored through the auspices of the United Prayer Track of the A.D. 2000 and Beyond Movement, headed by Dr. C. Peter Wagner. Prophetic people span the globe, praying against Satan's power and for world evangelization.

A VISION OF HEALING

The same year Rolland Smith had his vision of the angels, two significant things happened to me. One was an inner vision and the other an open vision. The first came when I was alone in a hotel room in Temple, Texas. It was the first time I had ever been by myself in a strange city in a hotel room, and I was a little nervous. Finally, I was able to fall into a light sleep. The next morning at six o'clock, I was awakened by a knock on the door. In my half-dazed condition my heart started beating wildly and my thoughts raced. *Who could it be at this hour?* I wondered.

After a moment, I got up my courage and peeked out the door window. (Mighty woman of faith and power that I am!) No one was there. I laid down, wondering if I had imagined the knock, when it occurred to me that maybe the Lord had awakened me.

"Lord," I asked, "is there something You want to show me?"

I closed my eyes and immediately saw a vision. It was of a river—a very beautiful river. I thought, *Oh, Lord, thank You for waking me up to see Your river.* The vision was so glorious. I was really enjoying myself when all of a sudden I saw a terrible sight. People were getting into the river and throwing up! They also were tossing the garbage from their houses into God's river.

The next thing I knew, they were jumping into the river and acting very religious. "Oh, hallelujah!" they shouted. "Isn't this water wonderful?" I knew they represented the Body of Christ. Why, they even erected a large pediment sign that announced "River of Living Water." I asked the Lord what had polluted the river and He said in my heart, "Judgmentalism, criticalness, sectarianism, strife and divisions. These have polluted My river."

After a while, I saw people coming to the bank of the river. I sensed that they represented the unsaved world. They looked at the sign, the people in the river who appeared to be having a fabulous time, and they decided to try the water. Kneeling down, they started to drink. It only took one taste and they spat the water out of their mouths with disgust and went away. Meanwhile, the Church hardly noticed what had happened. Nobody could tell the water was polluted because they had tasted it so long that they thought it was good. No one was able to tell the difference between polluted and clean water.

Later, they all got out of the river and fell asleep on either side of the bank. The army of God was fast asleep and no one cared what happened to God's river. As time passed, a couple of the sleepers awakened, looked up astonished at the river, and tried to shake the others awake but were unsuccessful. (I believe they stood for the prophets and prophetesses in the Church.) At last, two angels from heaven came down and put little pots of eye salve in their hands and instructed them to put it on the eyes of those who were asleep.

The two prophetic people applied the salve to each person, one at a time. Each person had the same response after having the medicine put on their eyes. They sat up, looked at the river and declared, "Oh, what has happened to the river of God! How did we let this happen?" Finally, they all stood up in one accord and went into the river to try to clean it up. Alas, they sadly failed. It was too polluted to clean individually with their hands.

As I watched, I could see they had found a strategy. They were building a huge water purification plant. After they finished the plant, I saw a tiny trickle of fresh water flow out of the other side of the unit. Then, more and more water flowed, until the trickle became a stream, and at last, the stream became a mighty river, pure and clean.

The next sight I saw was puzzling to me. I saw trees on either side of the river bank, dropping their leaves into the river. (It was several years before I would come to understand what these leaves represented. More on this later.) The last part of the vision was the most precious. There were children in the river, laughing and playing. They splashed and dunked each other, having a perfectly glorious time. (I believe this is symbolic of a coming children's revival that will span the globe.)

The ending part of this scene was a great blessing. I saw the world come and look at the children in the river. Gazing at one another, they asked the question, "Should we try to drink one last time from the river?" Kneeling down, they put their mouths to the water and began to drink, and they drank and drank and drank as though they would never get enough of the pure river of life. At that moment, the Lord spoke to me and said this, "O taste and see that the Lord, He is good!"

Prayer and Healing for the Nations
A couple parts of the dream I have waited until now to interpret for you. They are strategic to this chapter.

The water purification plant represents the houses of prayer that are springing up all over the world. Isaiah 56:7 says, "Even them I will bring to My holy mountain, and make them joyful in My house of prayer....For My house shall be called a house of prayer for all nations." Twenty-four hour prayer watches and specially purchased houses for the sole purpose of prayer are being started in the nations of the earth. With this movement will come a revival of joy as His presence fills the house.

The river becoming fuller can be likened to the passage in Ezekiel 47 where water flows from under the Temple door. This passage has often been used to preach about revival. Remember the leaves falling into the river? Read verse 12:

> Along the bank of the river, on this side and that, will grow all kinds of trees used for food; their leaves will not wither, and their fruit will not fail. They will bear fruit every month, because their water flows from the sanctuary. Their fruit will be for food, and their *leaves for medicine* [italics added].

God wants to heal nations. The Bible also talks about this in

Revelation 22:1,2 where God showed John a pure river of water of life, and trees whose leaves were used for healing nations.

GOD'S LOVE FOR NATIONS

The second unusual visitation came to me at the end of 1984 and links to the experiences Rolland Smith had while in Sweden and the former Yugoslavia. This second visitation involved an angel that appeared in my living room late one night and gave me instructions on ministering to the nations and their churches.

Within a few months of this open vision (i.e., the angel looked like a physical being sitting in my living room), during a period of fasting and prayer, the Lord gave me a strategy to heal nations as I was praying for America. I wrote about this more at length in *Possessing the Gates of the Enemy.*

During that season of prayer, the Lord gave me a commission. He wanted ed to use me to minister healing to my nation and subsequently the nations of the world. This connected with the angelic visitation. When He said, "I want you to minister to the nation," I immediately asked Him, "How do you do that? How do you minister to an entire nation?" You probably have guessed by now that I am a very simple person. God has to make things easy for me. He rejoined, "How do you minister to an individual?"

This, I understood. For several years, I had been involved in deliverance ministry. I knew a person had to find the entrance that allowed the demon to come in and close it up in order to maintain his or her freedom. The person could have had bitterness or relational problems that opened the door for demonic oppression. If a person is rejected at birth, this also can allow a spirit of rejection to enter his or her life.

The Oppression of Nations

As I studied nations in this light, I began to see similar patterns to what I had learned. Whole nations can be oppressed by the demonic powers listed in Ephesians 6:12. I remember thinking one day, *The Bible says we wrestle against these powers and not flesh and blood, and I don't have any idea how to do that.* Growing up in church, I never heard a single sermon on the healing of nations or wrestling against powers of darkness for nations. *There must be a way to wage war in this way for nations,* I reasoned, *or the Bible wouldn't say to do so in Ephesians 6:12 and 2 Chronicles 7:14.*

Dialoguing in prayer with the Lord I asked, "Lord, what are the sins of my nation?" Satan cannot oppress areas with high-level territorial powers without being given a legal right through sin by those who live in the region. The answer didn't come in an audible voice but by the Holy Spirit speaking inside me, "The sins of America are the sins against the American Indians, the treaties broken against them. Other sins include slavery, the oppression of the Jews through anti-Semitism and the internment of Japanese Americans during World War II." The list goes on and on.

Looking at the nations of the world, I came to some conclusions, many of them interrelated:

- Nations are sick and need healing.
- Nations have relational problems with other nations.
- Nations have sin between nations.
- Nations have generational sin that causes problems that are reaped by the current generation.
- Nations have sinned against the people groups who live within their boundaries.
- God holds these nations responsible for their sins.
- These sins have caused people groups to be resistant to the gospel.

Prophets and Nations

The prophetic voices in the land will cry out for these sins to be repented of by God's people. They are, in a way, spiritual recollectors (or "remembrancers") of the generations of a nation. Moses was a type of spiritual recollector to his nation in the book of Deuteronomy. Prophetic people are agents of change—particularly those who are prophets and prophetesses to the nations and thus the watchmen we talked about earlier.

Prophetic people aren't always popular because they tend to remind rulers and nations of things they would rather forget. Right now, many prophetic voices in the Church in the United States are reminding us of our sins against the Native American Indians. We have just recently begun to come to grips with our sins against the host people of the land. Reports indicate that more than 350 treaties have been broken with them. Sadly, many times the Church itself was the cause of wounding.

John Dawson has done a masterful job of voicing the need for healing

America's wounds in his book by the same title. His writing is a prophet-ic call to repentance and reconciliation. *Healing America's Wounds* is a trum-peting wake-up call to the United States, which stands on the precipice of strong discipline by God for its sinful state. Dawson brings us face-to-face with the issue of corporate sin, which is something the prophetic voices throughout the Word of God repeatedly cried out against. One of the strong statements he makes is important for us here: "God disciples nations, He shapes nations; there is already a history of God dealing with the nation in which we live, whether we know it or not."[3]

Recently when I was speaking in a Latin American nation, the Lord spoke to me: "This generation is suffering because 40 years ago the Church in this nation quenched the moving of the power of the Holy Spirit and it has been wandering in the wilderness ever since. The 40-year period is almost over and the Church is about to experience incred-ible revival as it will not turn away My visitation in this generation." Checking with some of the leaders who had been around for 40 years, they concurred. This type of quenching by the Church was exactly what had happened in the 1950s when the leaders decided to repent in order to reopen the door for God's visitation.

The healing of a nation requires monumental courage, prophetic intercession and faith. And faithful, prophetic intercessors are present in every nation because He who is the creator of such nations wants them for His own. Psalm 24:1,2 declares, "The earth is the Lord's, and all its fullness, the world and those who dwell therein. For He has founded it upon the seas, and established it upon the waters."

Today, those who have prophetic voices similar to Joshua and Caleb give good reports that God's people are more than able to possess the promised land. They challenge others who, when looking at the natural circumstances surrounding what God has said to do, declare, "The job is too big. We are just grasshoppers!"

George Otis Jr. gives the heart-essence of those who have the Joshua and Caleb calling:

> It may have been the mention of seeing the Anak giants that brought Caleb to his feet to silence the first murmurs of con-cern among the people. Whatever it was, Caleb clearly sensed it was time to steer the house of Israel in the direction of faith. For this captain of Judah there had been enough talk about what had been *seen*. It was time to consider what must be *done*!

> "Let us go up at once and take possession [he declared], "for
> we are well able to overcome it." (Numbers 13:30)[4]

The prophetic Joshuas and Calebs are very much "now" kind of people. They don't like to wait around for others who are slower than themselves. In the case just cited, the "now" word needed to be heeded. These action-minded prophets, however, need to be willing to have their prophetic gifts tempered by other leaders in the Body of Christ. For those who give prophetic words to their pastors, once they deliver the words they need to rest in the Lord and trust their pastors. They need to pray and ask God to guide their pastors so that, if the prophetic words are from God, the pastors will receive them.

Many young prophetic people become highly offended if their pastors don't implement immediately what they believe they have heard from God. What those prophesying need to take into consideration is that the pastors may know more about the church situation than they do. Timing is critical for implementing a prophetic word—or it could blow up the church.

Just as in the story of Caleb, God will use militant intercessory prayer—often expressed through a prophetic word—to target specific sin that affects the land. Thank God for the promise in 2 Chronicles 7:14, "If My people who are called by My name will humble themselves, and pray and seek My face, and turn from their wicked ways, then I will hear from heaven, and will forgive their sin and heal their land."

FORGIVENESS FOR CORPORATE SIN

The word "heal" is the Hebrew word *rapha*, which is the same as that used for physical healing in the Bible.[5] How do you find out the things God wants to heal in your nation? A form of spiritual investigation is used that gives information to pray intelligently for the strongholds that corporate sin has allowed.[6] The term coined by George Otis Jr. for this kind of research is "spiritual mapping." It enables people to see their cities as they really are, not as they appear to be.

Daniel understood about praying and asking for forgiveness for corporate sin. He didn't have to do spiritual mapping to find out about the sins of his people. The prophets had clearly pointed out the people's sins again and again. In fact, Daniel was in exile along with the Israelites for the sins he enumerated in Daniel 9:5-7: wickedness, rebellion, departing from God's precepts and judgments, and not heeding the prophets.

Identificational Repentance

What did Daniel do so God would release the people? He repented on their behalf, by admonishing, "We have sinned and committed iniquity" (see v. 5). This kind of praying was also done by Ezra and Nehemiah and is called "identificational repentance." Identificational repentance occurs when a person repents for the corporate sin of his or her nation. Does this mean that each person is not personally responsible before God for his or her own individual sins? Of course not. Each person must come to Christ for his or her own sins (see John 3:16; Rev. 20:13). However, *corporate* sin allows Satan to blind the eyes of whole nations, according to 2 Corinthians 4:4: "Whose minds the god of this age has blinded, who do not believe, lest the light of the gospel of the glory of Christ, who is the image of God, should shine on them."

Historically, Japan has been extremely closed to the gospel and Western Christianity. This is changing dramatically and I believe identificational repentance has played a major role in a closed people group becoming open to the gospel.

Repentance Toward Japan

In 1990, the Lord gave me a prophetic prayer that essentially said Peter Wagner would be used as a spiritual bomb to undo what had happened in Hiroshima and Nagasaki in 1945 when the atomic bombs were dropped. The second part of the prophecy stated that the Lord would arise with healing in His wings over the Land of the Rising Sun.

As a result of this prophecy, Peter went to a meeting in Japan and repented to those who had suffered loss of loved ones during the bombings. He knelt down and with a voice full of tears and sorrow he said, "On behalf of the United States of America, will you, Japan, forgive us and forgive me for the dropping of the bombs on Hiroshima and Nagasaki?" When the thousand or so Christians in attendance heard these words, they began to weep. Actually, it sounded more like a mournful wail. This is very unlike the Japanese, who are not given to crying in public.

After Peter prayed, a Japanese leader jumped up and started speaking. Because Peter doesn't understand Japanese, he had no idea what the man was sharing. Later, he learned the leader had said, "Our sin is much greater..." and then proceeded to repent to Korea, the Philippines and other nations that were victims of the Asian holocaust.

A few years later, my husband, Mike, and I went to Kyoto with Peter and Doris Wagner. Paul Ariga, a well-known Japanese Christian leader, and other Japanese leaders formally repented for the Asian holocaust. We met in an outdoor amphitheater with about 1,200 Japanese Christians. They humbly asked God to forgive them for giving their sons in worship of the emperor as Kamakazi pilots and for their ensuing deaths. Nation after nation was called out as they repented to God. Tears flowed so freely that one of the brother's feet were soaked from his crying.

New Blessing in Japan

What did this do? This was powerful warfare in the heavenlies. Satan's legal right to blind the eyes of the Japanese people was broken. A receptivity to the gospel, unheard of previously, came upon Japan. This, however, was only a beginning.

The next year, the Japanese held a campaign called "All Japan Revival Koshien Mission" in a baseball stadium in Osaka. For many years, a lady pastor had climbed to the top of a hill overlooking this stadium, asking God to one day use it for His glory. She shared this with other Japanese leaders and they agreed it was the Lord's desire for a crusade to take place on that site.

A prayer strategy was developed and leaders such as Takimoto Sen Sei and his sons, along with Paul Ariga and others, spread the word. Prayer was mobilized with the idea of compiling 180,000 hours of intercessory prayer: one hour for each night of the meetings for each of the 60,000 seats in the stadium.

This kind of endeavor was unheard of in a nation such as Japan where less than 1 percent of the population claim to be Christians and probably only a third of those are actually born-again believers. Each time someone prayed for 10 hours, the person would send in a card to be entered in a central computer. Approximately 300,000 hours of intercessory prayer was eventually logged for the mission!

What happened? The three nights of the evangelistic meetings saw about 30,000 people accept the Lord Jesus as Savior. A Billy Graham crusade was to have similar results. The intercessory prayer had created an open heaven over the stadium and the people were free to hear the good news. The warfare in the heavenlies was successful!

Paul Ariga has this message of reconciliation and identification repentance imbedded so deeply in his heart that the Lord is using him as an ambassador to bring healing between Japan and the nations it wounded during World War II. When John Dawson and I were speaking at a conference in Brisbane, Australia, Paul called through a phone link and asked forgiveness for the atrocities committed against the Aussies during the war. The large crowd listened with a sense of awe, and history was in the making through the crackled line, and these infamies were dealt with. Then Ben Gray, the Australian leader, forgave on behalf of all the Australians who were hurt by the Japanese. It was deeply moving.

The next day after the phone call, reports of changed lives were already coming in. One pastor who had been horribly tortured by the Japanese during World War II was on his deathbed. The wounds were deep in his soul. His daughter had been at the meeting and went to visit him afterward in the hospital. She told him what had happened and for the first time, he was able to truly forgive the Japanese before he went home to be with the Lord.

PRAYER FOR YOUR CITY

For many years, prophetic people in local communities have received pieces of insight concerning the strongholds over their areas. Through the years, I've had many people share with me the pictures they have seen of the strongman looking like a black octopus that has tendrils reaching into the churches, government and so forth. Another person said that the demonic darkness looked like a huge elephant. Sadly, the knowledge of what these prophetic people were discerning was so vague that they rarely had any sort of major breakthrough.

Pastors and leaders have come to me, saying, "Cindy, my town is the hardest there is. It is so dark here, I preach my heart out with little results. I want souls to be saved but we are not impacting our community at all." These pastors know that something is terribly wrong but they don't have a clue what to do about it. The information in this chapter will give some spiritual insights and provide practical ways to pray for your city.

When a pastor comes to me to talk about his city, I first talk to him about his own church. Before we begin to pray for his city, it is necessary to deal with the corporate sin of the church. Christians cannot begin to war in the heavenlies for a city until they have secured the borders of their own churches. Churches can have generational sins that corporately affect the work of God today.

Neil Anderson and Charles Mylander have written an excellent book on this subject entitled *Setting Your Church Free*. In their book, they give a prayer of action to help identify the past sins of the church that have produced modern-day strongholds. They also write about ways to find the church's strengths or—to use this chapter's terminology—its redemptive gifts. Additionally, they suggest a time of corporate *renunciation* of sins (this renunciation has the effect of binding the enemy) and corporate *announcing* (which has the effect of loosing or releasing God's provision and power into the church). Here are a few examples:

We renounce...	We announce....
We renounce forsaking our first love.	We announce that Christ is our first love because He first loved us and gave Himself an atoning sacrifice for our sins.
We renounce our false pride in financial "security" that blinds us to our actual spiritual needs.	We announce that Christ is our true wealth, security and insight—and outside of Him we are wretched, pitiful, poor, blind and naked.[7]

Once the perimeter of your church is secured, then you can move to identify the corporate sins of your city and nation. This is what Daniel was doing in Daniel 9:4,5. Many times, pastors do not understand that ungodliness in their own cities' histories has a direct influence on whether or not people are receptive to the gospel. Because of such lack of understanding, Satan has major footholds in communities. Some of the smaller communities have some of the biggest strongholds. I've found that witches, covens and New Age leaders often adopt out-of-the-way places to "hide out."

The Story of One City
Pastor Bob Beckett lives in the city of Hemet, California, which has a population of around 80,000. On the surface it appears to be a sleepy retirement village. As Bob started studying the past of his community, however, he found some shocking things. His study included the physical, spiritual and political realms.

First of all, the Lord started opening Bob's eyes to things that were common knowledge, but held tremendous pull for the kingdom of darkness. One local phenomenon was something called the "navel of the earth," which turned out to be a sort of demonic epicenter for the Transcendental Meditation (TM) people who would go there to meditate. Bob talks about a guide taking him to visit this navel in his chapter in *Breaking Strongholds in Your City*:

> One of their highest spiritual exercises for those at the TM retreat center would be to go the waterfall [the navel of the earth] any time the rains would fill the canyon. They would meditate at the vortex of the waterfall until the water no longer swirled in a clockwise motion, as water naturally does above the equator, but in reverse of its natural course....My guide went on to point out that the walls of the canyon had been scarred over time in a clockwise motion, but the sand and earth of the dry streambed had clearly been marked in a counterclockwise motion.[8]

Another thing Bob discovered was that the Maharishi Yogi had purchased property in the community of Hemet because he was told, "This area is very conducive to meditation and has a spiritual aura about it."[9]

In researching the past, Bob uncovered many other things about his community. Hemet has a canyon known as "Massacre Canyon," where one Indian tribe, the Temeculas, slaughtered the local Sobobas. This location, tainted by the sin of murder, became a breeding ground for violence and gang activity. The Soboba reservation was known as one of the most violent in the United States, having at least one murder a month. Even other Indians didn't want to go there.

Bob worked hard to obtain unity among the pastors and spiritual leaders of Hemet and one day several of them went together to the site of the massacre. They asked some of the Soboba Christians if they would join them. There, the Soboba Indians forgave the Temeculas for the massacre. Then they gathered stones and went back to the reservation where they piled them up in an altar to the Lord and prayed to break the power of the spirit of violence over the reservation. Since that day (and at the time of this writing), not one murder has occurred on the Soboba reservation. In fact, the tribal leader recently rededicated his life to the Lord and made an open declaration that Jesus is Lord of the reservation.

BREAKING STRONGHOLDS THROUGH PRAYER

Many Scriptures point to the pollution of the land and curses that came upon it from the sins of the people who lived there. Leviticus 18:25 says, "For the land is defiled; therefore I visit the punishment of its iniquity upon it, and the land vomits out its inhabitants."

But how are curses broken? The blood of the Lamb needs to be applied through intercessory prayer and identificational repentance. In the case of specific American Indian tribes, healing occurs when white Christians repent to the Indian leaders for violating their territories. And if necessary, restitution must be made. The repentance needs to be done in the name of Jesus; then the curse is broken.

Another Scripture to examine regarding the land is Ezra 9:11. It warns the Israelites, "The land you are entering to possess is a land polluted by the corruption of its peoples....they have filled it with their impurity from one end to the other" (*NIV*).

Many of us live on land that is polluted by sin. Some people move into houses that are built on polluted land. They may pray through the house itself to cleanse it, but they still have major problems with things breaking down, bizarre sicknesses and so on. They may need to ask forgiveness for the sins of the people who previously lived on the land in order to break any curses from these former situations.

Breakthrough in Argentina

A couple of months ago while I was writing this book, I was asked by Harvest Evangelism to go to the city of San Nicholas, Argentina. Harvest Evangelism is headed by Ed Silvoso, one of the foremost authorities on the subject of reaching entire cities for God. His book *That None Should Perish* is a classic on prayer evangelism. He tells in his book how as a 13-year-old boy, he would ride his bicycle to the western shore of the Parana River, and for a precious hour he would meet with the Lord and pray for his skeptical city of 100,000 souls.[10] But it seemed as though no one was interested in becoming a Christian.

Some 35 years later, Ed's heart still longed for a breakthrough in his home city. The pastors in the city had been in disunity, and strife had been rampant. San Nicholas was a tough place to try to pastor a church.

In the fall of 1994, as I was reading Ed's book, the Lord spoke to me, "Cindy, I want you to go to San Nicholas. I'm going to answer the prayers Ed prayed when he was a 13-year-old boy. In addition, My people are crying out to me and San Nicholas is a very special city."

As I traveled to the city with Dan and Elaine Jue, missionaries with Harvest Evangelism, they shared with me how San Nicholas was known as "the graveyard of evangelists." That was certainly a faith-building bit of information! But upon our arrival, I discovered some good news. The intercessors and some of the pastors had been on a 40-day Daniel fast (i.e., vegetables and water), and it was to end the second day of the meetings. (I was only there for a two-day seminar, coteaching with Ed Delph.)

We met for the first session at the Harvest Evangelism campground outside the city. It was so packed that people were standing outside looking into the windows! I felt led to share about the redemptive purpose God had in mind for the city of San Nicholas. By redemptive purpose, I mean the reason God created the city, and His plans and destiny in the Kingdom for it.

The name Nicholas comes from the Greek word *nikao* and means overcomer or victor. The word *nikao* is used in two significant places in Scripture related to prophetic warfare. First, in Luke 11:22, Jesus Himself talked about overcoming the strongman. The second reference is found in Revelation 2 and 3 and is addressed to the *churches in the cities* concerning their need to overcome. A particularly powerful promise was given in Revelation 2:26 to the church in Thyatira, "And he who *overcomes,* and keeps My works until the end, to him I will give power over the nations" (italics added).

I believe it is no mistake that the name Nicholas was given to this city in Argentina. From the looks of things, however, the city was not experiencing the victory God meant for it. Why was this? The pastors were working as hard as they could and loved the Lord.

As the local leaders studied the city, one major thing was apparent. A stronghold of the Queen of Heaven was present in the city. This demonic spirit that counterfeits as Mary had appeared there and told the locals she wanted a grand cathedral built. People came from all over the world to worship her there. Many of the walls of the city were painted with pictures of her, declaring it to be her city.

As I read the Scripture from Jeremiah 7:16-19 to the meeting, about how the worship of the Queen of Heaven brings God's wrath upon a city, it was very quiet. I was thinking how similar their situation was to the city of Rosario, which I wrote about in the chapter dealing with strongholds in the book *Breaking Strongholds in Your City.* Rosario had also been given to the Queen of Heaven. Explaining that the Queen of

Heaven was not the Virgin Mary and that Mary would be very unhappy to be given the title of a demonic power brought great understanding to the local leaders.

That night, the church, held in a theater, was packed. The pastors came prepared by the Holy Spirit. This is how I led the meeting:

I taught on God's purpose for the city.

We looked at the stronghold of the Queen of Heaven. It seems wherever we have found this kind of idolatrous worship, the city's economy has dropped dramatically. This had happened in San Nicholas. It used to have a big factory that brought large amounts of revenue. After the appearance of the Queen, poverty hit the city; the factory closed down and many were out of work. This directly correlates to Deuteronomy 28 that lists the curses that come from idolatry.

It is irresponsible to take people into spiritual battle without—as much as possible—making sure the "holes in their armor" are closed. Such "holes" are openings where Satan has legal right to hit them because of sin issues such as unforgiveness, relational problems between churches and so on. We had taken care of these issues earlier in the day by taking time for repentance. During this time, the pastors had knelt down and wept because of their strife and division. I'll never forget one pastor who prayed, "Perhaps this is why the fire has gone out in my heart. It is because I have spoken against my brothers."

Another area we covered was personal generational sin. Repentance was needed for those who had participated in the worship of idols or their ancestors. We had to shut the door to anything Satan would try to do to "backlash" against them after we prayed. This was a major spiritual battle and I had the fear of the Lord upon my life as I led them into war.

That day, the leaders repented of various kinds of generational sin: sins of witchcraft, consulting occultic healers, reading the astrological forecasts, participation in secret societies such as freemasonry, the worship of the Queen of Heaven and other idols. I then prayed that God would break the curses of poverty, insanity, infirmity and others that come with such worship. (Again refer to Deut. 28.)

The last step was to ask the pastors to come forward to repent for the sin of the worship of the Queen of Heaven in their city. Many came to the platform. I did not pray because it was not my place of authority to do so. Those who live in the city are responsible for the sin. Also, the pastors and spiritual leaders are the "spiritual gatekeepers" for their city and they have great power in the Spirit to deal with the city's strongholds. The pastors knelt, as did everyone else in the church. This kind of humility is important because it is part of the 2 Chronicles 7:14 pattern. A holy hush filled the room. Many began to weep as the pastors chose who would pray and represent them.

After the leaders of San Nicholas repented for idolatry and the worship of the Queen of Heaven, they stood to their feet and with loud voices of victory, entered into their redemptive destiny as overcomers! They proclaimed before the host of heaven, the demons in hell and those assembled that Jesus was Lord over San Nicholas. They pronounced that it was God's city and that it did not belong to the Queen of Heaven. To use Neil Anderson's terminology, they *renounced* the hold of the Queen of Heaven and *announced* the Lordship of Jesus Christ over the city! They took away the keys and legal right the prince of darkness had used to lock up their city spiritually. Chills ran down my back that night as these repentant people stood up in the power and authority given them through the King of kings.

As I looked around the church, my spirit discerned myriads of angels with bright swords warring over the city. Hosts and hosts of mighty warring angels fought back the dark angels surrounding the strongman until at last he left in defeat.

At the end of the service, the Holy Spirit gave me a prophetic word that a businessman attending the meeting was going to start putting signs all over the city stating, "San Nicholas, where Jesus is Lord!" I exhorted the people to paint the outer walls of their homes with this declaration, thus welcoming the King into their city. Later, a young leader came to me and said he felt he was the one who would lead the campaign to fill the city with signs declaring the lordship of Christ. Already, I could tell the anointing of the overcomer was filling his heart.

After the service, some of the leaders asked me, "Cindy, how will we know that the power of this demonic strongman is broken?"

I answered, "People will not worship her here anymore. She will leave."

Exactly one week later, on November 25, 1994, the headline of the San Nicholas newspaper read, "The Virgin has moved to Tucumán." Tucumán is about 600 miles away from San Nicholas. Evidently, it was said she appeared in the freezer of a poor peasant. One of the Harvest missionaries, Dan Jue, put it this way in his report:

> The demon *behind* the virgin found things so hot in San Nicholas that it literally went into a deep freeze. The spiri-

tual significance is that the demonic stronghold in San Nicholas has been battered down! The grip of the forces of darkness has been broken! This is really a new day for this area! Gloria a Dios! The city is in the process of being transformed from the city of Maria (Queen of Heaven) to the city of Jesus Christ. You may find it strange that a Baptist should wax so mystically over what has occurred in the past few weeks in San Nicholas. But I have no other explanation except that God has done something supernatural in this area. Hallelujah to the King of kings!

That same month, the pastors of San Nicholas got together. Usually, only about three pastors would come and conduct a sort of business meeting. This time it was different. Twenty-one pastors came and they prayed for each other and blessed the work of God in each other's churches. Pastors who had been bitter enemies were hugging and praying for reconciliation.

Remember Luke 11:22? The stronger (the Church of Jesus Christ) overcame the strongman, took from him all the armor in which he trusted, and divided his spoils! The city of San Nicholas is fulfilling its destiny and becoming a city of God.

OVERCOMING TERRITORIAL SPIRITS

It is possible to totally break the power of an Ephesians 6:12-type territorial spirit through warfare prayer.

A certain area in Guatemala was ruled by a demonic strongman called Maximon. Guatemala's Spiritual Warfare Network (SWN) representative, Filberto Lemus, has a church in Quezaltenango and the congregation has done warfare against the powers behind Maximon for years. (The SWN is a worldwide network under the A.D. 2000 United Prayer Track made up of those who are leaders in the spiritual warfare movement and do strategic-level intercession.)

In addition, Harold Caballeros, pastor of El Shaddai church, sent out four teams to cardinal points (strategic places) in Guatemala on the Day to Change the World, June 25, 1994. On the same day, seventy-thousand people participated in the March for Jesus in Guatemala City, declaring to the principalities and powers (see Eph. 3:10,11) that Jesus, not the

Mayan spirits (in which category Maximon falls), is Lord of Guatemala.

One week later, *Cronica,* a Guatemalan periodical along the lines of *Time* magazine, ran a cover story showing a picture of the idol of Maximon and had the following headline:

THE DEFEAT OF MAXIMON
Protestant Fundamentalism Alters the Culture
of the Altiplano and Turns the Native Religions
into Tourist Attractions

Here is one of the interior headlines: "The Evangelical Church, in all of its different forms, represents the most important force for religious upheaval since the Spanish conquest." A paragraph from the article states:

> The fraternity of Maximon and its followers has been reduced to a mere handful of individuals and, due to his downfall, the men of the city of Santiago de Atitlan in western Guatemala no longer drink liquor because of their evangelical faith and therefore the annual festival to the idol is now financed only by money collected from sightseeing tours of Japanese, Germans and Americans.[11]

I was teaching on this subject in Malaysia recently and a Chinese leader approached Mike and said, "You know, what Cindy's teaching really works. My friend and I were planting a church in Argentina and were experiencing absolutely no breakthrough. We got Cindy's tapes, listened to them, applied the principles of spiritual warfare and we had an incredible breakthrough. (For more detailed study on the subject of spiritual mapping I suggest you read *Breaking Strongholds in Your City.*)

PROPHETIC ACTS

Throughout the Scriptures, we see that certain prophets would literally act out the prophetic messages God gave them. At other times, God would ask His people as a whole to do something that not only was prophetic, but also had great power as a form of intercession to bring profound change when obeyed.

For example, Ezekiel was told to make a map out of a clay tablet and "lay siege" to the map. The Lord gave him specific instructions to portray on it the city of Jerusalem (see Ezek. 4:1,2). His next instructions were unusual. He was told to lie on his left side as a prophetic act for the house of Israel for 390 days! Then he was to turn on his right side and lie on that side 40 days: a day for each year of Israel's iniquity. His arm was to be uncovered during that time. God told him that He would restrain Ezekiel so he could not turn from one side to the other until he had finished the days of his siege. Not only that, but God also had a special diet for him to eat and told him how much water to drink.

Just looking at these raw facts, they seem pretty strange. Would God ask His prophet to do such a thing? Evidently. In truth, these acts are very powerful.

Each prophetic act is unique. Consider Jericho (see Josh. 6). If you've been reading the story of God's people marching around Jericho's walls since you were little, it doesn't seem too far out. However, read it as though it's the first time you have ever heard it. The march around Jericho was a prophetic act that incorporated prophetic praise (which we'll discuss in the next section) in order to bring down a mighty stronghold (compare Josh. 6:8,9 with 1 Kings 1:34; 1 Chron. 15:25,27,28; Ps. 81:1-3).

In 1990, a team from Women's Aglow went to Russia to intercede for that nation. We were led to perform several prophetic acts. Our trip came before the fall of Soviet communism and several things happened that led us to believe we were being monitored. Before we left, my friend Beth Alves had a dream that we had actually buried the Word of God in the ground. This was to result in a critical prophetic act later in the trip.

One strategy we used for intercession was to take a bus tour around the city. City tours are great because they take the visitors to all the historical sites. One place the tour visited was Moscow State University, a bastion of communist teaching. As we sat on a wall near the school, I suddenly remembered Beth's dream and thought of the "Four Spiritual Laws" tract I had in my purse. In a flash, I knew this was the place to do what Beth had dreamed about.

I quickly jumped up (we had just a few minutes before the bus was leaving) and said, "Come on, let's plant the Word in the ground!" Several of the ladies came after me. Huffing and puffing as we ran, I reminded them of Beth's dream and told them of the tract. I glanced around to find the shelter of some trees in which to do the prophetic act.

(We had encountered a person in Red Square that day whom we were pretty sure was a KGB agent, and since we weren't interested in a premature prison ministry we had to be careful!)

Finding a sheltered place, I knelt and started to dig. This was a dismal failure as I only succeeded in breaking my fingernails. Finally, I found a stick and dug a hole. Dropping the tract into the ground, I quickly covered it up while the ladies prayed. Pointing toward the university, I began to prophesy, "The seed from this tract will grow schools of evangelism, and theology will be taught here."

Later on, after the fall of Russian communism, Billy Graham did start schools of evangelism there. Sister Violet Kitely, a friend of mine, told me that a church has been planted in Moscow State University by Shiloh Christian Center (a large church in Oakland, California).

What happens through these prophetic acts? They are intercessory in nature. In fact, they might be called intercessory acts. Certain aspects of what happens might seem speculative in nature. We cannot prove a correlation between obedience in doing a prophetic act and, say, the starting of schools of evangelism. Time and time again in Scripture, however, we see where God spoke to His children to perform an intercessory, prophetic act, and He powerfully moved as a result

Prophetic Worship

Examples, other than Jericho, show how prophetic worship played an important intercessory role in victory for God's people (see Josh. 6:8,9; 1 Kings 1:34; 1 Chron. 15:25,27,28; Ps. 81:1-3). Second Chronicles 20 tells of a dire situation when Jehoshaphat had received word that a great multitude was coming against him from east of the Jordan River. As he prayed and cried out to God, the Lord spoke through the prophet Jahaziel, the son of Zechariah, that Jehoshaphat was not to fear or be dismayed for the battle was the Lord's.

The next day, Jehoshaphat made a powerful statement, "Believe in the Lord your God, and you shall be established; believe His prophets, and you shall prosper" (v. 20). God had spoken through His prophets and this great leader was going to act on what had been prophesied. As Jehoshaphat consulted with the people, he appointed singers who should praise the beauty of holiness and go before the army in worship. Verse 22 says, "Now when they began to sing and to praise, the Lord set ambushes against the people of Ammon, Moab, and Mount Seir, who had come against Judah; and they were defeated."

When earthly weapons are not powerful enough and the odds are overwhelming, a principle found in Psalm 149:6-8 releases heavenly power, "Let the high praises of God be in their mouth, and a two-edged sword in their hand, to execute vengeance on the nations, and punishments on the peoples; to bind their kings with chains, and their nobles with fetters of iron."

Prophetic worship is just as powerful a weapon today as it was in the days of Jehoshaphat. Worship teams are ministering around the world to break the power of Satan in the high places. Prophetic acts of worship release tremendous amounts of God's power and glory.

In May 1994, the worship team from Springs Harvest Fellowship led by David Morris, a gifted composer and worship leader, was invited to England by a group from a prayer house outside of London. The group was asked to come and demonstrate the redemptive gift of the majesty of God to England.

Do you recall the earlier story about the redemptive purpose of the people of San Nicholas being "overcomers," as this was part of their name? God has redemptive purposes for cities as well as whole nations. An aspect of the nature and attributes of God is displayed through every people and city—as well as nation. These redemptive attributes are then taught by the people of God to others.

Prophetically, when the redemptive purpose is displayed, a release of God's power into the nation is exhibited in amazing ways. Keying in on this, the Springs Harvest team made preparations in worship just as though it was welcoming an earthly king. The members purposely set their hearts, minds, souls and strength on ushering the majesty of God into England. With the agreement of two nations—England and the United States—they were making ready a fitting entrance for the King of glory. The group went from cathedral to cathedral, worshiping God. At last, the finale for ushering in the King's presence was to worship in London's Westminster Chapel.

As the team members prayed, they felt they were to bring beautiful banners to announce His arrival. Thirty-two banners were carried in a processional manner, each displaying aspects of His nature and character, as well as intercessory statements about how they believed God would manifest Himself in England.

In addition, dancers praised God unabashedly with all of their strength, just as David did when he danced before the Ark as it was brought up to Jerusalem (see 2 Sam. 6:14). Worshipers streamed in, magnifying the King of glory. As the last part of the processional was completed, no one moved. They just sat in the awesome presence of the King of glory. The King of the universe responded with a sweeping move through the praise of a thousand tongues singing thousands of angelic choruses to His Majesty.

Within a few weeks, a visitation from God was to pour into the churches in England. He had been duly welcomed, this King of glory. The declaration was fitting: "Lift up your heads, O you gates! And be lifted up, you everlasting doors! And the King of glory *shall* come in" (Ps. 24:7, italics added). He had been invited through a prophetic act, and in He came.

THE MOST MAJESTIC ACT

This reminds me of the most supreme intercessory act done for all mankind—when Jesus died as a substitute for all people. Of course, the intercessory acts He asks us to do cannot be compared with His redemptive sacrifice made on calvary. As we stand in the gap through prophetic acts, however, we release people from the powers of darkness through the power of the name of Jesus. The blinders Satan has placed on their eyes are ripped off, so they can behold the Lamb of God who takes away the sins of the world (see 2 Cor. 4:4). This is the reason— and the only reason—we ever do spiritual battle. We wage a holy war for the souls of humankind because He isn't willing that any should perish, and neither are we (see 1 Tim. 2:1,4,8; 2 Pet. 3:9).

God wants us to hear His Voice so we will be able to effectively wage strategic warfare until every tongue, every tribe and every kindred can hear unhindered the good news of the gospel of the Lord Jesus Christ. The Voice of God speaks to us today in ways that equip us to meet the ongoing challenges of world evangelization. Whether He has to speak through a dream, a vision, through a prophetic act or directly with His voice, He wants people to learn of Him and to accept His Son as their eternal Savior.

PROPHECY IN PRACTICE

1. Do you believe that God could use secular events, such as a soccer game, as a tool for spiritual warfare? Can you name any other instances when this has occurred?

2. Have prophets/prophetesses been used historically to do battle against unseen forces of evil? Give some biblical examples.
3. What do you think is God's redemptive plan for your own city? How does this fit into the larger picture for your nation as a whole?
4. Has anyone you've ever known seen an angel or had an angelic encounter of some kind? Do you think that person has a role in doing spiritual battle for nations?
5. How does repentance and forgiveness in the area of reconciliation of generational sins cause an openness for evangelization?

Notes

1. Clifford Hill, *Prophecy Past and Present* (Ann Arbor: Vine Books, 1989), p. 66.
2. Rolland C. Smith, *The Watchmen Ministry* (St. Louis: Mission Omega Publishing, 1993), pp. 8-15.
3. John Dawson, *Healing America's Wounds* (Ventura, Calif.: Regal Books, 1994), p. 48.
4. George Otis Jr., *The Last of the Giants* (Grand Rapids: Chosen Books, 1991), pp. 26-27.
5. F. Brown, S. R. Driver, and C. A. Briggs, *A Hebrew and English Lexicon of the Old Testament* (Oxford: The Clarendon Press, 1951), pp. 950-951.
6. See Ephesians 4:27, where the verb form is in the second person plural, addressing the corporate community of believers.
7. Neil T. Anderson and Charles Mylander, *Setting Your Church Free* (Ventura, Calif.: Regal Books, 1994), pp. 307-309.
8. C. Peter Wagner, *Breaking Strongholds in Your City* (Ventura, Calif.: Regal Books, 1993), p. 149.
9. Ibid., p. 150.
10. Ed Silvoso, *That None Should Perish* (Ventura, Calif.: Regal Books, 1994), p. 22.
11. Notes taken from a memorandum written by C. Peter Wagner. Quotes from magazine article, "La Quiebra de Maximon" by Mario Roberto Morales. *Cronical Semanal*, Guatemala, del 24 al 30 de junio de 1994, pp. 17-20.

APPENDIX

RECOMMENDED MINISTRIES

Elizabeth Alves
Intercessors International
P.O. Box 390
Bulverde, TX 78163

Julie Anderson
(Prophetic Intercession)
Prayer for the Nation
P.O. Box 236
High Wycombe, Bucks
HP112EX, United Kingdom

Rev. Bob Beckett
(Spiritual Warfare;
Spiritual Mapping)
The Dwelling Place Church
27100 Girard
Hemet, CA 92544

Rev. Harold Cabarellos
c/o El Shaddai Church
Guatamala City, Guatamala
U.S. Mailing Address:
P.O. Box 02-3289
Miami, FL 33102-5289

Ron Campbell
(Freemasonry Information)
Jeremiah Project
P.O. Box 445 C
East Cheyenne Mt. Blvd. #241
Colorado Springs, CO 80906

Christian Information Network
A Ministry of New Life Church
11025 State Highway 83
Colorado Springs, CO 80921-3471

Rev. Dick Eastman
(Intercession; Literature
Distribution)
Every Home for Christ
P.O. Box 35930
Colorado Springs, CO 80935-3593

Dr. Bill Hamon
(Prophetic Ministry; School
of the Prophets)
Christian International
P.O. Box 9000
Santa Rosa Beach, FL 32459

Walther Kallestad
Community Church of Joy
16635 No. 51st Ave.
Glendale, AZ 85306

Rev. Dick Mills
(Prophetic Ministry)
P.O. Box 520
San Jacinto, CA 92581

Rev. Steve Penny
(Prophetic Ministry)
Christian Growth Centre
7 Stapleton Avenue
Sutherland NSW 2232 Australia
Sydney, Australia

Cheryl Sacks
(Prayer Ministry for
Local Churches)
c/o El Shaddai Ministries
P.O. Box 31415
Phoenix, AZ 85046

John and Paula Sandford
Elijah House
1000 S. Richards Rd.
Post Falls, ID 83854

Sister Gwen Shaw
(Prophetic Intercession)
End-Time Handmaidens
P.O. Box 447
Jasper, AR 72641

Dutch Sheets Ministries
(Prophetic Teaching)
c/o Springs Harvest Fellowship
1015 Garden of the Gods Rd.
Colorado Springs, CO 80907

Kjell Sjöberg
(Prophetic Prayer Journeys)
Mistelvagen 18
197-34
BRO, Sweden

Rolland C. Smith
(Watchmen Ministry)
Mission Omega Publishing
P.O. Box 28506
St. Louis, MO 63046-1006

Wesley Tullis
(24-Hour House of Prayer;
Prayer Journeys)
Strategic Frontiers (YWAM)
P.O. Box 38369
Colorado Springs, CO 80937-8369

Kevin van der Westhuizen
Prophetic Ministries International
P.O. Box 9093
Colorado Springs, CO 80932

Dr. C. Peter Wagner
Doris Wagner
(A.D. 2000 United Prayer Track)
Global Harvest Ministries
215 N. Marengo, Suite 151
Pasadena, CA 91101

RECOMMENDED READING

■

Alves, Elizabeth. *The Mighty Warrior.* San Antonio, Tex.: Intercessors International, 1987.

Anderson, Neil T., and Charles Mylander. *Setting Your Church Free.* Ventura, Calif.: Regal Books, 1994.

Blomgren, David. *Prophetic Gatherings in the Church.* Portland, Oreg.: Bible Temple Publishing, 1979.

Brant, Roxanne. *How to Test Prophecy, Preaching and Guidance.* O'Brien, Fla.: Roxanne Brant Ministries, 1981.

Clinton, J. Robert. *The Making of a Leader.* Colorado Springs: NavPress, 1988.

Damazio, Frank. *The Making of a Leader.* Portland, Oreg.: Trilogy Productions, 1988.

Dawson, John. *Healing America's Wounds.* Ventura, Calif.: Regal Books, 1994.

Deere, Jack. *Surprised by the Power of the Spirit.* Grand Rapids: Zondervan Publishing House, 1993.

Eastman, Dick. *The Jericho Hour.* Altamonte Springs, Fla.: Creation House, 1994.

Edwards, Gene. *A Tale of Three Kings.* Wheaton, Ill.: Tyndale House Publishers, 1992.

Facius, Johannes. *Intercession.* Cambridge, Kent, England: Sovereign World Limited, 1993.

Grubb, Norman. *Rees Howells, Intercessor.* Fort Washington, Pa.: Christian Literature Crusade, 1952.

Grudem, Wayne. *The Gift of Prophecy in the New Testament and Today.* Westchester, Ill.: Crossway Books, 1988.

Hamon, Bill. *Prophets and Personal Prophecy*. Shippensburg, Pa.: Destiny Image Publishers, 1987.

———. *Prophets, Pitfalls and Principles*. Shippensburg, Pa.: Destiny Image, 1991.

Hansen, Jane. *Inside a Woman*. Lynwood, Wash.: Aglow Publications, 1992.

Hawthorne, Steve, and Graham Kendrick. *Prayerwalking*. Orlando, Fla.: Creation House, 1993.

Hill, Clifford. *Prophecy Past and Present*. Ann Arbor: Vine Books, 1989.

Jacobs, Cindy. *Possessing the Gates of the Enemy*. Grand Rapids: Chosen Books, 1991.

Kinnamen, Gary. *Overcoming the Dominion of Darkness*. Grand Rapids: Chosen Books, 1990.

Law, Terry. *The Power of Praise and Worship*. Tulsa, Okla.: Victory House Publishers, 1985.

Ludwig, Charles. *Mother of an Army*. Minneapolis: Bethany House Publishers, 1987.

Marshall, Catherine. *Something More*. New York: Avon Books, 1976.

Mills, Dick. *He Spoke and I Was Strengthened*. San Jacinto, Calif.: Dick Mills Ministries, 1991.

Nee, Watchman. *Spiritual Authority*. Richmond, Va.: Christian Fellowship Publisher, 1972.

Odon, Don. *School of the Prophets*. Orlando, Fla.: Daniels Publishing Co., 1976.

Otis Jr., George. *The Last of the Giants*. Grand Rapids: Chosen Books, 1991.

Penny, Steve. *Look Out, the Prophets Are Coming!* Sutherland, NSW Australia: Prophetic People International, 1993.

Peretti, Frank E. *This Present Darkness*. Westchester, Ill.: Crossway Books, 1986.

Prince, Derek. *How to Judge Prophecy*. Fort Lauderdale, Fla.: Derek Prince Publications, 1971.

Roe, Earl O., ed. *Dream Big: The Henrietta Mears Story*. Ventura, Calif.: Regal Books, 1990.

Sandford, John, and Paula Sandford. *The Elijah Task*. Tulsa, Okla.: Victory House, Inc., 1977.

———. *Healing the Wounded Spirit*. Tulsa, Okla.: Victory House, Inc., 1985.

———. *Restoring the Christian Family*. Tulsa, Okla.: Victory House, Inc., 1979.

Shakarian, Demos. *The Happiest People on Earth.* Grand Rapids: Chosen Books, 1975.

Sherrer, Quin, and Ruthanne Garlock. *A Woman's Guide to Breaking Bondages.* Ann Arbor: Servant Publications, 1994.

———. *The Spiritual Warrior's Prayer Guide.* Ann Arbor: Servant Publications, 1992.

Silvoso, Ed. *That None Should Perish.* Ventura, Calif.: Regal Books, 1994.

Sjöberg, Kjell. *Winning the Prayer War.* Chichester, England: New Wine Press, 1991.

Smith, Rolland C. *The Watchmen Ministry.* St. Louis: Mission Omega Publishing, 1993.

Wagner, C. Peter. *Breaking Strongholds in Your City.* Ventura, Calif.: Regal Books, 1993.

———. *Churches That Pray.* Ventura, Calif.: Regal Books, 1993.

———. *Lighting the World.* Ventura, Calif.: Regal Books, 1995.

———. *Prayer Shield.* Ventura, Calif.: Regal Books, 1992.

———. *Warfare Prayer.* Ventura, Calif.: Regal Books, 1992.

———. *Your Spiritual Gifts Can Help Your Church Grow.* Ventura, Calif.: Regal Books, 1979; revised edition, 1994.

White, Tom. *Breaking Strongholds.* Ann Arbor: Servant Publications, 1993.

Yocum, Bruce. *Prophecy.* Ann Arbor: Servant Publications, 1976.

SUBJECT INDEX

■

SCRIPTURE INDEX

More Resources from Generals of Intercesssion

Generals of Intercession, P.O. Box 49788, Colorado Springs, CO) 80949-9788 • 719-535-0977 • Fax 719-535-0884

Strategies For Spiritual Warfare Series

Tape Series 1
Teachings include: Wrestling With Principalities, Territorial Spirits, The Ministry of Angels an Breaking Demonic Strongholds. Includes 4 audio tapes

Tape Series 2
Teachings include: Closing the Holes in Your Armor, Tearing Down Sectarian Strongholds, Breaking Occultic Strongholds an Witchcraft, and The Iniquity of Generations. Includes 4 audio tapes.

Tape Series 3
Teachings include: Healing of the Nations, Biblical Remitting of Sins, Possessing the Gates of the Enemy and Models for Taking the Promised Land. Includes 4 audio tapes.

A U D I O

Basic Intercession 101
Series includes teachings on: the Language of Intercession, Manifestations of Intercession, and Flaky Intercession Part I and Part II. Includes 4 audio tapes.

S E R I E S

Defeating the Destroyer
This series is co-taught with Elizabeth Alves. It is a two tape series with teachings on: Breaking Curses and Witchcraft.

Encouragement for Difficult Times
The series includes teachings on: The God of All Comfort, Shipwrecked in Faith, Renewal of the Holy Spirit and The Making of a Clean Heart. Includes 4 audio tapes.

Flaky Intercession
This series is co-taught with Mike Jacobs. It includes teachings on: Safeguards in Private and Corporate Intercession, teaching on Absalom and Jezebel. This is the same teaching as sold in the Strategic Intercession tape series. Includes 2 audio tapes.

God's Hour for Women
This series includes teachings on: Women of Destiny-The High Life, Covenant of Friendship, Possessing Our Inheritance, and The Father Heart of God. Includes 4 audio tapes.

Pioneering A Nation in Intercession
This series includes teachings on: Pioneering A Nation in Intercession, Laying Siege to a City, A Challenge to Change Your Nation Through Prayer, and Stewardship of the Land. Includes 4 audio tapes.

Strategic Intercession
This series includes, Strategic Intercession, Prophetic Intercession and Intercession in Action Part I and Part II. Includes 4 audio tapes.

V I D E O

Strategies For Spiritual Warfare Featuring Cindy Jacobs is also available on 8 Videos!

POSSESSING THE GATES OF THE ENEMY, Cindy Jacobs

This widely acclaimed book will guide anyone who wants to join the battle of spiritual warfare through intercession. Whether you are a beginning "pray-er" or an experienced intercessor, you can learn to pray about matters that are on the heart of God -and possess the gates of the enemy.

ALSO AVAILABLE IN DIFFERENT LANGUAGES

Warfare Prayer Video Series featuring Cindy Jacobs

This Brand New Series Includes:

Video 1 The Language of Intercession
Video 2 The Greatest Commandment
Video 3 Challenge Canada! For the Year 2000
Video 4 Examining Our Culture in the Light of God's Word • and Part I– Establishing God's Rule in Your Culture
Video 5 Flaky Intercession • Ephesians– A Blueprint for Spiritual Warfare
Video 6 The Manifestation of Intercession Part II–Establishing God's Rule in Your Culture
Video 7 Laying Siege to a City through Intercession

★ ★ ★

Healing America's Wounds Conference

A Day to Change the World Conference held in Atlanta, Georgia was one of the most unique and powerful conferences ever held! Listen to historical, and groundbreaking national repentance take place. Speakers include: Dr. Corinthia Boone, John Dawson, Cindy Jacobs, Evelyn Christenson, Frank Kaleb Jensen, David Morris, George Otis Jr., and Ed Silvoso. 12 audio tapes Also available on 10 Video Tapes